Qualifications

Introduction to a concept

Sjur Bergan

Council of Europe Publishing

Cover: Graphic Design Workshop, Council of Europe
Layout: Jouve, Paris

Council of Europe Publishing
F-67075 Strasbourg Cedex
http://book.coe.int

ISBN 978-92-871-6125-3
© Council of Europe, August 2007
Reprinted November 2007
Printed at the Council of Europe

Contents

Preface.. 5

    Gabriele Mazza, Director of School, Out-of-School and Higher Education

Introduction... 7

Part I — Approaching a complex reality... 13

1 Setting the scene: the development of qualifications... 15

2 A complex reality... 30

3 Making sense of complexity: specific and generic competences 45

Part II — The components of qualifications... 69

4 Level 71

5 Workload.. 87

6 Quality 101

7 Profile... 118

8 Learning outcomes... 128

Part III — Making qualifications fit together 143

9 National qualifications frameworks 145

10 Overarching qualifications frameworks... 160

    The Overarching Framework of Qualifications for the European
    Higher Education Area (EHEA)... 160

    The European Qualifications Framework 166

11 Obtaining qualifications: learning paths.. 180

Part IV — Qualifications and education systems.. 197

12 National, European, international and transnational qualifications................. 199

13 Moving between education systems: the setting and legal framework for the
    recognition of qualifications 215

14 Moving between education systems: recognition procedures and issues 236

15 Qualifications: functions and further development... 254

Suggestions for further reading... 268

List of tables

2.1 European Language Portfolio, global scale: levels..38

2.2 European Language Portfolio, global scale: levels and functions..............................39

2.3 Dublin Descriptors: differentiating between cycles...43

9.1 Scottish Qualifications Framework (SCQF)..153

9.2 New Zealand Qualifications Framework (levels 2, 5 and 9).....................................154

10.1 European Qualifications Framework (draft version, 2005)......................................170

10.2 European Qualifications Framework (revised version, 2006)..................................172

Preface

I am pleased to present a new book in the Council of Europe Higher Education Series. This series, launched in late 2004, is now well established as a reference series for higher education issues and policies. This is illustrated by the range of subjects covered, from the recognition of qualifications and quality assurance, through higher education governance to the public responsibility for higher education and research and the responsibility of higher education for democratic culture.

The present book reviews qualifications, which are a key element in higher education policy. Qualifications are an essential element of the Bologna Process and of the Council of Europe's higher education programme, and much has been written about qualifications, but this book is, to my knowledge, the first systematic presentation of this important concept.

I therefore hope the book will fill a clear need and serve as a reference work for credentials evaluators and those in charge of developing and maintaining national qualifications frameworks as well as, in more general terms, for policy makers and practitioners in higher education institutions and public authorities.

In one way this book represents a new development in our Higher Education Series. Whereas previous books have been edited volumes, this is a monograph, the first in the series. I am particularly happy that this monograph has been written "in house", by the Head of the Department for Higher Education and History Teaching, Sjur Bergan. He draws upon his long experience with the Council of Europe's higher education activities, ranging from work with the Council of Europe/UNESCO Recognition Convention and our Steering Committee for Higher Education and Research to representing the Council of Europe in many areas of higher education policy debate in Europe.

I wish you pleasant reading, and I hope this book will help improve knowledge and understanding of a key concept in the current higher education debate in Europe and beyond.

Gabriele Mazza
Director of School, Out-of-School and Higher Education

Introduction

Reading a book on qualifications, as you are about to do, is an act that requires some courage. Qualifications are generally not considered a very stimulating topic, and there was a time when they were seen as the domain of a few highly specialised characters safely stored away in corner offices of higher education institutions, ministries or national information centres on recognition.

That was certainly an exaggerated view, but at the same time, though most higher education policy makers as well as the general public intuitively understood that qualifications were important, they also to a considerable extent took qualifications for granted. With some poetic licence, we may say that qualifications were thought of as what you obtained at the end of your studies – end of story.

This view may be exaggerated and overly simplified; if so, that would be a good thing. What is beyond discussion, however, is that our view of qualifications has developed considerably over the past few years. From being a concern for specialists, qualifications have moved to the centre of higher education policy debate. In Europe, the Bologna Process – aiming to establish a European Higher Education Area by 2010 – has defined qualifications as one of its key aspects, and two other aspects – recognition and quality assurance – are intimately linked to qualifications.

Not only have qualifications moved to the centre of the policy debate, but our perceptions of and thinking about qualifications have evolved at considerable speed. In Europe this rapid reappraisal is reflected in the development of national and overarching qualifications frameworks, in discussions of subject-specific and transversal competences and in a focus on learning outcomes, which may be defined as what learners can be expected to know, understand and do on the basis of a qualification. It is also reflected in a more developed view of the elements that make up a qualification, where the previous emphasis on the years it took to earn a qualification is being replaced by an emphasis on workload, and this is being complemented by consideration of other elements. Not least, the link between quality assurance and qualifications is becoming increasingly clear.

While our thinking has advanced considerably, to my knowledge there has so far been no attempt to provide a comprehensive overview of these developments. That is the reason why I have written this book: to try to present the concept of qualifications as they are reflected in current thinking and debate. I hope I have succeeded in doing so in an accessible form, yet I am painfully aware that not all issues concerning qualifications make for easy reading. This is hopefully a book that will not put readers to sleep, but it is also not a book to take to the beach. It requires a fair degree of commitment and interest from the reader, and I hope to reciprocate by providing an interesting if not always easy journey through a fascinating concept.

The book is divided into four main parts. Part I outlines the complex reality that we will be exploring, in part through a brief and selective historical overview – or rather synopsis – and in part by exploring some of the complexities involved. In particular, this is where we will meet the concepts of subject-specific and transversal competences.

Part II dissects the concept of qualifications by considering each of their five elements: level, workload, quality, profile and learning outcomes.

Part III seeks to put things back together again and to put them into context. This part considers national and overarching qualifications frameworks as well as learning paths.

In Part IV, we look at the relationship between qualifications and education systems. Not all qualifications are linked to national education systems, and we look at some qualifications that are not. We also consider how learners can move from one education system to another without losing the real value of their qualifications. In other words, we discuss the recognition of qualifications. Finally, we close by looking at why qualifications are important and link that to some developments we are likely to see in the future.

In writing this book, I have often thought about the kind of introduction to qualifications I would have liked to have had at my disposal when I started working with the recognition of qualifications some fifteen years ago. I had a background in higher education administration, but I had not worked much with qualifications until I came to Strasbourg in 1991 to take on responsibility for, among other things, the Council of Europe's recognition activities. Little was available in terms of introduction, and I had to learn by failing and doing, and by discussing with more experienced colleagues, many of them from various national information centres.

However, this book could not have been written fifteen years ago, and not only because I did not have the necessary knowledge and understanding at the time. Many of the developments that are described in this book have taken place over the past decade or so, and had this book been written fifteen years ago, it would not only have been very different but also much less interesting.

Secondly, though the early focus of my activity in the Council of Europe – recognition of qualifications – is of great importance as well as a frequent source of frustration, this is not a book about recognition. It is a book about qualifications, and recognition is just one aspect of them. Recognition will, however, be greatly facilitated if we arrive at a better understanding of the very concept of qualifications. This will help us move away from a legalistic emphasis on comparable procedures to a more qualitative approach, in which we seek to assess knowledge, understanding and abilities, and not just the formal procedures that have brought learners to where they are.

I believe that much progress has been made in the recognition of qualifications as well as in the understanding of the concept of qualifications itself over the past decade, and that here is a clear relationship between the two. Yet, much remains to be done. We need to develop our understanding further, and we need to encourage more policy makers and practitioners to share this understanding. That is one of the main aims of this book.

Qualifications may appear to be a technical topic, even if they are a key element of current policy debates, and one cannot deny that technical considerations are important. Yet understanding the technical aspects should enable us to place the issues in context and to use transversal skills like analytical ability and communication skills to develop and assess qualifications. Technical aspects are important, but those who limit their consideration to the technical aspects have missed a great deal. Few things in life are entirely technical, and qualifications are no exception. Knowledge is important, but it is even more important to marry knowledge and understanding. Understanding without knowledge may be impossible, but knowledge without understanding is at best an opportunity missed.

Qualifications are also about attitudes. They need to be approached not from a purely mechanistic and technical point of view, but with understanding and respect for those who hold them. Very often, considerations of qualifications are important to the further activities of those who hold them. In considering qualifications, we may open or close opportunities for individual learners: we may enable them to make use of their full potential or deny them the opportunity to do so. The best approach to qualifications that I can think of is found in the title of one of the most famous and influential political pamphlets of all time: Tom Paine's *Common Sense*. In working with qualifications, the prevailing attitude should be that of trying to make things possible rather than to make them impossible. We should seek to identify opportunities rather than restrictions, even if both are of course a part of our reality.

No author can write a book of this length without revealing something about himself. We write more easily about things we know than about things we are less familiar with. By the end of the book, readers will be in no doubt that history, linguistics and social sciences are closer to my heart than natural sciences, and I hope they will bear with my choice of examples, which at times will undoubtedly seem exotic to some. However, exotic examples may be better illustrations since we are not tied up in our preconceptions.

It is also obvious that no author can write a book like this without being indebted to many people. I have benefited from the encouragement and wisdom of many colleagues from all over Europe and beyond. They are recognition specialists at national information centres, academic and administrative staff from higher education institutions and policy makers working with public authorities. They are engaged in the European networks for the recognition of qualifications, in the Bologna Process aiming to establish a European Higher Education Area by 2010, and in a variety of other contexts in Europe and beyond.

They are too numerous to name, but some nevertheless deserve special mention. In my early days working on the recognition of qualifications, I learned a lot from Graça Fialho, Marianne Hildebrand, Chantal Kaufmann, Kees Kouwenaar and the late Tibor Gyula Nagy. From the late 1990s onwards, Cloud Bai-yun, Yves Beaudin, Carita Blomqvist, Christoph Demand, Jindra Divis, E. Stephen Hunt, Erwin Malfroy, Polona Miklavc-Valenčič, Eric Schvartz, Timothy Thompson, Nadežda Uzelac, Gunnar Vaht and many others have been invaluable colleagues and friends in my work on recognition. So have Stephen Adam and Andrejs Rauhvargers, from whose immeasurable knowledge and great common sense I have benefited both on recognition issues and on far broader issues of higher education policy.

That naturally leads me to the Council of Europe's Steering Committee for Higher Education and Research (CDESR), where those who deserve a heartfelt thanks are again too many to name, but where I cannot imagine what our work would have been like without the competence and friendship of successive committee chairs Krzysztof Ostrowski, Per Nyborg, Věra Šťastná and Luc Weber, as well as Bureau members Radu Damian, Michael Daxner, Jürgen Kohler, Evangelos Livieratos, Virgílio Meira Soares and Gro Beate Vige.

In the Bologna Process, I am again faced with the problem of having too many friends and colleagues to thank and too little space in which to do so. Purely in alphabetical order, Heli Aru, Gottfried Bacher, Fr. Friedrich Bechina FSO, Mogens Berg (who chairs the working group on qualifications frameworks), Yvonne Clark, Germain Dondelinger (who is now also a member of the CDESR Bureau), Hans-Rainer Friedrich, Éva Gönczi, Rachel Green, Birger Hendriks, Fr. Franco Imoda SJ, Dionyssis Kladis, Hélène Lagier, Jan Levy, Pedro Lourtie, Lela Maisuradze, Ian McKenna, Ann McVie, Seán Ó Foghlú, Annika Persson Pontén, Seámus Puirsell, Louis Ripley, Sverre Rustad, Norman Sharp, Athanassia Spyropoulou, Bjørn Stensrud, the late Roland Vermeesch, Barbara Weitgruber, Peter Williams and Lesley Wilson receive particular thanks, also on behalf of those who cannot be mentioned here. With Staša Babić, David Crosier, Lewis Purser, Srbijanka Turajlić and Pavel Zgaga I have shared unforgettable moments as well as intense discussions, in South-East Europe and elsewhere. Martina Vukasović represented European students in a spectacular way as President of ESIB – the National Unions of Students in Europe – in 2000 and has been a valued expert and friend ever since.

Jan Sadlak and Lăzar Vlăsceanu of UNESCO-CEPES as well as David Coyne and Peter van der Hijden of the European Commission have shared very generously of their insights without undue regard to organisational turf. With Stamenka Uvalić-Trumbić, now of UNESCO Headquarters, formerly of UNESCO-CEPES, I shared the unforgettable experience of seeing both the Lisbon Recognition Convention and the ENIC Network (about which, more later in this book) from early ideas to functioning realities. Last, but not least, some colleagues in the Council of Europe deserve particular thanks. Maitland Stobart and James Wimberley helped me in my early years here, and our current Director of Education, Gabriele Mazza, as well as Sophie Ashmore, Katia Dolgova-Dreyer, Angela Garabagiu, Josef Huber, Ólöf Ólafsdóttir, Jean-Pierre Titz and Mireille Wendling have provided continual encouragement, advice and support.

Stephen Adam and Athanassia Spyropoulou read and commented on the whole manuscript, and Carita Blomqvist, Josef Huber and Lewis Purser read and commented on parts of it. Andrejs Rauhvargers also provided valuable discussion. The responsibility for any remaining mistakes, omissions and misinterpretations of course remains with the author.

Qualifications become a reality to us at different stages of our lives: when we meet them as students and hopefully also as lifelong learners, when we meet them as requirements in our professional lives, when we meet them as parents and also at other stages. This book is dedicated to Gabriela and Catalina, for whom qualifications are a bit closer to their daily lives than they would sometimes wish as they make their way through the school system, as well as to Margarita, who helps them cope. May our joint multicultural background – with one leg in Europe and one in Latin America, as well as at least a hand in North America, and our joint experience as immigrants belonging in more than one place – be a source of strength rather than of problems.

Part I

Approaching
a complex reality

1 Setting the scene: the development of qualifications

In the beginning

It would be difficult to identify a society that did not in some way value qualifications, and this seems to have been true for as long as we can determine. Even those prehistoric societies that were the least advanced in terms of social organisation and technical development seem to have valued group members who had extraordinary skills in hunting animals or distinguishing edible plants from non-edible and poisonous ones. Special skills seem to have granted special status. At an early stage of their development, societies have also tended to value individuals who could communicate with their deities. It would perhaps be preposterous to identify the skills thus valued as qualifications in zoology, botany, theology and medicine (since those with an ability to communicate with the deities also often seem to have been entrusted with recovering the health of suffering group members), but we do seem to be describing a social situation in which individuals with specialised qualifications were more highly regarded than unskilled group members. Physical strength may well have been a criterion for the selection of group or society leaders, but it is unlikely that other criteria – such as the ability to understand the environment in which the group lived or knowledge of its religious traditions – would not have played an important role as well.

As societies developed, so did the kind of qualifications those societies valued. Both Iceland and Greenland were settled in the mid- to late ninth century by Norse who brought considerable cultural baggage with them, but had to adapt to a new and often harsh environment. Norse settlers in Iceland did so successfully, whereas those in Greenland did not.[1] Early Icelandic settlement was essentially rural, so people were farmers and fishermen and often did double duty as part-time warriors. Even if the country was sparsely populated, it was well organised politically, and regional grandees met at Thingvéllir to legislate and solve disputes. In view of the importance of the law, knowledge of legislation was a very highly respected qualification, and the *lögsögumaðr* (literally: law-sayer-man),[2] who had committed the whole body of laws to memory and could recite the appropriate law that would apply to the dispute at hand, played an important role. Poets and storytellers were also highly valued as they were the carriers of the community's culture. It is worth noting that in early Icelandic society, before the sagas were written down,[3] the legal and literary qualifications that were so highly valued were essentially oral. The Norse settlers in Greenland, on the other hand, were faced with an environment quite different from the one they were used to, and they did not learn how to adapt to it from those who had settled there before them. On the contrary, they treated the Inuit with hostility and contempt.

---

1. See Jared Diamond, *Collapse: How Societies Choose to Fail or Survive* (London 2006: Penguin), pp. 178–276.
2. I am grateful to Ólöf Ólafsdóttir for giving me the correct term in Icelandic.
3. The most famous of the authors of the sagas, Snorri Sturluson, lived from 1179 to 1241.

Iceland was not, of course, the socially most complex or technologically most sophisticated society the world had seen by the tenth century, and writing came into being much earlier. Many societies of the Middle East and the Mediterranean, as well as of South and East Asia, had complex written codes that required advanced, specialised qualifications. However, writing was not a necessary precondition for the development of advanced social organisation, as was seen in many African and American societies. The Inca Empire, for example, clearly valued qualifications, but these were not based on a knowledge of writing.[4] Some Meso-American cultures did develop writing systems or communications systems reminiscent of writing systems. The clearest example of a writing system is that of the Maya,[5] who also developed advanced knowledge of arithmetic and astronomy.[6]

Where writing had developed, the ability to use it was a valued qualification and one inaccessible to the vast majority of the population. The value was, however, not necessarily expressed in social terms: in ancient Rome, many scribes were slaves. Although their qualifications were valued by their owners, this was largely because of the service they could then render to the advantage of their owners. The slaves possessing specialised writing skills may have enjoyed better living conditions than slaves employed in the fields, but highly regarded free members of Roman society they were not. In Athens, where the culture of writing was well developed, oratory was very highly valued and the subject of what we would today call special training programmes.

At some stage, societies felt a need to codify qualifications and to organise preparation for them. One of the earliest and best known examples of this is the ancient Chinese civil service examination, which required advanced knowledge of philosophy, calligraphy and other disciplines far removed from the daily lives of the people, and this remoteness was reflected in the kind of language used by those who must have been among the world's earliest professional administrators. The remoteness was also reflected in the practice that once they had passed the necessary examinations – once they were "qualified" – civil servants were in general not posted to their home region.

In Europe, the first organised – or at least institutionalised – forms of advanced learning emerged in Ancient Greece, primarily in Athens.[7] The first academy was established by the rhetorician Isocrates in 392 BC, to be followed five years later by Plato's

---

4. A good introduction is Waldemar Espinoza Soriano, *Los Incas: Economía, sociedad y estado en la era del Tahuantinsuyo* (Lima 1997: Amaru Editores).
5. However, it was reported in September 2006 that a stone had been found in Mexico with what may be the oldest writing yet found in the Americas, possibly dating back as far as 3 000 years. The inscription has yet to be deciphered, but it has been suggested it is related to the Olmecs.
6. An excellent introduction is Robert J. Sharer, *The Ancient Maya* (5th edn, Stanford, California 1994: Stanford University Press).
7. See Stephen Lay, *The Interpretation of the Magna Charta Universitatum and its Principles* (Bologna 2004: Bononia University Press/Observatory for Fundamental University Values and Rights), on which this paragraph is based.

academy, which focused on philosophy. Aristotle's academy, the Lyceum – which has given rise to the generic term for secondary school in some languages (*lycée, liceo*) – was established in 335 BC. While Ancient Greek philosophy and rhetoric are often considered as the archetype of the pursuit of learning for its own sake, they were not divorced from the societies in which they functioned. Philosophy and rhetoric were key competences in city-states in which citizens – still a minority of the population and exclusively male – made major political decisions following debate. The academies were also the first examples, at least in Europe, of the organisation and institutionalisation of advanced learning. This included not only providing the intellectual effort with a physical seat and a minimum of organisational form, but also establishing a corpus of learning that students were expected to master – in other words, to earn a qualification.

The organisation and formalisation of education programmes and qualifications started in ancient Greece, but came to be associated with the medieval Church. Schools grew up in the major cities and, since they were run by the diocese and associated with the seat of the bishop, they became known as cathedral schools. Their target group was young boys, who received training to prepare them ultimately for the priesthood. This was the main occupation for which a theoretical education was required. In a sense, ordination to the priesthood was a formal recognition that the candidate had the necessary qualifications to exercise his vocation, even if the distance between theory and practice was often considerable. By virtue of their literacy and theoretical knowledge, many of the better qualified – or higher ranking – priests also fulfilled important functions in civil society.

Another feature of medieval urban society was specialisation in trades and occupations, and their organisation in professional bodies or guilds.[8] These were associations of people working in the same trade, such as smiths, tanners or carpenters, and each guild had its own social organisation. Each association had its hierarchy, from apprentice to master, and advancement to a large extent depended on a member gaining adequate qualifications and proving these through some kind of public examination.[9] Although social and economic factors may well have played a role in advancement to the highest ranks of a guild, earning adequate qualifications was normally a requirement.

The organisation of higher education qualifications: the universities

While the diocesan clergy[10] were often barely more than literate – and sometimes less – there were examples of great learning in medieval European society. Some

---

8. Again, occupational specialisation and the specialised knowledge that goes with it emerged in most slightly complex societies, and medieval Europe was far from the first example.
9. See Jacques Verger, *Les universités au Moyen Age* (Paris 1999: Quadrige/Presses Universitaires de France, first published in 1973), p. 21.
10. The Catholic Church distinguishes between diocesan (or secular) and regular clergy. The first serve the needs of their diocese, primarily in parishes, though some work in the diocesan administration or other

of these examples were laymen, and since the nobility formed the only social group with the time and money necessary to develop a culture of learning, the educated layperson was more often than not a nobleman, even if the emerging commercial classes also needed numeracy and literacy skills. There were also examples of educated laywomen, and what they had in common with the educated laymen was that their learning was largely informal. It was developed through a combination of independent study and tutoring – often individual – but even if there may have been broad agreement on what constituted a suitable education, there were no formal study programmes completed by examination and certified through a formal degree or diploma.

The high seat of learning, however, was in the Church, and especially in some of the religious orders. The Benedictines[11] are an example of a traditional monastic order whose members are bound to their houses, where – according to the motto of their founder – they work and pray in relative isolation from the society around them. The Benedictine monasteries were often great houses of learning, and monks spent the better parts of their lives at the service of God and knowledge. A distinguished but hardly unique example is the Venerable Bede (673–735), who arrived at the Benedictine monastery of Jarrow in the north of England as a boy of seven and stayed there for the rest of his life.[12] He is still known today as the author of the *Ecclesiastical History of the English People*, which was a very early attempt at writing the history of England. As the author of a book that was highly appreciated by contemporary society as well as by later generations, the Venerable Bede communicated well beyond the walls of his monastery and he transmitted at least a part of his vast knowledge to society. He may perhaps be considered an early example of a researcher, but a university teacher he was not. He most probably taught, but his students would be younger members of his own monastic community, who would also spend most of their lives at Jarrow or another Benedictine monastery. Some of them would receive a kind of formal qualification through ordination to the priesthood, whereas others would remain lay brothers who would make perpetual vows of obedience, poverty and chastity in the monastic tradition but would not become priests.

The Dominicans[13] represented a new kind of religious order, active in the expanding medieval cities around their monasteries. The Franciscans are another example of this new kind of order, often called mendicant (begging) orders, but whereas the

---

functions. They are incardinated in (belong to) a specific diocese and are under the authority of the bishop. Regular clergy belong to a religious order (e.g. Dominicans, Jesuits, Franciscan, Cistercians or Carthusians) and their tasks reflect the mission of their order. Their tasks might include parish work, other missions "in the world" such as teaching, research or charitable work, or a secluded life in contemplation. Some regular clergy served under the authority of bishops, some solely under that of the superiors of their order. Some orders, notably the Dominicans, Jesuits and Benedictines, have a history of valuing academic qualifications very highly.

11. http://www.osb.org/
12. See http://www.bedesworld.co.uk/academic-bede.php
13. http://www.op.org/

Franciscans' mission was chiefly to practise Christian charity by serving the poor and unfortunate, the Dominicans' main mission was to spread the word of God. For this reason, they were known as the Order of Preachers, and to succeed in their mission they needed to develop advanced learning. It is no coincidence that the first universities grew up around this kind of order. The fact that the new orders were largely urban also links in with the view that the emergence of the universities was linked to the growing urbanisation of Europe at this time. Religious, intellectual and social factors probably combined in bringing forth the early universities.

The University of Bologna is considered as the oldest one in Europe, and it is generally accepted that it was founded in 1088, even if the precise date or even year is difficult to establish. The universities of Oxford and Paris were established almost a hundred years later, and in the thirteenth century they were followed by other universities in England, France, Italy, Portugal and Spain. Among these we find Vicenza (1204), Palencia (1208), Cambridge (1209), Padua (1222), Napoli and Salamanca (both 1224), Toulouse (1229), Montpellier (1289) and Lisboa (1290).

In the fourteenth and fifteenth centuries, further universities were founded in these countries, and the university model was adopted in other parts of Europe: Scotland (St Andrews and Glasgow in the fifteenth century),[14] the German-speaking lands (including Wien, Heidelberg and Köln in the fourteenth century and Würzburg, Leipzig and Rostock in the early fifteenth century), what are now Polish, Czech and Hungarian territory (Praha 1347, Kraków 1364, Pécs 1367) and the Nordic countries (Uppsala 1477, København 1479).[15] By 1500, there were some 70 universities in Europe, whereas there had been about 15 in 1300.[16]

Toward the end of this period, the university models had already diversified to some extent, and in the sixteenth century the university was influenced by and also became a battlefield of the Reformation and Counter-Reformation, where Tübingen, Wittenberg, Genève and Strasbourg were all important Protestant universities. In Catholic areas, the Jesuits played a prominent role in laying the intellectual foundation for the Counter-Reformation and founded universities, for instance Vilnius (1579).

For the purpose of this book, the most significant aspect of the European university model was that it provided an institutional framework for qualifications. Thus, universities fulfilled the same function as the academies of Ancient Greece, but with an important new element: institutional autonomy.[17] Students followed a formal study programme, and the successful completion of the programme led to a diploma or degree. In other words, a formal course of study led to a formal and certified

---

14. Scotland was politically independent from England at the time.

15. For details, see Nuria Sanz and Sjur Bergan (eds), *The Heritage of European Universities* (Strasbourg 2002: Council of Europe Publishing). See also the multi-volume history published by the CRE (now the European University Association), Walter Rüegg (gen. ed.), *A History of the University in Europe*.

16. Verger, op. cit., p. 105.

17. See Lay, op. cit.

qualification, and this was a very significant development. This meant that a graduate's skills and knowledge were certified and would in principle not need to be proved anew every time the holder of the qualification moved. It also meant that there were now established norms for the skills and knowledge required of those who wanted to enter certain occupations.

The early universities were not divorced from the labour market, engaged solely in noble pursuits of the spirit without regard to the use to which the intellectual pursuit could be put. Rather, university studies, in addition to developing academic knowledge and satisfying the intellectual curiosity of students, also prepared them for the parts of the labour market for which advanced theoretical knowledge was required. Unlike the literate but enslaved scribes of Roman times, university graduates acquired formal qualifications that were highly valued in social and financial terms.

The early academic labour market focused on theology, law and medicine, and in addition students studied the *artes liberales*, often as a preparation for one of the three professional fields. In fact, the teaching of law and medicine marked early tensions between the secular and ecclesiastical orientations of higher education, since some Church officials considered the disciplines of law (at least secular, as opposed to canon, law) and medicine as too mundane.[18] Higher education qualifications did, however, provide entry tickets to lucrative careers in the Church and in civil society.

The range of academic fields was largely identical at all early universities, and their qualifications were easily recognised. The doctorate or *licentia ubique docendi* gave the right to teach at any European university.

It would be justified to think of the early academic labour market as regulated in the same way that trades were controlled by guilds. Regulated professions stipulated requirements for their practitioners that were intended to protect the public from malpractice, for example from incompetent lawyers or medical doctors. At the same time, however, these requirements served to regulate the number of new entrants into the profession and hence to protect the academic labour market – or at least to protect those who were already employed in that labour market. This was not particular to academic professions – medieval society was one of guilds for many occupations, including crafts like tanners, carpenters, cobblers or goldsmiths. Guilds had positive effects in that they provided training and education as well as security for their members, but they also had the negative effects of creating virtual monopolies and hence of limiting supply, and in many cases also of at least indirectly hindering innovation by emphasising the existing methods and professional outlooks of the guilds.

---

18. See Verger, op. cit. p. 27.

Towards diversified qualifications

The Renaissance and Enlightenment broadened the field of human knowledge, including those parts of it deemed fit for academic study. The Renaissance "rediscovered" the classics of Ancient Greece and Rome and acquired new knowledge, for example in mathematics from Arabic scholars – "algebra" is a word of Arabic origin. Renaissance humanism emphasised the value of the human being, the importance of human dignity and the centrality of the human being in the world. Humanists also emphasised the need to study original sources rather than contenting oneself with secondary sources, and this pointed to later developments in the Enlightenment and modern thought. The dissemination of knowledge was radically altered by the development[19] of the printing press, which allowed the wide circulation of books and the ideas they described well beyond what had been possible with manuscripts.

In the eighteenth century, the Enlightenment emphasised rational enquiry and reliance on empirical data. These are key elements of modern scientific thought, but they were largely developed outside the universities, by philosophers and publicists such as the French *Encyclopédistes*.[20] In many cases Enlightenment philosophers worked with official patronage, and in some cases were in conflict with the establishment of their times. Some leading Enlightenment figures, like Immanuel Kant, also held university positions. The Enlightenment emphasis on enquiry and empiricism was important for developing a concept of qualifications that emphasised actual knowledge and ability, something that is a clear trait of current considerations of qualifications.

Over time, then, the academic labour market changed, and the universities changed less fast. This at least is what many felt, and in the seventeenth and eighteenth centuries a substantial part of the intellectual development in Europe took place outside universities, which were often reduced to teaching yesterday's curriculum to people preparing for yesterday's society, or to people who felt no great need to prepare for any particular walk of life, since they had the money and the social position to do without. In the words of one prominent historian of universities, referring to the seventeenth century: "The universities had fallen to the ranks of (glorified) boarding schools for the sons of the rich who spent their time taking courses on subjects that were completely outmoded – that is medieval – taught by uninspired and uninspiring masters … Real research was done outside the universities in academies or other specialised institutions".[21] This development was not uniform, but the tensions between traditional form and new requirements were felt throughout the parts of Europe that had adopted the university model.

---

19. This is not the place to go into whether the printing press was invented in Europe – and if so, whether by Johann Gutenberg or by others – or whether it originated in East Asia.
20. For an interesting view of a less well known aspect of the Enlightenment, see Arthur Herman, *The Scottish Enlightenment: The Scots' Invention of the Modern World* (London 2003: Fourth Estate).
21. Hilde de Ridder-Symoens, "The intellectual heritage of ancient universities in Europe", in Nuria Sanz and Sjur Bergan (eds), op. cit., p. 78.

The university, along with the Church and Parliament, is among the oldest surviving institutions in Europe, and it has survived in large part because it has managed to adapt to changes in the society of which it is a part while managing to preserve its core values. At times, however, the required adaptation has taken an unduly long time to accomplish, and few if any periods would be a better example than the seventeenth and eighteenth centuries.

It was only in the nineteenth century that the university seriously adapted to the considerable changes that had taken place outside its walls. This adaptation was particularly slow in terms of university teaching and study programmes. At the same time, though it is true that much scientific research and innovation took place outside the universities during those centuries, many university staff were at least up to date on developments and some also contributed to the development of new knowledge.

While the development of research in the modern sense of the word may be dated to the sixteenth century,[22] these developments were not reflected in university curricula and study programmes until much later. Many university teachers found themselves in the unenviable position of having to teach according to the established canon while being able to present their own views and contribution to knowledge only outside the classroom, mainly in publications.[23] In the nineteenth century, the Humboldt model of the university emphasised the unity of teaching and research, and this model is an important component of the European university heritage. It has dominated the nineteenth and twentieth centuries and has only recently come under serious attack.

Even then, the attack does not so much concern the validity of the model for *some* universities as its validity for *all* universities – and whether in fact it corresponds to the reality of European higher education. The assertion that European higher education should be research-based may be understood in two ways, and the balance between the two is largely what the discussion is about. Traditionally, the assertion has been taken to imply that higher education programmes should be given by staff who are themselves actively engaged in research, and who can therefore transmit to their students not only their working methods but also the newest research results. An alternative interpretation is that higher education programmes should be given by staff who have a research training, but who are not necessarily actively engaged in research any longer.

The latter model would break with a European tradition of equal opportunities to do research for all staff – and to learn from active research for all students – but the counter arguments are in part that such a high number of research institutions might not be economically viable, and in part that a number of universities – or at least individual members of staff – are in fact not actively engaged in research to any significant extent.

---

22. See John Gribbin, *Science: A History 1543–2003* (London 2003: Penguin).
23. Hilde de Ridder-Symoens, op. cit., p. 82.

With the Humboldt model, universities in the early nineteenth century diversified their range of academic disciplines. The traditional four faculties (humanities, theology, law, medicine) diversified, in the first instance by splitting the humanities faculty into one that we would today recognise as humanities (letters and philosophy) and one that we would today call natural sciences. University chairs were established in chemistry, physics and other natural sciences (mathematics had long been an academic discipline), and the study of classical languages was complemented by chairs in modern languages.[24] These chairs not only opened up new horizons in research; they also offered new opportunities for students to earn qualifications in disciplines that had so far not been considered of sufficient academic value.

The massification of higher education: a wealth of qualifications

The diversification of academic disciplines continued throughout the nineteenth and twentieth centuries; it reflected both the development of knowledge in new academic areas and, not least in the area of modern languages, the development of knowledge about "new" areas of the world.

This development accelerated greatly in the second half of the twentieth century and was related to at least two separate but parallel developments: on the one hand the increased democratisation of society in several parts of the world, in particular in Europe[25] and North America, and on the other hand the growing complexity of modern societies.

One consequence of the democratisation of society, which was uneven but also fairly widespread, was that access to higher education became broader in terms of absolute numbers as well as social background. Student numbers increased dramatically, and, even if the student body was still much more middle- and upper-class than society as a whole and even if minority groups were generally under-represented, the student body was more socially diverse than it had been less than a generation earlier. The transition from elite to mass higher education may not have been complete, but it became very much a reality.

This transition also led to a need for a more precise definition of what the outcomes of education would be. The model that had been predominant until halfway through the twentieth century was assumed to provide learners with a set of competences in their field of study as well as in more general terms – what we will later in this book call

---

24. A knowledge of modern languages had, of course, been valued for centuries and had been the object of organised training. The *grand tour* of the European upper classes included language training, and a working knowledge of French – often also Italian – was generally assumed in noble circles. The Ottoman Empire had an early example of a specialised school set up to train interpreters; in France, what is now the Institut National des Langues et Civilisations Orientales (popularly known as "Langues 'O'") was founded in 1795.

25. In central and eastern Europe, this development was delayed until after the fall of Communist regimes.

subject-specific and generic competences – but study programmes rarely described these in precise terms. The current emphasis on – and efforts to define – level, learning outcomes and competence, and for that matter qualifications as a concept, is to a large extent a consequence of the relatively loose model that had characterised higher education in the nineteenth and early to mid-twentieth centuries.

Modern, complex society – regardless of political regime – requires a substantial number of people who are highly qualified in a wide diversity of fields. Whereas, in more traditional societies, those without specialised qualifications constitute a significant share of the population and have a range of opportunities for meaningful employment, their numbers as well as their opportunities are significantly reduced in technologically complex societies.

Higher education sought to meet this need both through institutional diversity and by diversifying study programmes within existing institutions. In addition to establishing many new institutions modelled on the classical universities, many governments also established a new kind of higher education institution whose main purpose was to provide specialised education at higher education level. These institutions offered study programmes that had a more professional and employment focus than classical university programmes, that were often of shorter duration and that were often to be found in technological and business disciplines, such as several branches of engineering, marketing or accounting, but they also extended to areas such as translation and journalism. In some countries, certain disciplines and study programmes could be found in both classical universities and the new type of higher education institutions, for which the German name *Fachhochschulen* came to be used as the generic name in international contexts. In their national contexts, the institutions had a variety of names, such as *hogescholen* in the Netherlands and the Flemish Community of Belgium, *főiskola* in Hungary and *distriktshøgskoler*, later *statlige høgskoler* in Norway. In the United Kingdom, the new institutions were known as polytechnics, but the polytechnics were, for the most part, transformed into universities in the 1990s. Even if reference is sometimes still made to "old" and "new" universities, the United Kingdom essentially moved from a binary to a unitary higher education system.

In some countries, students and graduates could transfer directly from *Fachhochschulen* to universities, whereas in other countries some additional work was required of students who wanted to continue their studies in a university. This difference in practice may reflect an opinion about a difference in the level of the two different strands of higher education, but it may also reflect different – if often unarticulated – views of what really constitutes a qualification. As we shall see later in this book, this point is highly relevant to our main consideration of qualifications.

The diversification of qualifications and study programmes also led to increasingly specialised qualifications, and sometimes to highly specialised institutions as well. In some countries, especially in central and eastern Europe under the former regimes, there were a good number of highly specialised institutions, such as universities of forestry or of petroleum engineering. In many western European countries, such institutions would have been considered to be *Fachhochschule* rather than universities.

This strong diversification of qualifications underlines the importance of advanced knowledge and skills in modern societies, as well as the need for documenting such knowledge and skills. However, the high degree of specialisation also raised concerns, in particular as to whether many of those who are highly specialised, not least in technical disciplines, might not have lost the ability to put their knowledge and skills in their proper context. These concerns were reinforced by developments in research, where in some areas of technology and medicine the limiting factors were no longer so much technical possibilities as financial and ethical considerations. Are medical doctors who are highly specialised in surgery also equipped to make difficult decisions about the ethical implications of their activities or to explain those implications to patients and their kin? Is it ethically defensible to carry out every experiment in biotechnology that it is technically possible to do? What are the consequences for the environment of certain production technologies?

As the amount of knowledge in specific disciplines increased and the degree of specialisation of most higher education graduates with it, concerns were raised that the proportion of true intellectuals among higher education graduates actually decreased, as did the role of intellectuals in society. The point here is not that intellectuals as a group should exercise authority alone. Rather, the point here is that intellectuals – as opposed to those with highly specialised knowledge of single disciplines – are skilled in putting knowledge into context and in raising deeper issues that are in the long term as critical to the survival of our societies as is specialised technical knowledge.

Maybe this is also a question of perspective. While universities have never – with the possible exception of their darkest hours during the seventeenth and eighteenth centuries – been entirely detached from the societies of which they are a part, in the last decades of the twentieth century they found it increasingly difficult to argue the case that, even in the age of the sound bite, society needs institutions and individuals that are committed to taking the longer view and examining the broader issues. There is little in the first decade of the twenty-first century to indicate that these concerns will not persist.

In our context, this is an important point because modern society seems to favour subject-specific over transversal skills: the ability to perform specific tasks or solve compartmentalised problems rather than put them in context. This is also an issue to which we shall return in our consideration of qualifications.

Qualifications without borders?

Until the 1990s, qualifications were earned within national education systems, and diplomas and degrees were national in the sense that one could comfortably refer to Austrian, Greek or Polish qualifications, and those with a knowledge of education systems and qualifications would have a reasonable idea of the qualification in question. There were some exceptions, notably the International Baccalaureate[26] (a secondary school leaving qualification giving access to higher education in most European countries), but these were relatively few and far between.

In the course of the 1990s, this situation changed drastically. True, most graduates still earned their qualifications within national higher education systems, and in these cases one could still comfortably refer to, say, Austrian, Greek or Polish qualifications. However, a rapidly increasing number of providers issued qualifications that were not a part of a national system, and this challenged the way we see qualifications.

These new qualifications are generally referred to by one of three terms: transnational, cross-border and borderless. There are slight differences in connotation, but these need not concern us here, except to note that the terms "transnational" and "cross-border" indicate that a course or programme is based in one country and given in another – it crosses the border – whereas "borderless" indicates that it is difficult to pinpoint the physical location of the providers, and therefore there is no physical border to cross. However, all three are generic terms, and they refer to education provided through a variety of means. In some cases, a higher education institution based in one country and belonging to the education system of that country establishes a branch campus in another, but without necessarily having this branch campus approved by the authorities of the host country as belonging to its education system. In other cases, the provider is based in a given country without belonging to the education system of that country, or sometimes without even offering education programmes in that country, and provides education in one or more other countries without belonging to the education systems of the host countries either. In yet other cases, education provision is entirely virtual, such as through the Internet, physical location is diffuse and perhaps irrelevant, and the provision belongs to no specific system.

Whereas in the previous parts of this chapter, we have referred to universities and, in a more generic sense, higher education institutions, here we refer to "higher education providers". Strictly speaking, this is also a generic term covering all kinds of higher education, whether provided by institutions or otherwise. In practice, however, the term has come to denote the kind of higher education given by non-traditional providers who often operate independently of national systems and often for profit.

The background for this development is manifold. In some cases, transnational or borderless education is seen by governments as a means of extending education opportunities for their citizens without massive government investment. In other cases, the demand for higher education is higher than the capacity of traditional higher education institutions to satisfy these demands, and in some cases individuals are more interested in higher education qualifications than in the education that is supposed to sustain the qualifications, and they buy qualifications from non-serious providers.

---

26. See http://www.ibo.org/ (accessed 30 April 2006).

This is not to say that all borderless education is non-serious. However, the fact that some of them are degree mills points to a major problem with such qualifications. Whereas national education systems provide a framework within which qualifications can be assessed and also some guarantee of the quality of the institution and its qualifications, such information is much more difficult to obtain and assess in the case of cross-border providers. Organised external quality assurance is now a prominent feature of many national systems, and establishing quality assurance is one of the requirements of the Bologna Process aiming to establish a European Higher Education Area by 2010.[27] Few cross-border providers, however, have undergone independent quality assessment and few describe their qualifications in ways that facilitate recognition. As we shall see, these are also highly relevant points in our consideration of qualifications.

Qualifications without papers

Traditionally, higher education qualifications – as well as qualifications giving access to higher education – are granted to those who satisfy the requirements of organised education programmes, and the qualifications are documented by diplomas or other written documentation.

However, knowledge and skills can be obtained in many different ways apart from traditional study programmes, and some countries accept alternative learning – such as work experience – for access to higher education. Some also accept alternative learning as counting towards higher education qualifications, and France has recently established a system allowing, in principle, a higher education qualification to be granted entirely on the basis of such experience.[28] Other countries are far more reluctant to accept alternative learning for access to higher education or in gaining higher education qualifications.

The discussion around the recognition of non-traditional learning illustrates that a given qualification can be reached through various learning paths. In other words, various roads can lead to the same goal. This is also important in the context of lifelong learning. One often hears references to "lifelong learning qualifications" as if these were entirely separate from other qualifications. A much more appropriate image of lifelong learning, however, is that of a set of alternative learning paths leading to "ordinary" qualifications.

---

27. For information on the Bologna Process, see http://www.bologna-bergen2005.no/ (to the end of June 2005) and http://www.dfes.gov.uk/bologna/ (July 2005 onwards). See also the Council of Europe's higher education website, http://www.coe.int/t/dg4/highereducation/Default_en.asp (all accessed 30 April 2006).
28. The French experience is outlined in the report *A Framework for Qualifications of the European Higher Education Area* by a working group within the Bologna Process, chaired by Mogens Berg (Copenhagen 2005: Ministry of Science, Technology and Innovation). In the printed version, the French experience is outlined – in French as "La validation des acquis de l'expérience" – on pp. 117–37. The report is also available at http://www.bologna-bergen2005.no/Docs/00-Main_doc/050218_QF_EHEA.pdf.

The issue of "qualifications without paper", then, points to yet another important issue that will be addressed in this book: how can we determine the real qualifications that an individual has earned? What are the knowledge and skills that person has acquired?

The concept of learning paths also points towards an important recent development: the emphasis on qualifications frameworks. Put briefly and perhaps too simply, qualifications frameworks describe the various qualifications that make up an education system, with an emphasis on what people know and can do on the basis of a given qualification, as well as how the various qualifications relate to each other and how learners can move between them. At this stage, "learning paths" may sound like a diffuse concept, but one of the aims of this book is to clarify this important concept by trying to outline current thinking about how qualifications should be understood.

From procedure to content

It may be worth touching briefly on yet another point before we begin our examination of qualifications in earnest. Traditionally, discussions about qualifications have tended to focus on their formal characteristics, such as the content and length of study programmes. As the discussion of non-traditional learning indicated, there is now an increasing emphasis on identifying the knowledge and skills acquired through a given study programme or other learning experience – what are often referred to as the learning outcomes associated with a qualification. While there is increasing agreement on the desirability of assessing qualifications on the basis of learning outcomes, arriving at a proper methodology for identifying learning outcomes still requires much work and will be a challenge to policy makers and specialists, such as curriculum designers and those responsible for the recognition of qualifications, for several years to come. This work is important, and hopefully this book will contribute to making some of the ideas behind this development a little clearer.

Qualifications: a definition

The attentive reader will have seen that in this first chapter, the term "qualifications" has been used somewhat loosely. It has often been used in the same way that we tend to talk about qualifications – and hence someone who is qualified – in everyday language, something like:

Qualified: Competent, suited or having met the requirements for a specific position or task.

Qualification: 1. a. The act of qualifying b. The condition of being qualified 2. Any quality, accomplishment, or ability that suits a person to a specific position or task.[29]

We have, however, avoided the sarcastic definition offered by Ambrose Bierce:

---

29. Both definitions are taken from *The Illustrated Heritage Dictionary and Information Book* (Boston, MA 1977: Houghton Mifflin). The term "qualification" is of course often used in a second sense, viz as restricting or limiting something (as in a "qualified majority"), but we are not concerned with this sense of the term in the present book.

Qualification, n. Being a cousin of the President's tailor.[30]

When discussing higher education policy in a European context, however, and especially when discussing the recognition of qualifications, there is a stricter, more technical definition, taken from the Council of Europe/UNESCO Convention on the Recognition of Qualifications concerning Higher Education in the European Region, also referred to as the Lisbon Recognition Convention or the Council of Europe/UNESCO Recognition Convention since it was adopted in Lisbon in April 1997:

Qualification

A. Higher education qualification

Any degree, diploma or other certificate issued by a competent authority attesting the successful completion of a higher education programme.

B. Qualification giving access to higher education

Any diploma or other certificate issued by a competent authority attesting the successful completion of an education programme and giving the holder of the qualification the right to be considered for admission to higher education (cf. the definition of access).[31]

This is the accepted definition of the term in the Bologna Process, and it is the one which will guide our discussions in this book.

---

30. Ambrose Bierce, *The Enlarged Devil's Dictionary* (Harmondsworth, Middlesex 1984: Penguin American Library).
31. The text of this convention and its explanatory report as well as a continually updated list of signatures and ratifications may be found at http://conventions.coe.int/ – search for ETS No.165.

2　A complex reality

A first approach

When we think of a qualified carpenter, we tend to think of someone who knows how to handle wood and a certain set of tools. We assume a professional driver is someone who knows how to drive a vehicle with great skill. Mention a medical doctor, and our expectations go more towards someone with a profound knowledge of the human body, whereas a teacher is someone with good knowledge of certain disciplines taught at school as well as the skills needed to transmit this knowledge. A priest is someone with a thorough knowledge of the Bible as well as of Church teachings and ceremonies.

Reality is, of course, more complex. A first illustration is offered by the example of the teacher: how broad and how deep his or her knowledge is, will probably depend on what level of school the teacher serves. In many countries, primary school teachers cover most of the subjects taught, whereas those in secondary school typically teach only a few subjects, sometimes only one. At higher education level, they may teach only a specific aspect of a discipline, such as medieval European history. If we think about it, many of us probably distinguish carpenters who build houses from those who make furniture. Some languages have specific terms for carpenters who specialise: my native language, for example, has the term *møbelsnekker* (literally: furniture carpenter) where English has the term cabinet maker. The difference between general knowledge and specialised competence is perhaps best illustrated by the famous quip that researchers know more and more about less and less, whereas journalists know less and less about more and more.

If we think a little further, however, we realise that qualifications are an even more complex reality. Carpenters need a variety of knowledge and skills to succeed in their trade: they must know not only how to handle their tools and wood in general, but they must also have an intimate knowledge of the material with which they work, since various kinds of wood are fit for various purposes. They must also know construction techniques, and they must have a good practical knowledge of mathematics. Drivers must have not only driving skills, but also a measure of technical skill to maintain their vehicle and carry out at least basic repairs. Perhaps more importantly, they must know traffic regulations, be able to read maps and not least to judge spatial relationships and speed: will I be able to pass the slow car in front of me before the fast car coming in the opposite direction reaches me? Like carpenters and medical doctors, professional drivers also tend to specialise. The skills and knowledge required of taxi drivers and long-haul truck drivers may have much in common, but there are also clear differences.

Medical doctors must know not only biology but various other natural sciences, and the knowledge they require is not only theoretical. Depending on their specialisation, medical doctors must be able to apply a variety of techniques, popularly illustrated by the surgeon who "did not know how to cut". They must also be well aware of their legal obligations and, if they have their own practice, they must know enough book-keeping to run their office. Not least, medical doctors must be able to relate to patients and their family: to show understanding for patients' predicaments, even if their fears may not always appear rational to someone trained in medicine, and to explain ill-nesses and suggested treatments in terms that laypeople will understand.

Communication skills are also of vital importance to teachers. If we think back to our school days, the good and bad teachers who crossed our paths were possibly distin-guished more for their communication skills – or lack of them – than their knowledge of the subject they were teaching. There are of course teachers with insufficient knowl-edge of their subject, but the knowledgeable teacher who is utterly unable to convey even the basics of his or her subject is probably a more common figure. The classic defence of university teachers – that a good researcher is automatically a good teacher – will not stand up. Good teachers must be able to explain, and explain in a way that arouses students' interest in the subject. This is a formidable challenge because, in the average class, students have a variety of backgrounds, levels of interest and individual learning styles. The teacher must be able to relate to all of them, and also to their par-ents, fellow teachers, school officials and often the public at large.

For priests, personal piety and a deep faith are essential, but the public image of the priest is not unlike that of the teacher: it probably depends more on communication skills and the ability to relate to people in different circumstances than on anything else. To show compassion in grief, to transmit a feeling of joy at baptisms and wed-dings and, even if most churches disapprove of divorce and remarriage in differing degrees, to be able to talk with parishioners in difficult marital circumstances with sympathy and understanding are all essential skills, as is the ability to explain complex theological issues in accessible terms. Even if theology to many may seem a highly theoretical subject, the life of a priest has many practical aspects. As has been said about a distinguished Dominican: when he entered the novitiate, he had not reflected on the fact that being a friar also implied standing several hours a day in church.[32] This Dominican became an excellent communicator and a much appreciated public figure, but his public image did not include the more mundane aspects of the life of his Order.

Even if we have tried to nuance our image of the qualifications of carpenters, driv-ers, medical doctors, teachers and priests, the pictures presented here are far from complete. All five groups require far more complex sets of skills and knowledge than can be described in a few lines. That, however, is the main point of this chapter and the next: to show that qualifications are a complex reality, and that to assess whether someone has adequate qualifications requires taking into consideration a variety of factors.

---

32. Hans Fredrik Dahl, "En munk for sin tid" in Bjørg Jønsson (ed.), *Pateren: En minnebok om Hallvard Rieber-Mohn* (Oslo 1983: Aschehoug), p. 21.

In the course of this chapter and the next, we will try to spell out some of the complexity of qualifications and look at some ways of describing them. In later chapters, we will consider some specific elements of qualifications in greater detail. The fact that three of our five initial examples are from higher education is not coincidental, since we will mainly consider higher education qualifications. Even if most of the examples are specific, however, the underlying principles are not. Consequently, we will seek to look at general principles of qualifications as well as specific subjects or levels.

Describing knowledge and skills: an example from Norway

Study programmes will normally specify the skills and knowledge they are intended to convey to students, but they will do so in different ways and with various levels of detail. These specifications are normally referred to as learning outcomes, a concept that we shall consider in more detail in a later chapter. Our first example dates from 1980 and outlines what students are expected to learn from what would now be called a study programme of 30 ECTS credits in a foreign language.[33] It may well be argued that the description is not properly speaking of learning outcomes, but rather of intentions for the study programme on the part of the teachers and/or course designers:

• Good practical knowledge of modern Serbo-Croatian language and practice in using it orally and in writing. Translation skills.
• Theoretical knowledge of the Serbo-Croatian language. The main emphasis will be on modern grammar, in particular syntax. In addition, students should gain an overview of dialects and know the main aspects of the developments of the Serbo-Croatian written language from the past century until today, in order to understand the present language situation. Students should also have an overview of the classification of Slavic languages.
• Linguistic and literary study of a selection of Serbian and Croatian literature. Students should arrive at an understanding of the specificity of individual works, in terms of both content and form. They should be able to explain the stylistic particularities of the works read, and they should have a general overview of the history of Serbian and Croatian literature of the nineteenth and twentieth centuries. Students should also be acquainted with the relationship of literature to the development of culture and society in general.
• Knowledge of the main aspects of Yugoslav geography, history, culture and society.

While this description is 25 years old, it has not been radically changed in that it answers the question "What will you learn?" for the current study programme in Bosnian-Croatian-Serbian language at the same university, though it has since been complemented by a description for each course. For example, the basic course provides

---

33. Serbo-Croatian at the University of Oslo, referred to as Bosnian/Croatian/Serbian in the current study programme, but that is immaterial to our present purposes. The example is from *Studiehandbok for Det historisk-filosofiske fakultet, Universitetet i Oslo, 1980–81* (Oslo 1980: Universitetsforlaget), pp. 610–11). The original text is in Norwegian; the translation is the author's. The text is paraphrased rather than quoted in its entirety. This particular description has been chosen because it is more developed than most other descriptions of study programmes in the same book.

students with an overview of basic Bosnian-Croatian-Serbian grammar, an ability to read basic texts and conduct simple conversation, and a basis for further study of the language. The fourth semester course in the history of the language provides students with a knowledge of the main development of Bosnian/Croatian/Serbian language as well as of a number of key older texts, preferably literary.[34]

From reading this description, it is clear that in this particular study programme, students will take a "holistic" approach to the foreign language. They will not concentrate uniquely on acquiring the ability to understand, speak and write the language, but they will also be required to study literature as well as the broader cultural, historical and societal context of the language.[35] The published programme is fairly general in its reference to the level of language skills that students are expected to obtain as well as the exact emphasis of their literary, historical and cultural studies, but this information is likely to be communicated to students in other forms.

For our purposes, it is more important to underline that this description focuses entirely on skills and knowledge related to the discipline itself. It says little about broader skills and knowledge that studies at higher education level might be expected to provide. In the study programme of 25 years ago, these are hardly referred to, whereas the current programme provides a measure of such description through its goals for the bachelor programme in languages, which specifies that students:

> will gain knowledge of how language functions in human communication, how languages are constituted, how they are learned and acquired, how they have developed and how they vary. ... In addition, students will develop the ability to work independently, to analyse complex problems and to express themselves orally and in writing.[36]

This last sentence describes skills that are characteristic of all higher education programmes at bachelor degree level (or, in generic terms, first degree) rather than specific to the study of a given language or to language studies in general.

Educational standards: an example from the Russian Federation

The State Committee of the Russian Federation for Higher Education in 1995 issued comprehensive state educational standards for higher professional education in a wide

---

34. See http://www.uio.no/studier/program/sprak/presentasjon/HFB-SPR002-hva-laerer-du.html (accessed 15 August 2005) for the current study programme and its expected learning outcomes. The structure of the current programme is quite different from that of 1980, as the University of Oslo has carried through a major reform of all its study programmes as a part of its implementation of the Bologna Process. The description of the study programmes has also been considerably improved.

35. Historically, the issue was the opposite: the main focus in foreign language at Norwegian universities until about two generations ago was the study of the literature of the language in question, and actual language learning was largely geared to this purpose. Hence, university graduates in foreign languages were not necessarily skilled speakers of the languages they had studied.

36. See http://www.uio.no/studier/program/sprak/presentasjon/hva-laerer-du.html (accessed 15 August 2005). The text is paraphrased rather than quoted in its entirety.

range of disciplines or fields of study. These standards are quite detailed and encompass the legal basis establishing the field of study, the required time of study (stipulated in years), general and specific requirements for the field in question and a compulsory minimum list of topics or courses to be included in the given field of study.

The preceding paragraph uses the terminology in the English-language version of the standards issued in Russia,[37] which differs somewhat from the terminology generally used now in international debate. Nevertheless, the standards offer several interesting features, not least the division into general and subject-specific requirements. Taking politology (political science) as an example, the general requirements are worth quoting *in extenso*:

[A graduate at] Bachelor [level] must:

• know fundamental studies in the field of humanities, social and economic sciences; be able to analyse scientifically social problems and processes and to apply the methods of these sciences in different spheres of his professional and social activities;
• know ethics and legal regulations controlling the relations: man to man, man to society, man to environment and be able to take them into account while developing ecology and social projects;
• have a system notion about processes and phenomena occurring in living and non-living nature, understand and be able to use the opportunities of modern scientific methods of nature investigations;
• be able to continue his studies and be ready for professional activities in foreign firms and abroad;
• have a scientific notion about healthy way of life and master sports training;
• know the scientific basis of organizing his labour and be ready to apply modern information methods;
• be able to analyse his intellectual and practical professional possibilities;
• be able to acquire new knowledge and experience using modern education methods;
• understand the main point and social significance of the future profession and the main problems and the main problems of fundamental sciences and their intercommunication in his professional field;
• be able to create and apply models for analysing, characterizing and forecasting different processes in his professional field;
• be able to formulate the aims and problems dealt with [in] his professional sphere and to determine [the] optimal method of realisation;
• be ready for communal work, know methods of organizing and governing the personal, be able to make administrative decisions in different complicated situations; possess the basis of pedagogical activities;

---

37. *State Educational Standard of Higher Professional Education* (Moskva 1995: State Committee of the Russian Federation for Higher Education), in English; the original standards were, of course, in Russian.

• possess psychological and methodological readiness for changing the character and content of his professional activities, and for working out complex projects.[38]

While the language as well as the level of detail used to describe the standards may read oddly to those whose background lies in a different tradition, this should not detract from the interesting features of the Russian standards of 1995.

The first thing that strikes the reader is perhaps that, if taken literally, these standards are very ambitious. This impression is further underlined by the "requirements for knowledge and skills in discipline cycles",[39] some of which would best be characterised as general competences and some as specialised competences. For example, successful candidates for the first (Bachelor) degree should, among other things:

• be familiar with the scientific, philosophical and religious world views, the essence, purpose and meaning of human life, the diversity of human knowledge, the correlation between truth and error, knowledge and belief, the rational and irrational in human life and work, the specific features of the functioning of knowledge in today's society, with spiritual values and their meaning in the creative and everyday life, and be able to orient himself in the aforementioned;

and also

• understand and be able to explain the phenomenon of culture and its role in the development of civilisation, have a notion about ways of acquiring, keeping and transferring cultural values.

More importantly for our purposes, the standards say not only what students should know but also how they should be able to use their knowledge. According to the standards, holders of the Bachelor degree should be able to undertake scientific analysis and apply appropriate methodology, learn and acquire new knowledge, create and apply models for analysis, formulate aims and problems and identify solutions, engage in teamwork, make decisions and explain complex phenomena. In addition, the standards contain a number of points specific to the field of study. For politology, these are:

[A graduate at] Bachelor [level] must:

• be able to determine the specificity of political environment and activities of a "man of politics", their impact onto the evolution of society and its components;
• understand the world outlook on political level, fundamentals of political philosophy, interrelations between politics and ideology, politics and culture;
• know the conceptual-categorical apparatus and methodology of political science, basic branches (directions) of political knowledge, be skilful in handling tools of political analysis and forecasting;

---

38. Ibid., p. 141. The standards quoted are for politology (political science), but they are common to all study fields covered by the publication.
39. For politology, see ibid., pp. 141–5.

•know and be capable of identifying theoretical and applied, axiological and instrumental components of politological knowledge, its expertise, prognostic and other functions, comprehend the role of political science in preparing and substantiating political decisions;
•be able to identify institutionalised and out-institutionalised aspects of politics, rational and irrational elements in it;
•be in the know of main varieties of contemporary political systems and regimes;
•be versed in handling that circle of problems belonging to human measurement of politics, specific features of political socialisation of a person, political ethics, criteria and methods of humanisation of politics, correlation between what must and does exist, public weal and individual interests;
•be able to analyse international political processes, [the] geopolitic[al] situation; problems relevant to the place and status of Russia in the modern world;
•master the knowledge "about the world of politics" and its correlation with civil society, economics and sociocultural system.[40]

Again, the specific requirements emphasise analytical skills and understanding in addition to theoretical knowledge, and graduates must be able to put their knowledge to use.

Together, the specific and general elements of the education standards specify the range and variety of knowledge and skills that a holder of a first degree in politology is expected to have. These relate to the chosen discipline, but also to more general knowledge and skills in a wide area of disciplines. However, even if these standards apply to a given level of education – the first or Bachelor degree – they are not overly specific about the level of knowledge and skills the holder is expected to attain. Holders of a first degree in politology are expected to be able to analyse international political processes, the geopolitical situation; problems relevant to the place and status of Russia in the modern world, but at what level? The holder of a Bachelor degree should be able to create and apply models for analysing, characterising and forecasting different processes in his/her professional field, but again at what level? Surely, if they had completely mastered this, they would be at doctoral rather than first-degree level?

The description of a qualification should ideally illustrate not only what the holder knows and can do, by enumerating areas about which they are knowledgeable; it should also say something about the extent of the holder's possession of such knowledge and skills.

European language portfolio

To this author's knowledge, the best developed description of qualifications at international level is found in the field of languages with specific reference to foreign language learning. It was elaborated by the Council of Europe's Language Policy

---

40. Ibid., pp. 144–5. Quotation marks in the original.

Division between 1998 and 2000 and is known as the European Language Portfolio (ELP).[41] It aims to describe the competence of language learners in a way that makes their learning achievements readily understandable as well as comparable across borders. The ELP is simple enough to be understandable yet complex enough to be meaningful, and it is not rooted in any single national system. In the language passport, which is part of the portfolio, learners can describe their own learning achievements according to established criteria, or others – such as education institutions – can do it for them. As stated in the introduction to the portfolio, it "aims to document its holder's plurilingual language proficiency and experiences in other languages in a comprehensive, informative, transparent and reliable way. The instruments contained in the ELP help learners to take stock of the levels of competence they have reached in their learning of one or several foreign languages in order to enable them to inform others in a detailed and internationally comparable manner".

An individual language portfolio is the property of the learner. It is linked to a Common European Framework of Reference for Languages and a set of common principles and guidelines has been agreed for all portfolios. Institutions and others who provide language courses may submit portfolios for validation by an international expert committee. The cornerstones of the European Language Portfolio are two key elements of language proficiency: level (what learners can understand and express in a given language) and function (how learners use the language). There are three main functions: understanding, speaking, and writing. Understanding can be through listening or reading, and speaking can be through spoken interaction (typically through conversation) or spoken production (one example of which would be the monologue or a speech delivered to an audience).

Levels describe the degree of proficiency that learners demonstrate. The point of departure is the commonly used triad of basic, intermediate and advanced level, but each level is divided in two. The full level description, known as a global scale, is shown in Table 2.1. If we combine level and function, we get the grid shown in Table 2.2.

For our purposes, the European Language Portfolio points to two important aspects of qualifications. Firstly, qualifications need to be nuanced: we may refer to someone as "fluent in Spanish", but we may need to be specific about what this actually means. The different levels described in the European Language Portfolio and their use with regard to the different functions of the language are very helpful in this respect. One could imagine similar formats for describing learning achievements in other areas, such as mathematics, history or carpentry.

---

41. See http://culture2.coe.int/portfolio/inc.asp?L=E&M=$t/208-1-0-1/main_pages/welcome.html – the description here does not aim to be complete and is mainly concerned with the relevance of the European Language Portfolio in relation to the description of qualifications.

Table 2.1: European Language Portfolio, global scale: levels

User	Level	Abilities
Proficient	C2	Can understand with ease virtually everything heard or read. Can summarise information from different spoken and written sources, reconstructing arguments and accounts in a coherent presentation. Can express him/herself spontaneously, very fluently and precisely, differentiating finer shades of meaning even in more complex situations.
	C1	Can understand a wide range of demanding, longer texts, and recognise implicit meaning. Can express him/herself fluently and spontaneously without much obvious searching for expressions. Can use language flexibly and effectively for social, academic and professional purposes. Can produce clear, well-structured, detailed text on complex subjects, showing controlled use of organisational patterns, connectors and cohesive devices.
Independent	B2	Can understand the main ideas of complex text on both concrete and abstract topics, including technical discussions in his/her field of specialisation. Can interact with a degree of fluency and spontaneity that makes regular interaction with native speakers quite possible without strain for either party. Can produce clear, detailed text on a wide range of subjects and explain a viewpoint on a topical issue giving the advantages and disadvantages of various options.
	B1	Can understand the main points of clear standard input on familiar matters regularly encountered in work, school, leisure, etc. Can deal with most situations likely to arise whilst travelling in an area where the language is spoken. Can produce simple connected text on topics which are familiar or of personal interest. Can describe experiences and events, dreams, hopes and ambitions and briefly give reasons and explanations for opinions and plans.
Basic	A2	Can understand sentences and frequently used expressions related to areas of most immediate relevance (e.g. very basic personal and family information, shopping, local geography, employment). Can communicate in simple and routine tasks requiring a simple and direct exchange of information on familiar and routine matters. Can describe in simple terms aspects of his/her background, immediate environment and matters in areas of immediate need.
	A1	Can understand and use familiar everyday expressions and very basic phrases aimed at the satisfaction of needs of a concrete type. Can introduce him/herself and others and can ask and answer questions about personal details such as where he/she lives, people he/she knows and things he/she has. Can interact in a simple way provided the other person talks slowly and clearly and is prepared to help.

Table 2.2: European Language Portfolio, global scale: levels and functions

	A1	A2	B1	B2	C1	C2
UNDERSTANDING — Listening	I can recognise familiar words and very basic phrases concerning myself, my family and immediate concrete surroundings when people speak slowly and clearly.	I can understand phrases and the highest-frequency vocabulary related to areas of most immediate personal relevance (e.g. very basic personal and family information, shopping, local area, employment). I can catch the main point in short, clear, simple messages and announcements.	I can understand the main points of clear standard speech on familiar matters regularly encountered in work, school, leisure, etc. I can understand the main point of many radio or TV programmes on current affairs or topics of personal or professional interest when the delivery is relatively slow and clear.	I can understand extended speech and lectures and follow even complex lines of argument provided the topic is reasonably familiar. I can understand most TV news and current affairs programmes. I can understand the majority of films in standard dialect.	I can understand extended speech even when it is not clearly structured and when relationships are only implied and not signalled explicitly. I can understand television programmes and films without too much effort.	I have no difficulty in understanding any kind of spoken language, whether live or broadcast, even when delivered at fast native speed, provided I have some time to get familiar with the accent.
UNDERSTANDING — Reading	I can understand familiar names, words and very simple sentences, for example on notices and posters or in catalogues.	I can read very short, simple texts. I can find specific, predictable information in simple everyday material such as advertisements, prospectuses, menus and timetables and I can understand short, simple personal letters.	I can understand texts that consist mainly of high-frequency everyday or job-related language. I can understand the description of events, feelings and wishes in personal letters.	I can read articles and reports concerned with contemporary problems in which the writers adopt particular attitudes or viewpoints. I can understand contemporary literary prose.	I can understand long and complex factual and literary texts, appreciating distinctions of style. I can understand specialised articles and longer technical instructions, even when they do not relate to my field.	I can read with ease virtually all forms of the written language, including abstract, structurally or linguistically complex texts such as manuals, specialised articles and literary works.
SPEAKING — Spoken Interaction	I can interact in a simple way provided the other person is prepared to repeat or rephrase things at a slower rate of speech and help me formulate what I'm trying to say. I can ask and answer simple questions in areas of immediate need or on very familiar topics.	I can communicate in simple and routine tasks requiring a simple and direct exchange of information on familiar topics and activities. I can handle very short social exchanges, even though I can't usually understand enough to keep the conversation going myself.	I can deal with most situations likely to arise whilst travelling in an area where the language is spoken. I can enter unprepared into conversation on topics that are familiar, of personal interest or pertinent to everyday life (e.g. family, hobbies, work, travel and current events).	I can interact with a degree of fluency and spontaneity that makes regular interaction with native speakers quite possible. I can take an active part in discussion in familiar contexts, accounting for and sustaining my views.	I can express myself fluently and spontaneously without much obvious searching for expressions. I can use language flexibly and effectively for social and professional purposes. I can formulate ideas and opinions with precision and relate my contribution skilfully to those of other speakers.	I can take part effortlessly in any conversation or discussion and have a good familiarity with idiomatic expressions and colloquialisms. I can express myself fluently and convey finer shades of meaning precisely. If I do have a problem I can backtrack and restructure around the difficulty so smoothly that other people are hardly aware of it.
SPEAKING — Spoken Production	I can use simple phrases and sentences to describe where I live and people I know.	I can use a series of phrases and sentences to describe in simple terms my family and other people, living conditions, my educational background and my present or most recent job.	I can connect phrases in a simple way in order to describe experiences and events, my dreams, hopes and ambitions. I can briefly give reasons and explanations for opinions and plans. I can narrate a story or relate the plot of a book or film and describe my reactions.	I can present clear, detailed descriptions on a wide range of subjects related to my field of interest. I can explain a viewpoint on a topical issue giving the advantages and disadvantages of various options.	I can present clear, detailed descriptions of complex subjects integrating sub-themes, developing particular points and rounding off with an appropriate conclusion.	I can present a clear, smoothly-flowing description or argument in a style appropriate to the context and with an effective logical structure which helps the recipient to notice and remember significant points.
WRITING — Writing	I can write a short, simple postcard, for example sending holiday greetings. I can fill in forms with personal details, for example entering my name, nationality and address on a hotel registration form.	I can write short, simple notes and messages relating to matters in areas of immediate needs. I can write a very simple personal letter, for example thanking someone for something.	I can write simple connected text on topics which are familiar or of personal interest. I can write personal letters describing experiences and impressions.	I can write clear, detailed text on a wide range of subjects related to my interests. I can write an essay or report, passing on information or giving reasons in support of or against a particular point of view. I can write letters highlighting the personal significance of events and experiences.	I can express myself in clear, well-structured text, expressing points of view at some length. I can write about complex subjects in a letter, an essay or a report, underlining what I consider to be the salient issues. I can select style appropriate to the reader in mind.	I can write clear, smoothly flowing text in an appropriate style. I can write complex letters, reports or articles which present a case with an effective logical structure which helps the recipient to notice and remember significant points. I can write summaries and reviews of professional or literary works.

Secondly, the European Language Portfolio underscores that learning achievements need not be equal in all areas of a field – in our case, with regard to all language functions. Most learners of foreign languages find that it requires less effort to understand a foreign language in its spoken or written form than it does to express oneself in it orally, and that using a foreign language in writing is even more difficult. Therefore, at a given stage of language learning, it would not be unusual for a learner to have reached level C1 in comprehension, but only level B2 in speaking and perhaps level A2 in writing. Someone who is "fluent in Spanish" is likely to have reached one of the C levels in understanding the language and very possibly also in speaking it, but does the person necessarily have to master the language in writing at C level? By emphasising what someone can do with the language, the European Language Portfolio represents a different philosophy of competences and qualifications, a philosophy akin to learning outcomes. By defining different levels and by recognising that learners do not necessarily attain the same level for all languages and all functions, the European Language Portfolio opens up a new way of conceiving of plurilingual competences, which is also highly relevant in describing future learning outcomes in higher education.

The European Language Portfolio is intended for use in documenting learning achievement, but it also has a fundamental pedagogical function in so far as it changes the learning environment and learning experience substantially from the point of view of both teacher and learner: it defines understandable learning aims and criteria, and it underscores learner involvement and achievement. For our purposes it may be worth recalling that whereas native speakers may be expected to have advanced level in understanding and using the spoken language – even if the size of their vocabulary, the sophistication of their language use and their conformity with standard grammar may vary – there are native speakers whose ability to read and write the language is basic or intermediate. Functionally illiterate persons may well have level C2 skills in speaking their native language. In modern, industrial societies, illiteracy is normally an indication of low educational level, but as we were reminded in the first chapter, there have been – and still are – societies in which all knowledge is oral. There is no contradiction in terms in a person being fluent in several languages but literate in none.

Dublin Descriptors

The so-called Dublin Descriptors were elaborated by the Joint Quality Initiative, which is an informal network for quality assurance and accreditation of first and second degree programmes in Europe.[42] The Dublin Descriptors aim to provide generic descriptions of what holders of higher education degrees at various levels are expected to know and be able to do.

Currently, there are descriptors for four qualifications at three different cycles of higher education. In addition to the first, second and third level descriptors (commonly referred to as Bachelor, Masters and Doctorate), there is also a descriptor for

---

42. See http://www.jointquality.org/ – the quotations of the descriptors have been taken from this website.

so-called short-cycle qualifications, which are qualifications within and linked to the first cycle. It should be noted that while short-cycle qualifications are a reality in many countries, they are rejected as a separate level of qualifications by others, and – against the advice of the working group that had elaborated the proposal – they were not included in the overarching framework of qualifications of the European Higher Education Area at the ministerial conference in Bergen in May 2005.[43] We will return to the concept of qualifications frameworks in a later chapter.

The Dublin Descriptors outline the four different qualifications as follows:

Qualifications that signify completion of the higher education short cycle (within the first cycle) are awarded to students who:

• have demonstrated knowledge and understanding in a field of study that builds upon general secondary education and is typically at a level supported by advanced textbooks; such knowledge provides an underpinning for a field of work or vocation, personal development, and further studies to complete the first cycle;
• can apply their knowledge and understanding in occupational contexts;
• have the ability to identify and use data to formulate responses to well-defined concrete and abstract problems;
• can communicate about their understanding, skills and activities, with peers, supervisors and clients;
• .... have the learning skills to undertake further studies with some autonomy.

Qualifications that signify completion of the first cycle are awarded to students who:

• have demonstrated knowledge and understanding in a field of study that builds upon and supersedes their general secondary education, and is typically at a level that, whilst supported by advanced textbooks, includes some aspects that will be informed by knowledge of the forefront of their field of study;
• ....can apply their knowledge and understanding in a manner that indicates a professional approach to their work or vocation, and have competences typically demonstrated through devising and sustaining arguments and solving problems within their field of study;
• have the ability to gather and interpret relevant data (usually within their field of study) to inform judgments that include reflection on relevant social, scientific or ethical issues;
• can communicate information, ideas, problems and solutions to both specialist and non-specialist audiences;
• have developed those learning skills that are necessary for them to continue to undertake further study with a high degree of autonomy.

---

43. See the Bergen Communiqué at http://www.bologna-bergen2005.no/Docs/00-Main_doc/050520_Bergen_Communique.pdf, p. 2.

Qualifications that signify completion of the second cycle are awarded to students who:

• have demonstrated knowledge and understanding that is founded upon and extends and/or enhances that typically associated with Bachelor's level, and that provides a basis or opportunity for originality in developing and/or applying ideas, often within a research context;
• can apply their knowledge and understanding, and problem solving abilities in new or unfamiliar environments within broader (or multidisciplinary) contexts related to their field of study;
• have the ability to integrate knowledge and handle complexity, and formulate judgments with incomplete or limited information, but that include reflecting on social and ethical responsibilities linked to the application of their knowledge and judgments;
• can communicate their conclusions, and the knowledge and rationale underpinning these, to specialist and non-specialist audiences clearly and unambiguously;
• have the learning skills to allow them to continue to study in a manner that may be largely self-directed or autonomous.

Qualifications that signify completion of the third cycle are awarded to students who:

• have demonstrated a systematic understanding of a field of study and mastery of the skills and methods of research associated with that field;
• have demonstrated the ability to conceive, design, implement and adapt a substantial process of research with scholarly integrity;
• have made a contribution through original research that extends the frontier of knowledge by developing a substantial body of work, some of which merits national or international refereed publication;
• are capable of critical analysis, evaluation and synthesis of new and complex ideas;
• can communicate with their peers, the larger scholarly community and with society in general about their areas of expertise;
• can be expected to be able to promote, within academic and professional contexts, technological, social or cultural advancement in a knowledge based society.

The Dublin Descriptors also provide a useful contrast in expectations in five areas: knowledge and understanding, their application, making judgments, communicating and learning skills. Expectations for each of the three cycles (short-cycle qualifications are not included in this overview) are shown in Table 2.3.

Unlike the study programme and the educational standards referred to earlier in this chapter, and unlike the European Language Portfolio, the Dublin Descriptors have been designed to apply to all subjects at a given cycle. Therefore, they contain no references to knowledge of a given subject, and they may appear fairly general. One may even legitimately wonder whether a few of the descriptions are not too general to be of much use in distinguishing between educational achievements. Thus, holders of short-cycle qualifications are expected to be able to "apply their knowledge and

Table 2.3: Dublin Descriptors: differentiating between cycles

Cycle	Expectations
Knowledge and understanding	
1 (Bachelor)	[Is] supported by advanced text books [with] some aspects informed by knowledge at the forefront of their field of study
2 (Master)	provides a basis or opportunity for originality in developing or applying ideas often in a research context
3 (Doctorate)	[includes] a systematic understanding of their field of study and mastery of the methods of research associated with that field
Applying knowledge and understanding	
1 (Bachelor)	[through] devising and sustaining arguments
2 (Master)	[through] problem-solving abilities [applied] in new or unfamiliar environments within broader (or multidisciplinary) contexts
3 (Doctorate)	[is demonstrated by the] ability to conceive, design, implement and adapt a substantial process of research with scholarly integrity [is in the context of] a contribution that extends the frontier of knowledge by developing a substantial body of work, some of which merits national or international refereed publication
Making judgments	
1 (Bachelor)	[involves] gathering and interpreting relevant data
2 (Master)	[demonstrates] the ability to integrate knowledge and handle complexity, and formulate judgments with incomplete data
3 (Doctorate)	[requires being] capable of critical analysis, evaluation and synthesis of new and complex ideas
Communication	
1 (Bachelor)	[of] information, ideas, problems and solutions
2 (Master)	[of] their conclusions and the underpinning knowledge and rationale (restricted scope) to specialist and non-specialist audiences (monologue)
3 (Doctorate)	with their peers, the larger scholarly community and with society in general (dialogue) about their areas of expertise (broad scope)
Learning skills	
1 (Bachelor)	have developed those skills needed to study further with a high level of autonomy
2 (Master)	study in a manner that may be largely self-directed or autonomous
3 (Doctorate)	expected to be able to promote, within academic and professional contexts, technological, social or cultural advancement

understanding in occupational contexts" – but would that not be equally true of some-one with basic vocational training at secondary level, or even an unskilled labourer with a primary level general education, as long as nothing further is specified about the level and nature of the occupational context?

Nevertheless, it is important to note the carefully worded description of the skills and knowledge acquired within each cycle. Someone with a short-cycle qualification is expected to "have the ability to identify and use data to formulate responses to well-defined concrete and abstract problems", in other words to have relatively limited ability to operate independently, whereas someone with a doctoral qualification is expected to be "capable of critical analysis, evaluation and synthesis of new and com-plex ideas". Holders of a first degree are expected to "have developed those learning skills that are necessary for them to continue to undertake further study with a high degree of autonomy", whereas more is expected of holders of second degrees, as they should "have the learning skills to allow them to continue to study in a manner that may be largely self-directed or autonomous".

Therefore, while one may have reservations that some aspects of the Dublin Descrip-tors are overly general, they do provide a useful articulation of the increasingly com-plex body of knowledge and skills that learners are expected to acquire as they prog-ress from one higher education cycle to the next, of their increasing ability to acquire new knowledge and skills, of their increasing autonomy in learning and work and of their increasing ability not only to acquire new knowledge but to develop new knowledge themselves. From knowledge and understanding supported by advanced textbooks at first degree level, learners move on to acquiring a systematic understand-ing of their field of study and mastery of the methods of research associated with that field at doctoral level; from making judgments involving gathering and interpreting relevant data, they progress to critical analysis, evaluation and synthesis of new and complex ideas.

Another significant element of the Dublin Descriptors is that they are specific about various components of a qualification. As in the preceding examples, holders of a qualification are expected to have mastered not just one aspect of their field, but a complex whole. In the generic terms of the Dublin Descriptors, these aspects include learning skills, communication skills and the ability to make judgments as well as what would probably be the first association of many readers when they see the term qualifications: knowledge and understanding, and the ability to apply that knowledge and understanding.

In this chapter, we have made the point that qualifications describe a complex reality, and that this reality is considerably more complex than may appear at first sight. This has been illustrated by a number of examples that, while perhaps somewhat eclectic and far from giving a complete overview of the issue, have served to demonstrate some of the variety of knowledge and skills that may constitute a qualification. In the next chapter we will seek to consider this variety in a more systematic way.

3 Making sense of complexity: specific and generic competences

Introduction

As we have seen in the previous chapter, qualifications are a complex reality, and probably more complex than a first approach would lead one to believe. Complexity can be challenging and stimulating, but it can also give rise to despair or at the very least to a lack of comprehension – to a feeling that there are so many details that it is difficult to make sense of the whole. One cannot see the forest because of all the trees, as it were. However, making sense of complexity is a skill or competence that is required in many contexts. It is certainly a requirement in considering qualifications.

Therefore, it may be useful to try to analyse and systematise this complexity, to try to break it down into manageable parts. This is what we will seek to do in this and the next few chapters, and we will do so from several slightly different angles. These different approaches should be seen as complementary rather than as mutually exclusive.

If qualifications describe what individuals know, understand and can do, a first attempt at systematisation may involve asking whether this competence is specific to the discipline in which an individual has specialised or whether it is broader – something one might expect to find in many individuals with roughly the same level of education, even if they have specialised in different disciplines. The answer to that question is the classic "a bit of both".

What we are in effect asking is what subject-specific competences individuals have, and what their generic competences might be. As we shall see in this chapter, subject-specific competences describe what learners know, understand and can do in a specific academic discipline. If we think in terms of this book, we might define subject-specific competence as:

> On having worked through the book, the successful reader/learner will be able to demonstrate:
>
> • knowledge and understanding of the concept of qualifications as well as of the main components of this concept;
> • knowledge and understanding of the characteristics and functions of qualifications frameworks;
> • ability to apply this knowledge and understanding in assessing and developing higher education policies, e.g. in the implementation of the goals of the Bologna Process at the level of national education systems or at the level of higher education institutions;
> • ability to apply this knowledge and understanding in assessing foreign qualifications.

If we are faced with a group of individuals who have reached approximately the same level of education and have specialised in the same academic disciplines, we would probably expect that the answer to both questions raised above would be broadly similar for all members of the group. That is a fairly straightforward case, but we may be faced with a group of people who all have degrees in the same discipline, but at different levels: some people hold a first degree in political science, whereas others hold a second degree and yet others a doctorate. Quite apart from the fact that they may have specialised in different aspects of political science – for example, political theory, voter behaviour, international relations, public administration[44] – we would expect the degree of specialisation to increase with the level they have reached, and would expect much greater knowledge and understanding of the discipline from the holders of a doctorate than we would from those with a first degree.

If, on the other hand, the group comprises individuals who have reached approximately the same level of education, such as a second (Masters) degree, but who have specialised in various academic disciplines (say, a foreign language, mathematics, chemistry, history and economics), we would not expect them to know, understand and be able to do exactly the same things. Literary analysis would be for the language graduate (supposing he or she specialised in literature rather than linguistics), whereas the economics or chemistry graduates would be expected to undertake other kinds of analysis.

However – and this is an important point – at second degree level, we would expect all of them to be capable of undertaking fairly advanced analysis within their own discipline. If they were only able to repeat rote learning without applying this knowledge, we would be justified in wondering how they had managed to get their second degree. Any holder of a second degree, in whatever subject, should have some analytical skills as well as the ability to explain their analysis to others. They should also approach issues outside their academic specialisation with a certain degree of sophistication. This points to the existence of generic competences – competences that are expected of all holders of qualifications at a given level, whatever their academic specialisation.

A generic competence developed through reading this book might be:

> On having worked through the book, the successful reader/learner will demonstrate:
>
> • understanding of complex concepts;
> • ability to analyse them in terms of their content and function and not only in terms of structure;
> • ability to explain this kind of reasoning to learners who have not previously been exposed to it.

The notion of subject-specific and generic competences is hardly new, but in the European context it has recently been well developed within the project called Tuning Edu-

---

44. In some systems, some of these might be considered separate disciplines, whereas in other systems, they would be considered different specialisations within political science. This possible distinction is not essential to the purpose of our discussion here.

cational Structures in Europe and often simply referred to as the Tuning Project. The project was launched in 2001 with funding from the European Commission, and it is co-ordinated by the Universities of Deusto and Groningen. At the time of writing, the Tuning Project is in its third phase, but it addressed the issue of subject-specific and generic competences in its first phase. Much of what follows is greatly indebted to the first phase of the Tuning Project.[45]

Competence: connotations and synonyms

Before examining subject-specific and generic competences in greater detail, it may, however, be useful to look at the terminology. In this chapter, we will mostly use the term "competence", but other terms have also been popping up, such as skills, ability, capacity, knowledge and understanding.

Since we use the term "competence" most frequently, let us take this term as our point of departure. In English, the term comes from Latin through French and Middle English, but its Latin origin is also manifest in a large number of other languages. A major dictionary gives three definitions:

> Competence 1. The state or quality of being capable or competent; skill; ability. 2. Sufficient means for a comfortable existence. 3. Law. The quality or condition of being legally qualified, eligible, or admissible; legal authority, qualification, or jurisdiction.[46]

In this first definition, competence is partly defined though the terms "skill":

> Skill 1. Proficiency, ability or dexterity; expertness. 2. An art, trade, or technique, particularly one requiring the use of the hands or body. 3. *Obsolete.* Understanding.[47]

and "ability":

> Ability 1. The quality of being able to do something: physical, mental, financial or legal power to perform. 2. A natural or acquired skill or talent.[48]

The sense of "competence" that interests us here is of course this first one that has to do with skill and ability, but it is nevertheless relevant to note the connotation of legal authority, the origin of which has to do with a knowledge and understanding of legal

---

45. See http://www.relint.deusto.es/TuningProject/index.htm or http://www.let.rug.nl/TuningProject/index.htm. For the purposes of this book, the final report of the first phase of the project is particularly relevant; cf. http://www.relint.deusto.es/TUNINGProject/documentos/Tuning_phase1/Tuning_phase1_full_document.pdf.
46. *The Illustrated Heritage Dictionary and Information Book,* op.cit., p. 271.
47. Ibid., p. 1212.
48. Ibid., p. 3.

doctrine, systems and application, as well as the now obsolete connotation of "understanding" for "skill".

The same dictionary gives a number of synonyms with some further explanation:

> **Synonyms**: ability, capacity, faculty, talent, skill, competence, aptitude. These nouns name qualities that enable a person to accomplish something. Ability is the power, mental or physical, to do something and usually implies doing it well. Capacity refers to the condition that permits one to acquire that power. Faculty denotes an ability, inherent or acquired, in one area of achievement: a faculty for mathematics. Talent emphasizes inborn ability in a particular field, especially the arts. Skill implies recognized ability acquired or developed through experience. Competence suggests ability to do something satisfactorily but not outstandingly. Aptitude usually implies inherent capacity for, and interest in, a particular activity.[49]

This list of synonyms is useful in that it illustrates both the variety of terms used more or less as synonyms and the range of meaning associated with them. However, in the current higher education debate in Europe, the connotation given to "competence" in the list of synonyms above is clearly too narrow. Rather than a middle-of-the-road ability, competence has come to be used as the generic term, and that is how we have used it here and will continue to use it throughout this book, with the connotations of knowledge, understanding, values, attitudes and ability to put them into practice.

What you can do in your field: subject-specific competences

As we saw at the beginning of the previous chapter, competences relating directly to a speciality or academic discipline are perhaps what first comes to mind when we think about qualifications. It may therefore be reasonable to consider subject-specific competences before we move on to a consideration of generic competences.

Subject-specific competences, then, are what individuals are expected to know, understand and be able to do in relation to a given discipline. In higher education, the term "subject-specific competences" is normally used of those who specialise in a given discipline, but it could also describe competences achieved by non-specialists in the same discipline. For example, if a study programme in economics or physics were to include requirements of foreign language competence, it should specify the competence required in, say, "German for economists".

Such "non-specialist" competence may perhaps also be described as general or generic competence. For example, an economist may be expected to be able to speak and write his or her native language as well as at least one foreign language at a given level. Whether one prefers to call such competence subject-specific or generic is perhaps a matter of choice, and any attempt at drawing a clear line will tend to be arbitrary.

---

49. Ibid., p. 3.

One possible guideline could be to characterise such competence as generic if it is an underlying assumption of the qualification – so the organised study programme contains no study course intended to develop the competence – but to define a competence as subject-specific if there is such a study course.

For example, if economists are expected to be able to read, speak and write German as a foreign language at a given level but it is assumed they will have this competence as a part of their general education, it may be reasonable to consider knowledge of German as a generic competence. If, on the other hand, the study programme specifies a given level of German as a requirement and provides for the study of German as a foreign language for students to acquire this competence, there may be a case for considering this as a subject-specific competence.

The difficulty of drawing a clear line between subject-specific and generic competences is illustrated in the descriptors of the Tuning Project. For example, the capacity to solve problems and the capacity to apply knowledge in practice may safely be called generic skills,[50] yet "solving numerical problems using computer and non-computer based techniques"[51] and the ability to solve problems using mathematical tools[52] are indicated as subject-specific competences in Earth sciences and mathematics, respectively. There is no inherent contradiction, however: to some extent, subject-specific competences are a specific application of broader, generic competences to a given discipline, and to some extent they are made up of methodologies, mind sets and a body of knowledge specific to that discipline.

Another example is what we often refer to as "general culture", which is shorthand for our perception of what, in very general terms, an educated person should know and be able to do. Perceptions of what constitutes an educated person develop over time and vary among cultures, but they would include basic competence in a range of humanities, social sciences and natural sciences. An educated person would, for example, be expected to have a general knowledge of literature. If we were to try to describe this knowledge in terms of learning outcomes and competences, would it be general or subject-specific? It would perhaps be convenient if we were able to draw impenetrable borders between subject-specific and generic competences, and assign any given competence neatly into one category or the other, but our inability to do so is not an obstacle that cannot be overcome in practice.

Subject-specific competences will, however, refer at least primarily to the academic speciality in question, and we will focus our discussion on this. A description of subject-specific competences will need to take account of the level of the qualification, as one would not expect the same competences at first degree as at second degree or doctoral level. The description will also need to consider how far holders of a qualification

---

50. Tuning Project, op. cit., Phase 1, pp. 72–3.
51. Ibid., p. 144.
52. Ibid., p. 167.

should have a broad overview of the discipline as well as how much they have specialised. Those elaborating the description also need to consider how detailed to make
it. Considerations of this kind can easily get overly abstract, so at this stage let us draw
on a number of illustrations from different areas. For our purposes, it may be useful to
start with a well-defined, traditional academic discipline, such as mathematics.

The mathematics group of the Tuning Project suggests that, whatever variations may
be found between mathematics programmes at first degree level at European universities, all programmes will include calculus in one and several real variables as well as
linear algebra.[53] These elements, then, would be the *sine qua non* of any qualification
in mathematics at first degree level. In addition, it is suggested that:

> graduates should normally be acquainted with most, and preferably all, of the fol-
> lowing:
>
> • Basic differential equations;
> • Basic complex functions;
> • Some probability;
> • Some statistics;
> • Some numerical methods;
> • Basic geometry of curves and surfaces;
> • Some algebraic structures;
> • Some discrete mathematics.[54]

This suggests that mathematics at university level[55] includes a limited number of areas
that should be found in all first degree programmes and, hence, qualifications. It also
suggests that there is a larger group of areas within the subject that would normally
be found, even if a specific programme or qualification might not include every one
of them. Also, whereas the language on calculus and linear algebra is definitive, the
list of almost compulsory elements includes the qualifying terms "basic" and "some",
indicating that while all or most elements will be included in a first degree, the actual
amount or level of these elements may vary between programmes.

A second example from the Tuning Project is business studies.[56] The group responsible for this area in the project defines five areas of competence, referred to as modules:

---

53. Ibid., p. 165.
54. Ibid., pp. 165–6.
55. All seven subject groups in the first phase of the Tuning Project made the point that the suggested
subject-specific competences refer only to universities and not to other higher education institutions. This
may reflect the composition of the working groups that elaborated the proposals as well as variations
between study programmes in different types of institutions. It must nevertheless be assumed that, in spite
of some differences, many of the competences would also be relevant to other higher education programmes
at the same level.
56. Tuning Project, op. cit., Phase 1, pp. 101–10.

Core modules, i.e. modules that will be represented in any Business qualification for it to warrant the name. An example is Business and Management;

Support modules, i.e. modules that complement the core modules and reinforce the competence of the degree holder in ways that are directly relevant to the discipline. Examples would include mathematics and statistics;

Organisation and communication skills modules, such as learning skills, time management, foreign languages or presentation skills;

Specialisation modules or electives, which allow students to pursue a specific field within Business Studies. Examples would cover almost any conceivable field of Business Studies, either in the form of further specialisation in core areas, in a specific field of business such as the beverage or aviation industry or in a geographical area, such as Latin America or South East Europe;

Transferable skills modules, which seek to bridge theory and practice.

The mix of elements or modules may vary between levels as well as between institutions and countries, even if it may be expected that the core modules will have a prominent place in first degree study programmes, especially in the early parts of those programmes, and specialisation modules will have a correspondingly greater place at advanced levels. In this example, the modules that seek to put theory into practice ("transferable skills modules") are also more likely to be found at advanced levels since, to put theory into practice, the theory first has to be acquired and mastered.

However, the working group for this area has been very careful not to make suggestions for prescribed courses within each module, even if it indicates a list of possible courses. It does, on the other hand, offer a list of subject-specific competences. For the first degree, these are the ability to:

• Use and evaluate tools for analysing a company in its environment;
• Work in a subject-specific field of a company, and be a specialist to some extent;
• Interface with other functions;
• Have self-awareness;
• Argue for the principles to be used in finding a solution to a problem mainly at an operational or tactical level;
• Defend the proposed solution;
• Prepare for decision making at mainly operational and tactical levels.

At second degree level, students should, in addition to first degree competences, have:

• Skills enabling them to participate in strategic decision making;
• Ability to do guided research;

- Ability to work independently;
- Skills to perform holistic judgment and abilities to make critical assessments on strategic solutions;
- Skills to manage change;
- International mobility and cultural understanding.

At third degree level, students should demonstrate the ability to perform independent, original and ultimately publishable research in one or more business or subject areas relating to business analysis, choice and implementation.[57]

An interesting feature of the description offered by the Tuning group for business studies is the inclusion of organisation and communication skills modules among the subject-specific competences. It is not difficult to see why this has been done, since it is difficult to imagine anyone working effectively in business without an ability to organise and to communicate. It is, nevertheless, another illustration of the fact that the line between subject-specific and generic competences can be difficult to draw and that certain generic competences can be so central to a given discipline that it may be reasonable to consider them subject-specific competences in given cases.

A third example, also from the Tuning Project, is history.[58] Whereas all academic disciplines are complex, it can well be argued that history is one of the most complex. Potentially, it covers all kinds of human activity from the earliest times to the immediate past, even if some aspects of human activity, such as creative arts, literature, scientific achievements, agriculture, warfare or religious and political ideas may be studied also or even exclusively in other disciplines. Since, in most traditions, history is closely tied to national identities[59] – an outgrowth mainly of the nineteenth century – and is in some contexts even used as an instrument in developing and maintaining national identity, study programmes in history show even greater variety from one country and institution to another than study programmes in most other disciplines. It is telling that the Tuning group responsible for history states that:

> Of all the subject areas involved in Tuning, History has turned out to present the most varied picture in the different countries represented. National university and school systems determine a context in which quite naturally a large part of the 'contents' taught in each country is linked to the national culture or vision of the past; furthermore, the History group has found that the theoretical and practical

---

57. Descriptions of subject-specific learning outcomes for all levels have been taken (accessed 13 January 2006) from: http://tuning.unideusto.org/tuningeu/index.php?option=content&task=view&id=96&Itemid= 123#learning.

58. Tuning Project, op. cit., Phase 1, pp. 147–59; see also http://tuning.unideusto.org/tuningeu/index. php?option=content&task=view&id=106&Itemid=133.

59. See e.g. Stefan Berger, Mark Donovan and Kevin Passmore (eds), *Writing National Histories: Western Europe since 1800* (London 1999: Routledge) and Michael Branch (ed.), *National Histories and Identity: Approaches to the Writing of National History in the North-East Baltic Region Nineteenth and Twentieth Centuries* (Helsinki 1999: Finnish Literature Society: Studia Fennica Ethnologica 6).

premises created by each national culture and teaching tradition differ, often very sharply. Hence the structure of studies, and ideas about what should be done at the beginning of degree programmes and what at a more advanced stage are quite different. For this reason, the History group did not consider it possible or useful to identify a core curriculum, but rather to create agreed reference points, based on both subject-specific and key generic competences, around which programmes can be built in all countries.

It is also significant that the Tuning group indicates that much history learning and teaching is conducted within study programmes in other disciplines, and that it therefore stipulates learning outcomes not only for degree courses in history, but also for history courses for students of other academic disciplines.

The approach taken by the Tuning group makes for a long and relatively complex list of subject-specific competences, but it is worth considering in some detail because it offers a very useful illustration of how subject-specific competences vary and develop between levels. For history courses for students of other subject areas, the learning outcomes and competences are stipulated as acquiring or experiencing:

- A critical view of the human past, and the realization that the past affects our present and future and our perception of them.
- Understanding of and respect for viewpoints moulded by different historical backgrounds.
- A general idea of the diachronic framework of major historical periods or events.
- Direct contact with the historians' [sic] craft, that is, even in a circumscribed context, contact with original sources and texts produced by professional historiographical research.

The next level is that described as "history as a relevant part of a degree in other or more general subjects", meaning programmes of which history is a more substantial component than just a limited number of courses with no strong relationship to the discipline in which the degree is obtained. Degrees in Letters and teaching degrees are mentioned as examples. Like subsequent levels, this builds on the preceding level, but it should be higher, the content broader and more detailed, and the emphasis on methodology stronger. Those who study history at this level should:

- Have general knowledge of the methodologies, tools and issues of at least two of the broad chronological periods into which history is normally divided (such as Ancient, Medieval, Modern and Contemporary) as well as some significant diachronic themes.
- Have demonstrated his/her ability to complete [and] present in oral and written form – according to the statute of the discipline – a circumscribed piece of research in which the ability to retrieve bibliographical information and documentary evidence and use it to address a historiographical problem is demonstrated.

Holders of a first degree in history should in addition:

• Possess general knowledge and orientation with respect to the methodologies, tools and issues of all the broad chronological divisions in which history is normally divided, from ancient to recent times.
• Have specific knowledge of at least one of the above periods or of a diachronic theme.
• Be aware of how historical interests, categories and problems change with time and how historiographical debate is linked to political and cultural concern of each epoch.
• Have shown his/her ability to complete and present in oral and written form – according to the statute of the discipline – a medium length piece of research which demonstrates the ability to retrieve bibliographical information and primary sources and use them to address a historiographical problem.

Holders of a second degree in history[60] should have acquired "to a reasonable degree" a set of subject-specific qualities, skills or competences and, building on the first degree, also have:

• Specific, ample, detailed and up-to-date knowledge of at least one great chronological division of history, including different methodological approaches and historiographical orientations relating to it.
• Acquired familiarity with comparative methods, spatial, chronological and thematic, of approaching historiographical research.
• Shown the ability to plan, carry out, present in oral and written form – according to the statute of the discipline – a research-based contribution to historiographical knowledge, bearing on a significant problem.

In this description of the different levels of competences in history, the first level – that of history courses for students of other subject areas – in a way sets the scene. The competences acquired here are fairly general and not very advanced, but they spell out four essential elements without which even a limited exposure to history would be incomplete.

With advancing levels, competences become more specific and indicate broadening as well as more specialised knowledge and understanding. Thus, even the second level (history as a part of another degree) requires general knowledge of two chronological periods. The first degree level also stipulates specific knowledge of a period or a diachronic theme; the second degree level adds specific, ample, detailed and up-to-date knowledge. Requirements as to methodological knowledge and understanding also increase, as does the expectation that those so qualified should be able to carry out and present independent work in history. This requirement is introduced for "history as a part of another degree" and is very demanding at second degree level, where the description uses terms like "ability to plan, carry out, present in oral and written form"

---

60. The group does not specify competences for a third cycle (doctoral) degree in history.

and "contribution to historiographical knowledge, bearing on a significant problem". At second degree level, the element of independent research is high; if there were a description of third degree competences, the research element would be even stronger.

In view of the strong national element in many history programmes, it is interesting to note that even the lowest level described in the Tuning Project calls for "understanding of and respect for viewpoints moulded by different historical backgrounds". This is a major element of the Council of Europe's work on history teaching, as seen in its political recommendations and publications.[61] This further illustrates that methodological knowledge and understanding are an important part of subject-specific competences, but also that attitudes and values have an important place in this context. As we have already seen, the dividing line between subject-specific and generic competences is not watertight, and this point provides a convenient transition to the perhaps more difficult issue of generic competences.

Another example is the European Language Portfolio. The subject-specific competences described in it are specific, in that they refer to learning a foreign language (as opposed to one's native language), but they can be applied to any language. As we saw in the previous chapter, the competences described in the portfolio are very precise, for instance:

I can use simple phrases and sentences to describe where I live and people I know. (Level A1, spoken production)

I can read articles and reports concerned with contemporary problems in which the witness adopts particular attitudes or viewpoints. I can understand contemporary literary prose. (B2, reading)

I can take part effortlessly in any conversation or discussion and have a good familiarity with idiomatic expressions and colloquialisms. I can express myself fluently and convey finer shades of meaning precisely. If I do have a problem, I can backtrack and restructure around the difficulty so smoothly that other people are hardly aware of it. (C2, spoken interaction)

In the United Kingdom, competences are expressed through subject benchmarking statements, and this approach is being adopted by some other countries. The Quality Assurance Agency for Higher Education offers the following explanation of subject benchmarking statements:

Subject benchmark statements provide a means for the academic community to describe the nature and characteristics of programmes in a specific subject. They

---

61. See the Council of Europe's Recommendation Rec (2001) 15 by the Committee of Ministers to member states on history teaching in twenty-first century Europe; see also Robert Stradling, *Teaching 20th-Century European History* (Strasbourg 2001: Council of Europe Publishing).

also represent general expectations about the standards for the award of qualifications at a given level and articulate the attributes and capabilities that those possessing such qualifications should be able to demonstrate.

[…]

Subject benchmark statements are used for a variety of purposes. Primarily, they are an important external source of reference for higher education institutions when new programmes are being designed and developed in a subject area. They provide general guidance for articulating the learning outcomes associated with the programme but are not a specification of a detailed curriculum in the subject. Benchmark statements provide for variety and flexibility in the design of programmes and encourage innovation within an agreed overall framework.

Subject benchmark statements also provide support to institutions in pursuit of internal quality assurance. They enable the learning outcomes specified for a particular programme to be reviewed and evaluated against agreed general expectations about standards.

Finally, subject benchmark statements are one of a number of external sources of information that are drawn upon for the purposes of academic review and for making judgements about threshold standards being met. Reviewers do not use subject benchmark statements as a crude checklist for these purposes however. Rather, they are used in conjunction with the relevant programme specifications, the institution's own internal evaluation documentation, together with primary data in order to enable reviewers to come to a rounded judgement based on a broad range of evidence.[62]

The UK subject benchmarking statement for the Honours Degree in history describes various components of the degree, such as the historian's skills and quality of mind, criteria for content, progression, teaching and learning. It also provides a summary of learning outcomes:

All graduates in history should demonstrate competence in the discipline and the purpose of schemes of assessment is to evaluate the level of competence achieved. In establishing and maintaining history degree programmes, departments should take into account the following summary of learning outcomes. They will not necessarily wish to include assessment of all these learning outcomes in degree classification:

i. command of a substantial body of historical knowledge;

ii. the ability to develop and sustain historical arguments in a variety of literary forms, formulating appropriate questions and utilizing evidence;

---

62. Quoted from the preface to the subject benchmarking statement for the Honours Degree in history, available at http://www.qaa.ac.uk/academicinfrastructure/benchmark/honours/history.pdf (accessed 24 July 2006).

iii. an ability to read, analyse, and reflect critically and contextually upon historical texts;

iv. an appreciation of the complexity of reconstructing the past, the problematic and varied nature of historical evidence;

v. an understanding of the varieties of approaches to understanding, constructing, and interpreting the past; and, where relevant, a knowledge of concepts and theories derived from the humanities and social sciences;

vi. the ability to read. analyse, and reflect critically and contextually upon historical texts and other source materials;

vii. the ability to gather and deploy evidence and data to find, retrieve, sort and exchange new information;

viii. a command of comparative perspectives, which may include the ability to compare the histories of different countries, societies, or cultures;

ix. awareness of continuity and change over extended time spans;

x. an understanding of the development of history as a discipline and the awareness of different historical methodologies;

xi. an ability to design, research, and present a sustained and independently-conceived piece of historical writing;

xii. the ability to address historical problems in depth, involving the use of contemporary sources and advanced secondary literature;

xiii. clarity, fluency, and coherence in written expression;

xiv. clarity, fluency, and coherence in oral expression;

xv. the ability to work collaboratively and to participate in group discussion;

xvi. competence in specialist skills which are necessary for some areas of historical analysis and understanding, as appropriate.[63]

An interesting feature of the subject benchmarking statement is that it specifies assessment criteria. For the Honours Degree in history, these criteria concern structure and focus, the quality of argument and expression, and the range of knowledge; and, in each category, the statement specifies expected learning outcomes for First Class,

---

63. Ibid., pp. 7–8. Internal references in the original text have been omitted.

Upper Second Class, Lower Second Class and Third Class Honours. In other words, the assessment criteria provide indications for grading. As an example, let us look at one part of the requirements concerning the range of knowledge expected.

For First Class:

> Relevant knowledge is both broad and deep. This will include knowledge of contemporary sources, historiography, secondary literature. The range of reading implied by the answer will be extensive.

For Upper Second Class:

> Knowledge is extensive, but might be uneven. Demonstrated knowledge will include reference to relevant contemporary and historiographical sources. The range of reading implied by the answer will be considerable.

For Lower Second Class:

> Knowledge will be significant, but may be limited and patchy. There may be some inaccuracy, but basic knowledge will be sound. The range of reading implied by the answer will be limited.

Finally, for Third Class:

> There will be sufficient knowledge to frame a basic answer to the question, but it will be limited and patchy. There will be some inaccuracy, but sufficient basic knowledge will be present to frame a basic answer to the question. The answer will imply relevant reading but this will be slight in range.[64]

What we can all do: generic competences

As their name implies, generic competences are those common to all. Yet, this statement clearly needs to be modified, as "all" is far too broad a category to be meaningful in this context. Generic competences are those that – at least in principle – do not depend on one's field of study, but rather are common to all higher education graduates. That, again, needs further clarification, as a good number of generic competences may be common to all or at least many fields of study, but will probably vary according to the level of qualifications attained. They may also vary somewhat from one study programme to another, from one institution to another, or from country to country.

We are, then, considering generic competences expected from someone with qualifications at higher education level, and these may vary from one level or cycle to

---

64. Ibid., pp. 9–11.

another within higher education. In a broader sense, however, our discussion will also be helpful for other levels.

The list of generic competences is potentially very long, and it would perhaps be overly ambitious to try to produce a definitive list. Besides, this is not our purpose here, since we primarily aim to explore and illustrate the many facets of the concept "qualifications", to which the concept of "competences" is, of course, of central importance. Nevertheless, the Tuning Project has elaborated a very extensive list of generic competences, and this list will be our starting point.[65]

As a first approach, it may be useful to look at the three broad categories of generic competences defined by the Tuning Project:

- instrumental competences
- interpersonal competences
- systemic competences.

The terms are partly self-explanatory; to the extent that they are not, they will become clearer when we look at the complete list from the Tuning Project. Nevertheless, a first attempt at explanation may be in order.

Instrumental competences are those that serve as instruments in applying subject-specific competences or, in broader terms, in putting one's whole range of competences to use. They may help us communicate, use technical aids, organise ourselves or make decisions.

Interpersonal competences help us relate to others and help us function in our social environment. They include what we are able to do as individuals, such as expressing our own ideas or assessing what we do with a certain critical distance, as well as what we are able to do in interaction with others, a typical example of which would be our ability to work as part of a team. Therefore, the Tuning Project sub-divided interpersonal competences into individual and social competences.

Systemic competences describe competences at system level or, put differently, ones that help us understand how elements fit into a whole – a system. They help us understand how specific elements fit into a whole and how changes in individual elements may change the system. The Tuning Project states that "[s]ystemic competences require as a base the prior acquisition of instrumental and interpersonal competences".

Let us look at them in turn. The Tuning Project's list of instrumental competences comprises:

---

65. The discussion here is based on Line 1 of the first phase of the Tuning Project; Tuning Project, op. cit., Phase 1, pp. 61–94.

- ability to analyse and synthesise[66]
- ability to organise and plan
- basic general knowledge
- grounding in basic knowledge of the profession
- oral and written communication in one's native language
- knowledge of a second language
- elementary computing skills
- information management skills (ability to retrieve and analyse data from different sources)
- problem solving
- decision making.

The interpersonal competences listed are:

- critical and self-critical abilities
- teamwork
- interpersonal skills
- ability to work in an interdisciplinary team
- ability to communicate with experts in other fields
- appreciation of diversity and multiculturality
- ability to work in an international context
- ethical commitment.

Finally, the systemic competences are listed as:

- ability to apply knowledge in practice
- research skills
- ability to learn
- ability to adapt to new situations
- ability to generate new ideas (creativity)
- leadership abilities
- understanding of cultures and customs of other countries
- ability to work autonomously
- project design and management
- initiative and entrepreneurial spirit
- concern for quality
- will to succeed.

The complete list is impressive, but it does give rise to some comments. The first one is that while the categorisation seems well justified, to some extent concepts overlap and other categorisations would have been possible, without necessarily being better. It is

---

66. For systemic skills, the Tuning Project actually uses the term "capacity" instead of "ability" for the first two instrumental as well as most, but not all, competences. We have preferred to use the term "ability" throughout.

easy to see why the abilities to solve problems and make decisions have been listed as instrumental competences, yet they also require an understanding of the whole – systemic competences – and in many situations the ability to make decisions also requires the ability to convince others, either because decision making is collective or because decisions, once made, have to be accepted by others in order to be effective. At least in some cases, decision making may also be seen to comprise interpersonal competences. This, however, is not to argue that the Tuning classification is wrong, but merely to point out that while it is convenient to categorise elements, this should not make us lose sight of the fact that they may be interconnected, and that various classifications may be justified.

The list also illustrates the point made earlier that some competences may be generic or subject-specific depending on the context. Our earlier examples were subject-specific skills that might also be considered generic, such as organisation and communication skills included as subject-specific competences for business studies. The list of generic competences gives us examples of the opposite: generic skills that might in some contexts be considered subject-specific skills. Knowledge and understanding of information technology and of a foreign language may be highly valued instrumental skills in many contexts, but – at least for those specialising in the relevant fields – they would also be subject-specific competences, in which case they would probably be further specified, for example in line with the levels of the European Language Portfolio.[67]

Foreign languages may illustrate the point further, in that for someone specialising in a given language, competence in that language may be subject-specific but competence in other languages may be instrumental. For example, for a native English speaker specialising in Caucasian linguistics – admittedly a restricted target group – competences in linguistics and in specified Caucasian languages such as Georgian, Ubykh or Abkhazian would be subject-specific competences, whereas proficiency in Russian would be a very useful instrumental competence. The point, again, is not to try to devise a list of situations and contexts in which a given competence is subject-specific or instrumental, but rather to stimulate reflection by pointing out that reality is often more complex than what can be committed to paper in a transparent and readable format.

It is also interesting to note that the ability to communicate orally and in writing in one's native language is listed – separately from the same ability in foreign languages – as an instrumental competence. This points to the fact that the ability to communicate is a complex competence. On the one hand, it encompasses skills that are independent of any specific language, such as the ability to express ideas clearly and the ability to formulate one's ideas appropriately according to the context. The latter point is not trivial: whoever uses the same level of language and style in a formal

---

67. As of 2006, the subject-specific competences in foreign languages in French primary and secondary schools will be based on the European Language Portfolio.

presentation to a boardroom or an academic audience as in a television interview aimed at a general audience or in a talk show would probably be well advised to upgrade his or her communication skills.

The difficulty of communicating even a simple message convincingly may of course also depend on other circumstances. Finding the balance between being serious enough to be given due consideration and lively enough to retain people's interest can be a formidable challenge and one that few speakers and presenters consistently manage to meet. Although most people would not find it difficult to win acceptance of the simple statement "I am not a crook", a good number of people have failed to do so, most notably in courtrooms. There was also a famous instance in the mid-1970s when a senior politician never tired of repeating the phrase – with the addendum "I shall not resign" – but ultimately to no avail. The addendum in the end turned out to be factually inaccurate since a large majority of his countrymen remained unconvinced of the veracity of the first statement. The reference, of course, is to Richard M. Nixon, who resigned as president of the United States in August 1974 over his role in the Watergate affair. The problem in these instances may of course not have been the communication skills of the persons involved but rather the circumstances surrounding the message, including, in some cases, the availability of massive contradictory evidence.

Communication skills also rely on competence in a given language, whether native or foreign. In principle, that distinction is not important for one's ability to communicate, even if one may be allowed a margin of error in a foreign language that one would not be granted in one's native language. But those using their native language to communicate with native speakers of other languages may well need to adjust their communication to this fact. This is a problem often faced by native speakers of languages such as English, French, German, Russian or Spanish, and one to which, alas, many speakers pay insufficient attention.

Even among native speakers, language skills vary considerably, and advanced mastery of one's native language is attained on the basis of hard work. In a previous job in my home country, and therefore in my native language, one of my tasks was to assess budget proposals from various university departments and faculties. I particularly remember two proposals, one of which argued for a new academic position because "corrosion is one of the main activities of the Department" and the other because "the current staff is totally outside of the norms in the field". In the first case, they meant that research on corrosion was a main field of activity and so the number of staff should be increased; in the second case, they were trying to say that the number of staff was below the norms for similar departments in neighbouring countries, but this was clearly not the only interpretation possible, nor the most tempting one.

The point about those communicating in their own language with speakers of other languages also illustrates the systemic competence listed as "understanding of cultures and customs of other countries". This requires knowledge of basic cultural norms and specificities, such as norms of formality and informality. In some cultures, people quickly move to address each other by first name, and not doing so is taken as a sign of reserve or even lack of appreciation of one's hosts, whereas in other cultures it is normal to address people by family name and/or by title. Such subtleties may be highly complex, since they may depend on factors (or a combination of factors) such as context, social background, age, gender or occupation.

For example, in Spain, the informal *tú* rather than the formal *Usted* ("you") is used much more readily than in Chile or Mexico, even if in all three cases one's interlocutor is a native speaker of Spanish.[68] Similarly, French-speakers from Québec use the informal *tu* instead of the formal *vous* much more readily than those of France. A different example is knowing what to do when you receive a wrapped gift. In some cultures, one should open it immediately to show that one appreciates it, whereas in other cultures doing so would imply one is more interested in the gift than in those who offered it. To complicate matters further, practice within a given culture may change over time. In Greece, older people would not open gifts immediately for fear of offending the giver, while younger people would open it in the presence of the giver, also to avoid offending him or her.[69]

In addition to such highly instrumental specific knowledge, however, "understanding of cultures and customs of other countries" also includes an awareness that behavioural norms may and do differ, and accepting that different norms may carry the same value. This is not an argument in favour of complete cultural relativism: certain values are fundamental to some cultures, and one may get into difficult and uncomfortable situations on issues such as the death penalty or the position and status of women. Nevertheless, an awareness and understanding of the fact that cultural norms may differ, and that one should also pay attention to them when visiting other countries, is a fundamental generic competence.[70] That, of course, is not limited to those who travel: understanding that cultural *faux pas* committed by foreign visitors to your own country may result from a lack of understanding of your culture and customs, rather than from ill will, is equally fundamental.

This systemic competence also illustrates that attitudes and values are included in the term "competences", at least to the extent that they are translated into practice. Those with a high level of "understanding of cultures and customs of other countries" are likely to place high value on interaction with foreigners as well as to accept that their own norms, values and beliefs are not the only ones possible or indeed of high value, albeit with the caveat as to cultural relativism expressed in the preceding paragraph.

---

68. Notwithstanding the fact other languages are also native to Spain (Basque, Catalan, Galician), Mexico (very many languages, including Maya or Huichol) and, to a very limited extent, Chile (primarily Mapuche).

69. I would like to thank Athanassia Spyropoulou for providing me with the example.

70. Again, these may perhaps be considered subject-specific competences for, say, anthropologists or area specialists, but that is not the main point here, since the possible overlap between subject-specific and generic competences has already been amply illustrated.

Other generic competences listed in the Tuning Project illustrate the point that attitudes and values are included in the term "competences". Ethical commitment implies that one has reflected on basic values and incorporated them into one's own attitudes and behaviour. The ability to work in an international context depends on instrumental competences, for example a knowledge of foreign languages, but also on systemic competences, such as understanding foreign cultures and customs. Initiative, entrepreneurial spirit and the will to succeed clearly include values and attitudes, as well as overlapping with other generic competences and subject-specific competences.

A final point to be made about generic competences is that to a large extent they refer to the abilities needed to put subject-specific competences to use. They indicate the ability to reason, to put together information from various sources, to assess the validity and relevance of this information and to take action on this basis. Generic competences also include the ability to draw broadly valid conclusions on the basis of specific phenomena and to predict behaviour or results in specific cases on the basis of broad knowledge; both these competences are central to research. They encompass the ability to think in abstract terms, and they include the ability to communicate with others, to inform them or to convince them of the validity of a view or position. Not least in this context, values and attitudes such as intercultural communication and ethical commitment are fundamental.

All these generic skills can be applied to specific academic disciplines, and in some contexts they may be subject-specific competences. However, the concept "generic competences" includes an ability to apply the competences to situations outside one's discipline. A linguist trying to reconstruct a language that is only partially attested, a historian trying to explain historical events, a biotechnologist working on stem cells or cloning, or a corporate lawyer trying to establish a business venture in a foreign country all need a high degree of subject-specific competence, but they also require generic competences – such things as research skills, the ability to learn and to solve problems, very possibly the ability to work in an interdisciplinary team and generate new ideas, and most certainly the ability to demonstrate concern for quality and ethical commitment.

Competence: absolute or relative?

One important remaining issue is whether competence is absolute or relative. Is competence something one has or does not have, or is the question rather how much competence one has? In some cases, of course, we have to admit that competence is entirely absent. This is perhaps most clearly illustrated by subject-specific competences. Someone without even basic knowledge of Chinese – someone who, in the terminology of the European Language Portfolio, has not reached even level A1 in listening, reading, spoken interaction, spoken production or writing – is clearly without competence in Chinese. Incidentally, such lack of competence seems to be so widespread in western Europe and North America that some languages use the phrase: "It is Chinese to me," to denote a lack of comprehension. Other languages refer to Greek for the same purpose.

On the other hand, even if most of us know people we consider to be devoid of common sense or to lack understanding of foreign cultures and customs – and lack any interest in learning about them – it is difficult to think of examples of absolute lack of a generic competence. For instance, with some medically determined exceptions, all people have some competence in their native language and some degree of communication skill, though not necessarily at the level needed for some kinds of employment. Few people desperately thirsty will be unable to communicate their desire for a glass of water, at least if they are in a familiar environment. Similarly, almost everyone has some kind of analytical skill and some decision-making ability, but again not necessarily at more than basic level.

Competence, then, is mostly not absolute. It is mostly neither entirely absent or entirely present, but present to various degrees. In formal education, grading scales seek to express to what extent specified competences have been acquired, and in everyday language we tend to do the same, but without necessarily thinking in those terms.

For higher education, it is clear that subject-specific competence is expected to increase with each cycle or level, and this is reflected in the description of subject-specific competences within the Tuning Project as it is reflected, in a broader education context, in the level specifications of the European Language Portfolio. However, the Tuning Project does not offer specifications of generic competences linked to the first, second or third degree. Does this mean that there is no expectation of improved generic competences as individuals progress in their formal higher education?

The answer would seem to be somewhat more complex. Higher education is clearly intended to provide generic as well as subject-specific competences, and there is every reason to believe it succeeds in this endeavour. However, the relationship between educational level and generic competence is much less straightforward than that between cycles and subject-specific competences. All – or at least most – generic competences identified in the Tuning Project are relevant to most forms of higher education, hence the term "generic"; but they are not equally central to all fields of higher education or equally well developed by all study programmes. Some generic competences, such as an ability to learn or to analyse and synthesise, are considered important in all kinds of higher education; others, such as leadership ability, may not be. One programme may value the ability to work in a team; another may place more importance on the ability to work independently.

The Dublin Descriptors, presented in Chapter 2, reflect this complexity. They provide level descriptors for each of the three higher education cycles and for short-cycle qualifications. Most of them refer to the field of study in which the degree has been obtained, but they do so in fairly general terms that could be applied to most fields of study, such as:

> [students] have demonstrated knowledge and understanding in a field of study that builds upon and supersedes their general secondary education, and is typically at a

level that, whilst supported by advanced textbooks, includes some aspects that will be informed by knowledge of the forefront of their field of study. (first cycle)

However, some of the level descriptors concern generic competences, albeit with some reference to the specific field of study, and they demonstrate that expectations increase from one level to the next. An example is communication skills:

[students] can communicate about their understanding, skills and activities, with peers, supervisors and clients. (short cycle)

[students] can communicate information, ideas, problems and solutions to both specialist and non-specialist audiences. (first cycle)

[students] can communicate their conclusions, and the knowledge and rationale underpinning these, to specialist and non-specialist audiences clearly and unambiguously. (second cycle)

[students] can communicate with their peers, the larger scholarly community and with society in general about their areas of expertise. (third cycle)

Degree holders' ability to learn is described with similar expectations of progress:

[students] have the learning skills to undertake further studies with some autonomy. (short cycle)

[students] have developed those learning skills that are necessary for them to continue to undertake further study with a high degree of autonomy. (first cycle)

[students] have the learning skills to allow them to continue to study in a manner that may be largely self-directed or autonomous. (second cycle)

[students] can be expected to be able to promote, within academic and professional contexts, technological, social or cultural advancement in a knowledge based society. (third cycle)

For some generic competences, such as the ability to learn, the ability to do independent work, research skills and some others, it seems possible to provide descriptors that differentiate expected competences according to the level or cycle, but this is hardly possible for all generic skills. One can also wonder to what extent it is possible – or at least meaningful – to develop descriptors for generic competences without also looking at subject-specific competences. Conceptually, it is very useful to make the distinction but, in practice, study programmes aim to develop both kinds of competence, which exist in a symbiotic relationship. Do concern for quality, ethical commitment or the will to succeed increase with each cycle? The ability to assess quality within one's academic discipline should reasonably be expected to improve, but that is not the same as a concern for quality. First-degree students may be as concerned about quality as doctoral students, but, at least within their academic field, they may not be in an equally good position to demonstrate their concern. It is difficult to see why the will – if not the means – to succeed would necessarily vary according to level, and the same applies to ethical commitment.

It therefore seems to be a reasonable assumption that, like subject-specific skills, many generic skills will increase with increasing levels of higher education. Yet, if we refer to the full range of generic competences, it may be no more than that: an assumption. It would in fact be an interesting research hypothesis to test; and, if research disproved the hypothesis, it should give rise to discussion of how the situation might be remedied. However, any such research and the possible ensuing debate would need to take account of the fact that different programmes develop various generic competences to an unequal extent. Devising reliable level indicators for all generic competences with general validity for first degree, second degree and third degree holders regardless of their field of academic specialisation is a challenge to which we are not yet ready to rise, and we may even doubt if the challenge can ever be met.

Part II

The components of qualifications

4 Level

In the previous chapter we looked in considerable detail at the concept of competences, and in particular at how they could be divided into subject-specific and generic competences. Yet, even if this distinction is clear in theory, we also saw that, in some cases, it is far from straightforward to determine whether in a specific context a given competence is subject-specific or generic. Nevertheless, these are useful concepts that help us come to grips with a complex subject, even if we may sometimes doubt how to classify a given competence.

We now turn to the components of a qualification, which may be outlined thus:

- level
- workload
- quality
- profile
- learning outcomes.

These are not all of the same order. In fact, it may well be argued that what really counts is the learning outcomes, and that the four other components should be seen either as part of the learning outcomes or simply as indicators in evaluating learning outcomes.

From a theoretical perspective, there is considerable virtue in this argument. Nevertheless, in practical terms, these components constitute important elements in determining the value of a qualification, and an examination of each element also provides an opportunity to reflect on the concept of "qualification". These five elements form a coherent whole.

We will therefore examine each component in turn, and the order in which we do so is not entirely accidental. We start with the component many people think of spontaneously when confronted with the term "qualification" and end with the most comprehensive but in many ways also the most difficult components.

Levels of education

Levels of education are part of our everyday vocabulary. Our children are first graders or in the sixth form, in the *Mittelstufe* or in CE (*cours élémentaire*) 2, attending *videregående skole* or *sredna škola*. In fact, some established terms stay in common use well after education systems and terminologies change, but that is hardly a particularity of education.

Education is often divided into three main parts:

- primary school
- secondary school
- higher education.

These three parts can be sub-divided, so that secondary education is sometimes divided into lower and upper secondary. The tripartite division has a long tradition, but the boundaries between the parts have changed over time, reflecting important changes in society. The division into three levels existed before mandatory schooling was introduced, but primary school largely encompasses what were until relatively recently the years of mandatory schooling. The age range of primary schooling has in some countries been extended in line with mandatory schooling, but over the past generation or so many countries have extended mandatory schooling well beyond primary school.

In many countries, mandatory schooling now encompasses all parts of secondary school. Nevertheless, the division into primary and secondary school is still felt to be meaningful, not least because the secondary level marks a higher degree of specialisation. Although in some countries specialisation may occur also in primary school, more extensive specialisation is normally reserved for secondary school. Some students go into vocational education and training specifically intended to prepare for employment at the end of secondary school; others follow courses that provide few subject-specific competences of immediate value on the labour market. Instead, these strands of secondary education – often referred to as theoretical – aim to prepare students for access to higher education.

This is, of course, a very cursory view of primary and secondary education, and its main purpose is simply to recall that a division into different levels is not the preserve of higher education. Since higher education is the focus of this book, however, let us turn now to a consideration of the levels of higher education.

The three levels of higher education

As education overall is broadly divided into three levels, so – in many countries – is higher education. Through the Bologna Process, which aims to establish a European Higher Education Area by 2010, what is often referred to as the three-tier structure is rapidly becoming the standard throughout the 45 countries making up the European Higher Education Area.[1] As for terminology, we saw in Chapter 2 that the European Higher Education Area uses the term "cycle" to denote the level within its overarching framework of qualifications; so a first (Bachelor) degree is a first-cycle qualification. We will examine the overarching framework itself in Chapter 10.

By the time of the stock-taking exercise for the 2005 meeting of the ministers of education of the Bologna Process, all but one of the 40 countries that had joined had at least started implementing the three-tier degree system. The 39 countries actually constitute 42 higher education systems, since some countries have more than one system. The example referred to most frequently is Belgium, where the Flemish Community and the French Community have their own systems. In Serbia and Montenegro, the

---

1. Status as of July 2006.

competent authorities for education were the Republics, so that Serbia and Montene-gro had separate education systems even before Montenegro declared independence in June 2006.[2] Of the 42 systems, then, 24 had already implemented the three-tier structure on a wide scale and nine were doing so on a limited scale, while the remain-ing nine systems were engaged in some kind of preparatory work.[3] This generalised move toward the three-tier degree system is one of the most significant reforms of the Bologna Process. Especially for countries that had traditionally had one, long univer-sity degree, this transition was a major undertaking.

Since, in some countries, these reforms were being prepared or had just been adopted, it could be expected that many or most students were still studying in the previous system. Yet, in 17 of the systems surveyed, more than 80 per cent of higher educa-tion students were enrolled in programmes within a three-tier system; in a further six systems, between 51 and 80 per cent of the students were studying in this kind of programme. So, in roughly half the systems included in the Bologna stock-taking, more than half of all students were enrolled in programmes with a three-tier structure. In 13 systems, less than a quarter of all students were enrolled in such programmes; three of these had no students at all in three-tier programmes. In some countries, the previous degree system continues to exist in parallel to the new one and may do so for a few more years, whereas in many countries a limited number of study programmes – notably medicine – may not be converted to the three-tier system. This does not chal-lenge the assertion that the three-tier system will be one of the main characteristics of the European Higher Education Area. Before we consider the present and the future, however, let us take a brief look at the past.

The three-tier system is rooted in the earliest traditions of the university, where spe-cialised studies at second degree level built on a foundation of general culture, the *artes liberales*. Therefore, both the three-tier system that is now being generalised again within the European Higher Education Area and the concept of liberal arts that is a cornerstone of US higher education go back to the earliest days of the university. Those defending the single, long university degree with arguments of academic tradi-tion might want to revise this particular line of argument.

The original university degree system had a first degree more or less common for all students, giving a general education of reasonably high standards. Of course the background to this was that primary and secondary education were less well organ-ised then, and in fact organised education – or theoretical informal education – at any level was a privilege of the few. This general first degree was the basis for specialised

2. Montenegro acceded to the Bologna Process on 17 May 2007.
3. *Bologna Process Stocktaking: Report from a Working Group Appointed by the Bologna Follow-Up Group to the Conference of European Ministers Responsible for Higher Education, Bergen, 19–20 May 2005*, pp. 33–5. See http://www.bologna-bergen2005.no/Bergen/050509_Stocktaking.pdf.

studies at second degree level, at first in the three classic professional fields of theology, law and medicine.

With the partial exception of theology, these studies can also be seen as the precursors of today's regulated professions, that is, those with specific laws and regulations requiring a licence to practise, which is granted on the basis of prescribed study programmes. Today, the list of regulated professions, varies somewhat from one country to another, but it typically includes law, medicine, dentistry and psychology – both developed from medicine along with architecture and certain types of engineering. In all these professions, those who practise can do substantial harm. The consequences may be serious and more or less immediate if medical doctors or dentists prescribe the wrong treatment or err in surgical interventions, if lawyers give clients wrong advice or misinterpret the law as judges, or if architects and engineers build unsafe buildings, bridges and roads. Teaching is also regulated in many countries, presumably on the reasoning that incompetent teachers may do great harm; even if the effect is less immediate, it may be even greater, for the individual and for society.

Paradoxically, in the discussion around the restructuring of the degree system in the context of the Bologna Process, many argue that while this may be a good reform for the humanities, social sciences and natural sciences, it is unfit for many professional study programmes. The argument has been advanced with particular force in the case of medicine. We will consider some of the arguments later, but it is interesting to note at this stage that in the earliest days of the university – and in a very different social and economic context – specialist professional studies at second degree level were based on a first degree of broad general education. This model was abandoned in most European countries. It has, however, to some extent been preserved in the United States, where access to professional studies, such as Law School or Medical School, is based on the Bachelor degree. That degree, however, is much more specialised than the medieval *artes liberales*. The US Bachelor degree has strong elements of general education, in particular in the first two years of study, but also ample opportunity for specialisation through majors and minors.

The second – *magister* – degree was, then, the degree that qualified the holder as a specialist. It is no coincidence that the first professional studies were in theology, law and medicine. This corresponded to the academic labour market of the day. These were broad fields: as we noted, medicine only later gave rise to specialisations such as dentistry. Law was a good preparation not only for work as a judge or legal adviser, but for all kinds of administrative work, as to some extent it still is today. Theology graduates were generally ordained priests, but their activities included many functions in what we now call the civil service.

Medieval graduates with a professional second degree went on to do a broad range of work; one reason for this was that academic study programmes – indeed, academic disciplines – were not yet highly specialised. Universities, incidentally, were then generally known as *studium generale*. Another important reason was that the pool of literate people who could fill administrative posts of any kind was not much broader than the pool of university graduates.

Even a first degree required long studies. In thirteenth-century France, students often spent six years obtaining their first degree.[4] Their starting point was, however, often low, as they entered university at age 14 or 15 on the basis of an often rudimentary education. The Bachelor graduate was then taught for two years under the supervision of experienced teachers holding the *magister* degree before he himself obtained the second degree. There do not seem to have been formalised courses for this degree, and there also do not seem to have been many exam failures. Rather, teachers were encouraged not to let students who were not sure to pass attempt to take the exam in the first place.

The third – doctoral – degree was obtained only after very long and costly studies, and required a public disputation or defence. The most extreme case was theology, where the doctoral degree in thirteenth-century France was rarely if ever granted to anyone below the age of 35. Medicine and law were quicker career paths, as in these disciplines one could obtain the doctorate at the youthful age of 28. In theology, the lower degrees also took longer, often five years for the second degree. Part of the explanation for the long years of study may be the low starting point, but in part it is also the emphasis on rote learning of enormous amounts of material. It should be kept in mind that the average life expectancy was considerably lower than in modern society, so that many doctors of law or medicine can have had professional careers of only ten or fifteen years.

The long years of study were not the only obstacle. Living conditions were often primitive, even by the standards of the day, and studies had to be financed. Not least, exams were expensive because the successful candidate was expected to throw a lavish banquet as well as to pay a gratuity to his teachers. Doctoral candidates had to give two banquets: one on obtaining the second degree and one when they received their doctorate. The doctoral banquet is still a tradition in some countries, but of course the length of study, the expense of the banquet – if there is one – and the study methods have become much more reasonable.

What do levels imply?

If we were to do a quick survey among the proverbial "men in the street", most people would probably equate academic level with competence, so the holder of a Master's degree would be considered more competent than a Bachelor, while the holder of a doctorate would be the most competent of them all. There is much to be said for this view, yet it is over-simplified.

---

4. These three paragraphs are based on Michel Rouche, *Histoire de l'enseignement et de l'éducation I; Ve av. J.-C. – XVe siècle* (Paris 2003: Editions Perrin; 1st edn Nouvelle Librairie de France 1981), pp. 378–83.

The equation arises from the use of levels to describe a hierarchy, in which a doctorate is a higher qualification than a second degree, and a second degree is more advanced than a first degree. Therefore, somebody with a Master's degree in mathematics will be expected to "know more mathematics" – be more competent in mathematics – than somebody with a first degree in mathematics. However, it is not a coincidence that the word "mathematics" occurs four times in the preceding sentence; that is the common element. As we might reasonably expect, a first, second or third degree primarily gives a broad indication of competence in the relevant academic field, as measured by a number of defined subject-specific competences.

As an example, with a first degree in mathematics at the University of Oslo:

> [y]ou will be a generalist in mathematics. You will be acquainted with some mathematical disciplines and develop the ability to acquaint yourself with new fields as the need arises. You will be trained in abstract thinking, and in analyzing problems of a mathematical character for which the methodology for the solution is unknown.[5]

As to the second degree:

> Through the study of advanced topics you will get in-depth knowledge within the mathematical areas with which you feel most at home. You will be able to formulate mathematical problems, analyse these and conduct independent proofs.

> You will develop the ability to understand new areas of mathematics quickly in order to treat problems that may arise.[6]

The first higher education level, as described above, is one where learners gain a broad, general knowledge of the discipline as well as sufficient understanding of it to approach new fields within it. They also gain analytical skills. In other words, they have broad knowledge and they can apply their knowledge for analysis and problem solving. They do not specialise in any part of the discipline. That is left for the study of advanced topics at second degree level, where students also have the opportunity to choose the fields in which they will specialise. At this level, they combine the broad knowledge of mathematics obtained through their first degree with specialised knowledge of certain fields at second degree level. In addition, they develop further their analytical and problem-solving skills, including the ability to conduct independent proofs, which is a significant development beyond the first degree. Finally, second degree holders can not only acquaint themselves with new areas of the discipline, but they can understand new areas and do so quickly. At least if interpreted literally, the difference between acquaintance with an area, which implies a rather superficial expo-

---

5. See http://www.uio.no/studier/program/mit/presentasjon/MNB-MIT_MAT-hva-laerer-du.html (accessed 18 January 2006). Original text in Norwegian.
6. See http://www.uio.no/studier/program/matem-master/presentasjon/hva-laerer-du.html (accessed 18 January 2006). Original text in Norwegian.

sure, and understanding the area, which implies not only knowledge but an ability to discern causality and to connect different elements of knowledge, is significant.

Therefore, in terms of the disciplines in which learners specialise, it seems reasonable to assume that the higher the level of education, the higher the competence. Yet, as we found in Chapter 3, competence is a complex phenomenon. Increased subject-specific competence in a given discipline does not automatically imply increased generic competences, nor of course does it imply increased subject-specific competences in other fields.

As we saw in Chapter 3, some generic competences are closer to some subject-specific competences than others. For example, since the second degree in mathematics described above aims to develop analytical and problem-solving skills beyond those obtained through the first degree, it seems reasonable to assume that second degree holders in mathematics will improve their analytical and problem-solving skills in general and not only in mathematics. It is a lot less obvious that a second degree in mathematics will increase learners' interpersonal skills, their appreciation of diversity and multiculturality, their leadership abilities or for that matter their ethical commitment. Of course, there may be study programmes in mathematics that develop such generic skills, but they do not seem to be inherent characteristics of mathematics programmes, or for that matter a wide range of other programmes. If a course in project development is included in the second degree in mathematics or is at least an optional course, students may very well improve their teamwork and leadership abilities, but that would be more because of this particular component of the programme rather than anything that had to do with mathematics as an academic discipline.

The point is of course not to examine in detail what generic competences may be developed to what extent at various levels of academic programmes in mathematics, but rather to point out that it is difficult to make valid sweeping statements about a specific level of competence being tied to a specific level of higher education. Many competences will increase, but they will not be the same for all study programmes and disciplines, and we need to be more specific about which they are.

This becomes even clearer if we consider subject-specific competences in fields other than the field(s) in which a given degree has been earned. Many mathematics students may well improve their reading knowledge of English if they study in countries where much of the literature is not available in the local language, but that again will have little to do with the discipline of mathematics per se. It is highly unlikely that their study of mathematics will improve their competence in, say, political science, history (perhaps other than the history of mathematics, for some study programmes) or less widely spoken languages, such as Dutch or Albanian.

We can possibly be accused of making a trivial point. Yet, at least in some cultures, those who have earned a higher education degree may be considered as universally wise and knowledgeable. Just think of the respect in which the teacher was held in many traditional villages. Granted, this was a context in which the level of formal education was generally low and the teacher something of a generalist who taught a whole range of subjects. Most villagers might never have met someone with a doctoral degree or professorial title, but if they did, they would certainly have held the person in very high esteem and considered them near universal geniuses – even if being a genius does not require a formal qualification. Nevertheless, the assumption that someone who has earned a degree in one field must also be knowledgeable about many other fields may well live on, even if it is expressed more subtly.

Even academic circles are not entirely free from the assumption. To some extent, it underlies our higher education governance. In European universities, students are represented on the institutional governance bodies, such as the academic senate. There are fewer student representatives than representatives of academic staff, however, even if the students are far more numerous at the institutions. On the other hand, there are generally more representatives of students than representatives of administrative and technical staff.[7] The traditional argument in favour of this distribution of seats on the governance bodies is that the academic staff have the highest competence in the two main missions of the university, research and academic teaching, but students have higher competence in these areas than administrative and technical staff. There is also a stakeholder argument, saying that academic staff have a higher stake in the institution than do students, administrators or technical staff, as well as an argument of citizenship, underlining the importance of the participation of representatives of all groups that make up the higher education institution. However, we need not consider these arguments for our present purposes.

The argument in favour of a given distribution of seats on the basis of competence gives rise to two questions. Firstly, is competence in research and teaching the competence that is most relevant for those governing the university? Even if we distinguish carefully between governance, which sets strategic goals for the institution and considers ways of reaching these goals, and management, which is concerned with the implementation of policy measures and requires a specialised technical competence, it is not obvious that competence in teaching and research automatically makes people good members of the academic senate. In some ways it may, such as a commitment to academic values and a willingness to consider a case on its merits (which is, however, not always a hallmark of debates in academic senates any more than in other and more overtly political bodies). Yet, in other ways, it is not certain that such competence makes much of a difference, such as in the ability to reach decisions or the ability to conduct meetings and votes. In fact, there is now a tendency to redefine the competence needed in academic leaders, as many universities move from the traditional model of rectors elected from and by the academic community to institutional leaders with solid management experience but not necessarily an academic career.

---

7. See Sjur Bergan (ed.), *The University as* Res Publica (Strasbourg 2004: Council of Europe Publishing – Council of Europe Higher Education Series No. 1), in particular the articles by Annika Persson and Sjur Bergan.

Whether this is a good thing is immaterial to our discussion. Personally, I believe it would be a good thing for higher education institutions to improve their management and policy-making competence, but only provided they do not lose sight of their purpose and academic values. In our context, however, the point is that an underlying belief in the universal value of high academic competence and a more explicitly stated belief that competence in research and teaching are the most relevant kinds of competence for members of academic governance bodies is now increasingly being challenged by those who emphasise a different kind of competence as most relevant.

The second question is whether competence in research and teaching – if, for the sake of argument, we accept this as the most valuable competence for members of higher education governance bodies – is universal. Sometimes people argue that it is – for example, when, in some institutions, student representatives do not have the right to speak or vote on certain issues. This is the exception rather than the rule, but that is not important to the validity of the argument. A typical example is that student representatives may not be allowed to vote on research-related issues. When I was a student representative in the academic senate of my home university in the 1980s, student representatives did have the right to speak and vote on all issues. This right was publicly challenged by a professor from another institution who in a newspaper article maintained that only professors were qualified to consider doctoral degrees.

The background for the debate was that a university had granted a doctoral degree in spite of a majority recommendation in the commission assessing the thesis that the thesis not be approved. The commission was over-ridden by the faculty senate, where the votes of the academic staff decide the issue, and the faculty recommendation was then approved by the academic senate, which was not even informed that the commission had given a negative recommendation. The student representatives then argued, and I still believe rightly so, that firstly, the competence that had been lacking in this specific case was organisational and procedural rather than research competence. Had the university senate known about the problems at faculty level, it might well have asked the faculty senate to reconsider the case. Secondly, and this is more relevant to our purpose, the assumption that research competence is universal is difficult to defend. If the governing body had really given detailed consideration to doctoral theses – which of course would have made no sense – and if the thesis in question had been in political science (which it was not), why would a professor of astronomy or dentistry have been better qualified to assess it than a second degree student in political science?

Therefore, the level of a qualification is a good indicator of the level of competence we can expect in the field in which the degree has been earned. The holder of a second degree in mathematics may reasonably be expected to be a better mathematician than the holder of a first degree in the same discipline. It is, however, much more hazardous to draw conclusions as to the level of generic competences an individual may have acquired through a first, second or third degree without giving much closer consideration to that particular degree. Finally, the level of a degree says next to nothing about the holder's subject-specific competences in disciplines other than the one(s) in which the degree was obtained.

Level descriptors

Level descriptors are what the name implies: descriptions of the skills and competences expected at different levels of qualifications. Again, we recall that the overarching framework of qualifications of the European Higher Education Area uses the term "cycles", so here the level descriptors relate to the three cycles of the higher education framework.

Level descriptors make explicit the learning outcomes associated with each level of qualification, and they tend to be limited to generic competences and skills. This is natural, in that descriptions tend to be provided for a given qualification regardless of the academic discipline. Level descriptors state what learners will typically know, understand and be able to do on the basis of a given qualification. This may relate to categories such as knowledge and understanding, practice (applied knowledge and understanding), generic cognitive skills, communication, information and communication technology, numeracy skills, and autonomy, accountability and ability to work with others.[8]

Level descriptors are an important element of qualifications frameworks, and we will take a closer look at the descriptors when we discuss national and overarching qualifications frameworks in chapters 9 and 10. It may nevertheless be useful to take a brief look at level descriptors here. In the Scottish Qualifications Framework, the holder of a Level 10 qualification, a typical example of which is the Honours Bachelor degree, is expected to demonstrate the following knowledge, understanding and abilities:[9]

Knowledge and understanding

Demonstrate and/or work with:

• knowledge that covers and integrates most of the principal areas, features, boundaries, terminology and conventions of a subject/discipline
• a critical understanding of the principal theories, concepts and principles
• detailed knowledge and understanding in one or more specialisms, some of which is informed by or at the forefront of a subject/discipline
• knowledge and understanding of the ways in which the subject/discipline is developed, including a range of established techniques of enquiry or research methodologies

---

8. These examples have been taken from the Scottish Qualifications Framework; other frameworks may use other categories. However, while details vary, the main thrust of the level descriptors is fairly similar from one qualifications framework to another.

9. See http://www.scqf.org.uk/downloads/IntrotoSCQF2ndEdition.pdf, p. 35 (accessed on 25 July 2006).

Practice: applied knowledge and understanding

Use a range of the principal skills, practices and/or materials associated with a subject/discipline

Use a few skills, practices and/or materials which are specialised, advanced, or at the forefront of a subject/discipline

Execute a defined project of research, development or investigation, and identify and implement relevant outcomes

Practise in a range of professional level contexts which include a degree of unpredictability and/or specialism

Generic cognitive skills

Critically identify, define, conceptualise, and analyse complex/professional-level problems and issues

Offer professional-level insights, interpretations and solutions to problems and issues

Critically review and consolidate knowledge, skills and practices and thinking in a subject/discipline

Demonstrate some originality and creativity in dealing with professional level issues

Make judgements where data/information is limited or comes from a range of sources

Communication, information and communication technology and numeracy skills

Use a wide range of routine skills and some advanced and specialised skills in support of established practices in a subject/discipline – for example:

• make formal presentations about specialised topics to informed audiences
• communicate with professional-level peers, senior colleagues and specialists
• use a range of software to support and enhance work at this level and specify refinements/improvements to software to increase effectiveness
• interpret, use and evaluate a wide range of numerical and graphical data to set and achieve goals/targets

Autonomy, accountability and ability to work with others

Exercise autonomy and initiative in professional/ equivalent activities

Take significant responsibility for the work of others and for a range of resources

Practise in ways which show a clear awareness of own and others' roles and responsibilities

Work effectively under guidance in a peer relationship with qualified practitioners

Work with others to bring about change, development and/or new thinking

Deal with complex ethical and professional issues in accordance with current professional and/or ethical codes or practices
Recognise the limits of these codes and seek guidance where appropriate.

Level descriptors may, however, also relate to a specific discipline, as we saw with the example taken from the mathematics programme of the University of Oslo above. The descriptors may even relate to a level within a qualification and thus, taken together, show the progress students are expected to make on their way toward the qualification. One such example is the level descriptors provided for levels within the undergraduate degree in law at the University of Manchester:[10]

Level One: Foundation and Exemption

Level One is the foundation level for undergraduate achievement: a period of initiation into disciplinary and intellectual cultures and of initiation into the substantive body of law which is required for professional exemption purposes.

Study will be

• structured within a well-defined framework of tasks
• limited in terms of autonomy for the students
The learner will

• acquire a familiarity with the concepts, information and techniques which are standard features of the discipline
• develop the basics of generic and subject-specific intellectual qualities
• develop and practise appropriate personal skills of communication and team work within seminars
• be guided to appreciate their strengths and weaknesses as learners become aware of professional boundaries and norms

Achievement will be measured by

• evidence of an ability to demonstrate knowledge of those concepts, information and techniques which are standard features of the discipline in conventional situations and be able to apply that knowledge to novel situations
• a range of techniques and activities that permit demonstration of a number of emerging abilities, skills and competencies
• work that is typically analytical in nature

Level Two: Development and Exploration

Level two is a period of development and exploration of the student's learning capabilities in and through the discipline.

---

10. See http://www.law.manchester.ac.uk/undergraduate/courses/level-descriptors.htm (accessed on 25 July 2006).

Study will

• be structured within a framework of tasks that provides breadth of study incorporating the application of concepts and techniques
• provide opportunities for students to develop interests and informed opinions

The learner will

• demonstrate a broad understanding of the concepts, information and techniques in a wide range of perspectives relating to the discipline
• consolidate and complement their range of intellectual qualities
• further develop and enhance their range of personal skills of communication and team work
• take greater responsibility for their learning

Achievement will be measured by

• evidence of an ability to apply a broad range of perspectives to the discipline
• work that draws on a wide variety of materials
• an ability to evaluate and criticise received opinion
• an ability to appreciate the nature of the discipline within a wider context

Level Three: Consolidation and Expertise
Level three is the full achievement of the undergraduate performance: a period of proficiency in, and consolidation of, the undergraduate curriculum.

Study will be

• partly autonomous
• monitored and supervised through structured support

The learner will

• demonstrate the ability to acquire, integrate and make flexible use of concepts, information and techniques in both complex and novel situations
• exhibit proficiency in the exercise of generic and subject-specific intellectual qualities
• deploy appropriate personal skills
• be effective and efficient, autonomous learners
• accept and conform to appropriate standards of professional conduct

Achievement will be measured by

• evidence of an ability to conduct independent, in-depth enquiry within the discipline
• work that is typically both evaluative and creative

Level descriptors are discussed in more detail in chapters 9 and 10.

Other levels of higher education

The three higher education levels often referred to as Bachelor, Masters and Doctorate degrees – in more generic terms as first, second and third degrees – are the most commonly found levels in higher education, but they are not the only ones. In particular, some systems include degrees at a lower level than the traditional first degree or Bachelor.

One example is the US Associate degree, earned on the basis of two years of higher education. It can count towards continuing studies for a Bachelor degree, which in the United States is a four-year degree, or it can be taken as a degree accepted in certain parts of the labour market. The USNEI, the official information centre on recognition of qualifications, based in the US Department of Education, describes the Associate degree as follows:

> The associate degree represents the successful completion of academic, professional, or vocational programs that are designed to require two full academic years of full-time study. Since many students enroll on a part-time basis or stop out temporarily, the actual time taken to complete an associate degree is often longer than two years.

> Associate degrees are awarded by community colleges, private junior colleges, and some 4-year colleges and universities that offer short programs at less than the bachelor's degree level. The credits earned in associate degree programs are generally recognized by 4-year institutions as fulfilling part of the requirements for the bachelor's degree. Many public colleges and universities have formal transfer agreements with community colleges located in the same state.

> Associate degree programs may consist of some general education requirements plus a concentration, or they may be entirely specialized in a single field. Specialized associate degrees are usually in professional or vocational fields such as nursing, allied health professions, business specializations, or technological subjects. Associate degrees in the academic areas are generally not specialized because the length of the program is too short. Instead they usually correspond to the general education requirements of a bachelor's degree program with a possible emphasis on a broad area such as the humanities. Persons who enter academic associate degree programs often intend to eventually transfer into a bachelor's degree program, and may sometimes do so without completing all the associate degree requirements.[11]

The Associate degree is an integral part of the US degree system, and it comes in two varieties. It can be granted on completion of vocational education at higher education

---

11. See http://www.ed.gov/about/offices/list/ous/international/usnei/us/edlite-underposted-credentials.html (accessed on 19 January 2006).

level providing competence in a specific field; this is generally geared to employment in positions that do not require higher formal qualifications and often give limited scope for independent work or decision making. As the lowest academic degree, giving a liberal arts education with little or no specialisation, it is often – but not always – a first step toward a Bachelor degree.

Higher education systems in Europe have no true equivalent to the US Associate degree, but several European systems have what is often referred to as short-cycle higher education. Typically, short-cycle studies are stipulated to last two years, though there is some variation. In the United Kingdom, for example, a Certificate of Higher Education may be obtained on the basis of one year of full-time higher education and a Diploma of Higher Education after two years. Some institutions in Switzerland have a *Vordiplom* granted on the basis of one or two years of study.[12] Generally, short-cycle studies provide qualifications in technical or vocational areas that are relevant for the labour market, but that generally do not qualify for leading positions.

Whereas the US Associate degree is considered a level in its own right, this is often not the case with shorter-cycle qualifications in Europe. Rather, these tend to be considered as falling within the first degree, even if students' possibilities to transfer from short-cycle programmes to full first degree programmes may vary.

In some systems, there are also degrees that are slightly different from the standard second or third degrees. For example, there the two tiers of Russian third degree, *kandidat nauk* and *doktor nauk*. Both are research degrees, but the requirements for the thesis at *doktor nauk* level are greater than at *kandidat nauk* level. In the Russian view, the *kandidat nauk* corresponds to most European doctoral degrees whereas the *doktor nauk* is at a higher level and has few corresponding degrees in other European higher education systems. Some European countries, however, while they recognise the stringent requirements for the *doktor nauk* degree, tend to consider the *kandidat nauk* as an intermediate degree between the second and third degrees. This view is, however, not accepted by the Russian higher education community. In a previous system, Norway had the degree *magister artium*, which was a second degree with a stronger element of independent research than the standard second degree. This was not a separate level, but rather a variation of the second degree. However, some members of the higher education community tended to consider it as a "superior" second degree.

In Ireland, an honours degree is considered a first degree but it is at the same time considered as more advanced and more demanding than an ordinary Bachelor degree. Consequently, the ordinary degree is a first degree, but one that does not quite fit the standard classification. This is underlined by its place within the Irish Qualifications Framework, where it is assigned to level 7, whereas the honours Bachelor degree is

---

12. *Schweitzer Universitätsqualifikationen/Qualifications universitaires suisses/Swiss University Qualifications*, issued by the Swiss ENIC, 2004, http://www.crus.ch/docs/enic/Publ/list.pdf (accessed on 20 January 2006).

level 8, and by the fact that the honours degree gives access to all second degree programmes, whereas the ordinary Bachelor degree gives only limited access to Masters programmes.[13] The Irish honours degree may perhaps be characterised as a first degree that in some ways goes beyond the most common requirements for a first degree, perhaps – at the risk of sowing confusion – as an "advanced first degree". Yet, it gives pause for thought that the ordinary Bachelor's degree does not, in general terms, give access to second degree programmes, but only to further studies for a second first degree.

There is also a whole range of specialist qualifications, in medicine for instance, which build on a completed second degree, but do not constitute a third degree. This brief overview does not pretend to be complete, but simply to show that while the most common higher education qualifications can be described as first, second or third degrees, there are some degrees that cannot easily be categorised. In terms of student numbers, the most important of these concern shorter higher education studies.

The concept of level, then, designates a degree of subject-specific competence in the field or fields in which the qualification has been obtained. It does not give a firm indication of what generic competences the learner may have, and how advanced these may be, though some such information may be deduced from the study programme. Similarly, it gives little or no information on subject-specific competences in areas not included in the qualification: the concept of "universal competence" is highly questionable.

It follows from our discussion that level is a useful concept in describing a qualification, but an indication of level does not by itself provide a sufficient description of a given qualification. We shall now pursue our examination of the elements that together make up a qualification by looking at the concept of workload.

---

13. See http://www.nfq.ie/nfq/en/TheFramework/DiagramTheNationalFrameworkofQualifications/larger/ (accessed on 29 January 2005).

5 Workload

In our discussion of the concept of level, we occasionally referred to study programmes of a given number of years. In the European Higher Education Area, a first degree is stipulated to take three to four years of study, a US Bachelor degree normally takes four years and short-cycle degrees require at least one and more often two years of study.

A year is a measure of time – 365 days, except in leap years – but, when we say a degree "takes three years", what we are really measuring is not time, but workload. This is made clearer if we are more specific and say the degree "requires three years of full-time study". Workload in study programmes has traditionally been expressed in terms of stipulated study time in years, and this remains an ingrained habit in universities and society at large. Yet, the time spent studying is hardly adequate to express workload, much less the results of the study. Let us first consider the implications of expressing workload in terms of time and then try to define some more reliable ways of measuring workload.

Time as a measure of workload

Simple measures of time are largely unproblematic: seconds aggregate into minutes, which aggregate into hours, which aggregate into weeks, which aggregate into months, which aggregate into years, and so on. All these measuring units are well defined, and the definitions are accepted and applied across most of the world.[14] An hour lasts as long in Russia as it does in Argentina or Malaysia. Granted, there is some imperfection in our time measures in relation to the actual movements of the earth in relation to the sun, and on astronomers' advice clocks are occasionally adjusted very slightly. The device of the leap year adjusts our calendar to the fact that the astronomical year is about 365.25 days.

There is also a looser concept of time, which has to do with how we use it. Local time can of course refer to standard deviations from Greenwich Mean Time (GMT), which are determined by geography. Every 15 degrees we move to the west, we have to set our watches back by one hour, even if there are some adjustments of convenience. For example, the city of Santiago de Compostela, in Spain, lies almost due north of Braga in Portugal, yet Santiago is one hour ahead, since it is in the same time zone as the rest of Spain, which is one hour ahead of Portugal. All Norwegian cities are in the same time zone, one hour ahead of GMT, yet Kirkenes is on roughly the same longitude as Sankt Peterburg, whereas Bergen is on a similar longitude to Amsterdam and, by purely geographical criteria, should be in the same time zone as the United Kingdom. China uses only one time zone, which causes considerable inconvenience in a country that spans more than 50 degrees from east to west. Local time, however, also has a different connotation, at least when used informally. In this

---

14. Some calendars use years of slightly deviating length, at least for certain purposes, often religious. Some such calendars are based on cycles of the moon.

sense, it designates a cultural habit in regard to timekeeping. If somebody tells you a meeting will start at "nine o'clock local time", you have no need to hurry to get there. If, on the other hand, they tell you that "here, 'nine' means nine o'clock sharp", you do have reasons to hurry.

Time used to express workload in higher education is hardly more precise than the second connotation of "local time". There is little agreement in higher education on standardised measures of time. When we refer to time of study, we most often refer to "years", but this is not an unambiguous measure. Like astronomical years, years of study can be broken down into months and weeks, but not all years of study contain the same number of weeks and months. The division into months and weeks of teaching, individual study, exams and vacations varies from country to country, and even from institution to institution. In Europe, school and university years start and end at different times; as a rule of thumb, the further north one goes, the earlier the school year starts and ends.

Occasionally, initiatives surface to "harmonise" academic terms, if not throughout Europe, at least within the European Union. Having the study year start and end at approximately the same time would have considerable advantages for exchange programmes and possibly also for those organising and attending conferences of researchers and teaching staff. However, all initiatives so far have faltered, and there seems little reason to assume they will succeed in the immediate future.

One factor is that the school calendar tends to be a deeply ingrained part of national culture. This again may well have to do with climate. In the Nordic countries, the end of June is known for its long days and correspondingly short, "white" nights and July is normally the month with the least unstable summer weather, whereas by mid-August, the weather can rapidly turn from summer to autumn. In southern Europe, on the other hand, August is still very hot and September can still be a nice summer month. To oblige Nordic students to work in July would border on depriving them of summer, whereas making students around the Mediterranean work in August would oblige them to study during the hottest time of the year and would hardly make for efficient study. Another important concern is that having the same dates for school and university vacations throughout the European Union would represent a formidable challenge to tourism, which would see its high season considerably reduced.

The school or study year, therefore, is considerably less than a calendar year, and, though the exact start and end of the school year may vary from country to country, there are definite traces of medieval agricultural society in the cycles of the school year that remain today.[15] One can also legitimately wonder how long into the twenty-first century the notion and practice of a common educational cycle will last. In the world of work, people are much more flexible about the time when holidays are taken than they were only a generation or two ago. This has to do with two main factors.

---

15. I am grateful to Stephen Adam for making this point.

Firstly, new technologies have led to more flexible ways of working, so that the pattern of fixed holiday periods, when factories close down and all employees go away at the same time, is no longer predominant. Secondly, people are no longer limited to taking their holiday at a time when they can expect sunny and warm weather at home, because they can now travel to places where the climate is more benign. As the technologies and practice of teaching and learning change in the coming generation, we can expect to see similar changes in the patterns of terms, semesters and school years, and that may ultimately have an impact on how we calculate study time and workload.

However, for our purposes, it is less important when study years start and end than how long they last. In the United Kingdom, schools must be open for 380 half-day sessions, the equivalent of 190 days, a year,[16] whereas the State of Vermont requires students to be in attendance for 175 days a year.[17] In 2001–2, the average length of the school year in the United States for primary and secondary schools was 180 days, with variations from 177.8 to 201.2 days.[18] According to the same survey, by the US Department of Education's National Center for Education Statistics, the average length of the school day was 6.7 hours, with variations from 6.1 to 7.0 hours. In higher education in Europe, the length of the study year varies between 28 and 42 weeks. This includes examinations as well as teaching periods.[19] However, the figures do not include periods designated exclusively for individual study, nor periods when students are widely if informally expected to undertake individual study. Nor do they measure the intensity of work during these study periods – when some learners may study very intensively, whereas others may be obliged to do paid work to support themselves – so the length of the actual learning year is very difficult to determine.

Even if we were to take weeks instead of years as the measure of study time, we would be hard put to find a uniform measure. Even within a given country or institution, the number of teaching hours varies considerably from one discipline to another, and from level to level within the same discipline. Beginners on a language course typically spend many hours a week absorbing the basics of their chosen language. They will do some individual study, but typically they spend a significant part of their week in class or in directed study in language laboratories. Natural science students in programmes that require laboratory work or practical training tend to do the same. By contrast, other disciplines rely on a significant amount of individual study. Law would seem to be one example. At second and third degree level, students again typically spend more time in individual study than they do at first degree level.

---

16. See http://www.teachernet.gov.uk/management/atoz/l/lengthofschoolday/ (accessed on 22 January 2006).
17. See http://www.state.vt.us/educ/new/pdfdoc/board/rules/2300_2343_2350.pdf (accessed on 22 January 2006).
18. See http://nces.ed.gov/surveys/pss/tables/table_15.asp (accessed on 22 January 2006).
19. The figures come from Högskoleverket (Swedish National Agency for Higher Education) PM Per Gunnar Rosengren 2005-06-23 *Terminslängd och ECTS*: http://www.hsv.se/digitalAssets/8310_PM_050623.pdf – or, in English – http://www.hsv.se/digitalAssets/8329_PM_050623_eng.pdf (both accessed on 22 February 2006).

The distinction between teaching time and individual study indicates that workload cannot be calculated in classroom hours only. Workload should really take into account all activities that are relevant to the study programme and the student's learning. Even so, however, the number of hours in a week varies according to the country, the institution, perhaps the discipline and certainly the student. This is, of course, not unique to the world of higher education. Work weeks tend to be harmonised within a country, or at least within a company or organisation, but working weeks vary between countries. Some countries, like France and Germany, have 35-hour working weeks; others have weeks of 37, 38, 40 or 42 hours. Many individuals work considerably longer hours than the standard working week, and the amount of work done within a given time also varies from individual to individual.

Even the smallest measure of study time, the hour, is not unproblematic. The chronological hour of 60 minutes is not much used in educational contexts, where a classroom hour tends to be from 40 to 50 minutes. A "double hour", a lecture lasting two teaching hours, will often be a 90-minute lecture with a break halfway through.

One further factor is worth considering. Even if we were to agree that a standard teaching hour was 45 minutes, this measure says little about the intensity of work. Some learners may work intensively for 45 minutes, while others keep to a far more leisurely pace. In some ways, this is similar to using time measures as a substitute for distance. Incidentally, I have heard the comment from Latin Americans that it seems to be an ingrained European habit to answer with a time measure when asked about distance. At least, it is one to which I readily admit. When asked how far away city A is, I often answer "two hours" rather than "150 kilometres", even though, strictly speaking, I am answering another question: "How long will it take me to get to city A by car?"

Such an answer may in some contexts be more useful, but it gives only approximate and indirect information on distance. Drivers drive at different speeds and, to paraphrase Henry David Thoreau, people walk to the beat of different drummers.[20] An engine propelling a car uphill may work as hard as one propelling a car on the level, yet the latter car will travel much faster and further in a given time. Similarly, learners will find some aspects of a subject – or even some subjects – more difficult to master than others. For example, whether we find a language difficult to learn, or not, in part depends on which other languages we know. Native speakers of English will find French or German easier to learn than Finnish or Chinese because the structures and vocabulary of Germanic and Romance languages are closer to English than are those of Finno-Ugric or Sino-Tibetan languages. Finnish has a reputation for being difficult, yet Estonians, whose language is related, will need less effort to master Finnish than English as their first foreign language. Someone studying James Joyce's *Finnegans Wake*, in which the author innovates terms based on many languages, is likely to read

---

20. We should note that Thoreau referred to far more than velocity – what he really meant was that people have different priorities, interests and outlooks on life.

far fewer pages in a given time than someone studying the writings of, say, Ernest Hemingway or Albert Camus.

While this has not amounted to a detailed examination of differences in teaching or study time, it has perhaps been sufficient to show that there is little agreement on common standards in this area. Even more importantly, the discussion above has contained little or no reference to the results of the time spent studying. Those arguing about workload in terms of years or weeks of study implicitly assume that all students do the same amount of work in the same length of time. In other words, the premise is that efficiency or productivity is equal in all systems, at all institutions and in all individuals. This, however, would treat the productivity and efficiency of higher education in the same way as in areas where they can be quantified easily, and more meaningfully. Education is not like those industries that rely on production lines, where one can measure the number of items produced in a day.

Study time may give a rough indication of workload, but for any more accurate comparisons of workload, other instruments are needed. The most common such instrument in higher education is the credit.

Credits

If we go back to our street survey, it is likely that few people would spontaneously associate the world of education with the word "credit". They are more likely to think of finance, where credit denotes a positive balance of payment or, in some languages, a loan. Yet a dictionary gives 13 meanings of the word, including the education credit:

> **Credit a.** Official certification that a student has successfully completed a course of study. **b.** A unit of study so certified.[21]

The term "credit" here also has the connotation of something earned or obtained.

In the world of education, it denotes a given amount of work achieved to a minimum standard. In a narrow sense, the term is based on classroom hours, teaching hours, contact hours or something similar. This means that only part of the learning experience is counted, namely organised interaction with teachers and learners. However, this often assumes that one hour of such activity requires a given time for preparation and follow-up through independent work. An educational credit is thus a means of quantifying learning achievements.

However, if a credit is truly to indicate workload, it should encompass all activities relevant to the study programme, including not only classroom hours, laboratory work,

---

21. *The Illustrated Heritage Dictionary and Information Book*, op. cit., p. 311.

seminars and discussion groups, but also independent study, the writing of theses and term papers, practice periods and even examinations.

In the United States, credit systems were developed in the late nineteenth and early twentieth century, for two different purposes. Firstly, as the number of high school graduates – and hence potential undergraduates – increased greatly, universities needed some way of comparing the work high school graduates had done. Secondly, the movement away from a standard university curriculum and the introduction of elective subjects pioneered by President Charles W. Eliot of Harvard led to the need for a system of quantifying the workload in different courses and study programmes; this also made them transferable from one institution to another within the USA. Charles Eliot chaired the Board of Trustees of the Carnegie Foundation, which became so closely involved in promoting the credit system that the standard educational unit came to be known as the Carnegie Unit. The system was broadly accepted within less than a generation, perhaps partly because Carnegie grants for retirement funds for academic staff were tied to the introduction of the credit system.[22]

One explanation of the US credit system is given by the Fulbright Commission:

> Generally, a class that meets for three hours of lectures or discussion a week carries three units of credit – one hour of undergraduate credit means one hour of lecture and two hours of homework, whereas one hour of graduate credit means one hour of lecture and five hours of homework. An average class-load at the bachelor's degree level is about 15 units per semester, which means about 45 hours of attendance and study are expected each week. At the graduate level the average class-load is about nine units per semester, so about 54 hours of attendance and study are expected each week.[23]

In this explanation, independent study in preparation and follow-up is explicitly included along with the classroom teaching, and the number of credits is related to the time an average student is assumed to spend. Of course, time spent in the classroom is equal for all students at a given lecture (assuming they arrive and leave on time), but time spent on preparation and follow-up is a calculated average, as some students will work faster and some more slowly, and some students will prepare thoroughly whereas others may do the bare minimum. If they do less than the bare minimum, they will fail and not receive credit for the course.

Although the credit system originated in the United States and was widely used by US institutions before it was well known in Europe, in a Google search[24] for "credit sys-

---

22. See John Harris, "Brief History of American Credit System: A Recipe for Incoherence in Student Learning" (2002) at http://www.samford.edu/groups/quality/BriefHistoryofAmericanAcademicCreditSystem.pdf and Jessica Shedd, "History of the Student Credit Hour", *New Directions for Higher Education* 122 (Summer 2003) at http://virtual.parkland.edu/todtreat/presentations/cetl03/shedd2003%20history%20of%20credit%20hour.pdf (both accessed on 24 July 2006) for brief overviews of the US system.
23. See http://www.fulbright.org.nz/studyus/uni.html (accessed on 28 January 2006).
24. Carried out on 28 January 2006.

tems education" the first five pages of links were almost all European. Credit systems are now being developed in Europe for the same reason that they were developed in the United States: to facilitate mobility. There has long been a high degree of internal mobility within the United States, students quite commonly taking their Master's degree at a different institution from the one where they earned their Bachelor degree. To do this, students needed a way to transfer qualifications between institutions, without having to repeat coursework they had already done, and the notion of credits was well suited to the task. In Europe, the same need has been felt as student mobility has increased.

Within one country, this was relatively easily done through national credit systems. These depended on one authority and one legislative framework within one education system. Yet, many students moved between systems and across borders. International student mobility has long been a feature of higher education in Europe, in Antiquity and in the Middle Ages, but it increased rapidly – in absolute numbers, though perhaps not as a proportion of all students – with the evolution from elite to mass higher education in most countries in the 1960s and 1970s. It increased dramatically with the development of organised mobility programmes in the 1980s and 1990s, foremost the European Union programmes like ERASMUS, but also regional programmes like NORDPLUS in the Nordic countries and CEEPUS[25] in central Europe.

The need to transfer credits gave rise to efforts to find a common system, and the European Union developed the European Credit Transfer System (ECTS).[26] ECTS was established in 1989 and has gradually won acceptance as the best system for credit transfer within European higher education. As late as 1999, the Bologna Declaration referred to the "establishment of a **system of credits** – such as in the ECTS system – as a proper means of promoting the most widespread student mobility" [emphasis in the original text], and the Prague Communiqué of 2001 referred to "a credit system such as the ECTS or one that is ECTS-compatible". However, no alternative systems have been developed, and ECTS – which is being extended to encompass credit accumulation as well as credit transfer – is now the only system widely used for the transfer of credits between education systems in Europe. It has also inspired the development of an Asian credit transfer system.

Two developments make the circle complete, as it were. On the one hand, although credits were originally devised to aid student mobility, they have proved highly useful also for indicating workload for students who take their entire degree at one institution. On the other hand, though ECTS was originally devised as a system to convert credits earned within one system to a universal "currency" that could in turn be

---

25. Central European Exchange Programme for University Studies, comprising Albania, Austria, Bulgaria, Croatia, the Czech Republic, Hungary, Poland, Romania, Slovenia, the Slovak Republic, Serbia and Montenegro and "the former Yugoslav Republic of Macedonia": http://www.ceepus.info/ (accessed on 29 January 2006).
26. See http://europa.eu.int/comm/education/programmes/socrates/ects/index_en.html#2 (accessed on 29 January 2006).

converted into credits in other education systems, some countries have now adopted ECTS as their national credit system. It is now a European system in at least three different ways. Firstly, its use extends well beyond the European Union to encompass almost all of Europe; secondly, it facilitates transfers of credits from one system to another; and thirdly, it has become a common system shared by several countries that do not use separate national credit systems.

The basic principle of ECTS is that an average full-time yearly workload is the equivalent of 60 ECTS credits. Actual working time differs from country to country, and ECTS does not base its credits on a given number of hours. This is why the working year has been adopted as the basis for calculating credits: it is assumed that students work 1 500–1 800 hours per year. This is certainly not a perfect measure of workload, and some of the problems of describing workload in terms of length of study also apply to credit systems. Ideally, credits should express workload and not the time spent in completing the workload, but the distinction is in practice less than complete. Without going to the extreme of calling credit systems a way of measuring time by other means, further research and development work would be welcome to enable us to better distinguish between time and workload. Not least, research is needed to test the assumption that an academic year consists of 1 500–1 800 working hours.

ECTS does implicitly make use of the concept of "substantial differences" as spelled out in the Council of Europe/UNESCO Recognition Convention,[27] which – as we shall see in a later chapter – states that foreign qualifications should be recognised unless it can be demonstrated that there are substantial differences between the qualification seeking recognition and the corresponding qualification in the country where recognition is sought. In other words, an Italian credentials evaluator should recognise a Finnish first degree as equivalent to an Italian first degree unless he or she can demonstrate substantial differences between the two degrees. "Substantial" in this context means something like "sufficiently important for the purpose for which recognition is sought to justify granting only partial recognition or non-recognition".

The ECTS system is based on the assumption that the workload of a full-time student is roughly equal in all European countries and the differences in working time are not sufficient to give rise to substantial differences in results or – in more technical language – learning outcomes. This is possibly not an entirely unproblematic position to take, but it is difficult to identify a more reasonable practical alternative. This is borne out by the very widespread acceptance of ECTS in Europe. It is also not obvious that a system that sought to describe credits in relation to working hours rather than working years would prove more accurate, as was shown in our discussion of time, above. If

---

27. Council of Europe/UNESCO Convention on the Recognition of Qualifications concerning Higher Education in the European Region, adopted in Lisbon on 11 April 1997 and therefore also referred to as the Lisbon Recognition Convention. The text of the convention and its explanatory report, as well as an updated list of signatures and ratifications, may be found at http://conventions.coe.int – search for ETS No.165.

we think of ECTS as a currency system, we should keep in mind that the allocation of ECTS credits in terms of working years is considerably more equitable than the remuneration of employees who do approximately the same work in different countries, where working hours and in particular salaries can vary substantially. The academic credits given to students accomplishing the same amount of work at the same level – say, a first degree course in mathematics – in, for instance, Albania and Sweden are much more equitable than the pay of workers in the same two countries doing similar work, perhaps in the construction industry or in office work.

Apart from the average yearly workload, ECTS is based on three further key principles:

• Credits in ECTS can only be obtained after successful completion of the work required and appropriate assessment of the learning outcomes achieved.
• Student workload in ECTS consists of the time required to complete all planned learning activities, including attending lectures, seminars, independent and private study, preparation of projects, examinations and any other relevant activities.
• Credits are allocated to all educational components of a study programme (such as modules, courses, placements, dissertation work, etc.) and reflect the quantity of work each component requires to achieve its specific objectives or learning outcomes in relation to the total quantity of work necessary to complete a full year of study successfully.[28]

Therefore, credits are more suitable expressions of workload than merely relying on time measures, and so far no better measures have been identified. Credit systems vary, but their common denominator is that they express the successful achievement of work that can reasonably be assumed to require a given workload. The definition of credit given by the Bologna Working Group on an Overarching Qualifications Framework for the European Higher Education Area may be used for all credit systems, viz:

Credit: a quantified means of expressing the volume of learning based on the achievement of learning outcomes and their associated workloads.[29]

In addition, credit systems make it easier for students to take on and gain recognition of a workload that deviates from the standard workload or the standard progression. Learners who work longer hours and/or who learn faster than the average learner may

---

28. Adapted from http://europa.eu.int/comm/education/programmes/socrates/ects/index_en.html#2 (accessed on 29 January 2006).
29. *A Framework for Qualifications of the European Higher Education Area* (Copenhagen 2005: Ministry of Science, Technology and Innovation), chapter 2.1, p. 29. The report is also available at http://www.bologna-bergen2005.no/Docs/00-Main_doc/050218_QF_EHEA.pdf. The Tuning Project uses the same definition, but with the addition "and their associated workloads measured in time". Julia González and Robert Wagenaar (eds), *TUNING Educational Structures in Europe: Universities' Contribution to the Bologna Process. Final Report Pilot Project Phase 2* (Bilbao and Groningen 2005: Publicaciones de la Universidad de Deusto), p. 380.

earn more credits in a year, whereas those who for various reasons work fewer hours or who need more time to complete a given part of a course may earn fewer credits, but without failing the study year.

Time, effort and level

As we have seen, the definition of credits is not entirely divorced from considerations of working time, yet it is also not limited to stipulations of working time. At this point, it may also be useful to link workload and level. As we know from many walks of life, different people need to make different efforts to accomplish the same task, and one person may not need to make the same effort to accomplish the same task at every stage of his or her life. The effort we need to make often depends on whether we are in good shape or not on a particular day. Reading a chapter in a book may be relatively easy on a normal day, but it may turn out to be something of a challenge if we are down with a fever. That, however, is a relatively trivial point for our purposes. In discussing qualifications and the workload needed to earn them, we are concerned with more general features, and in particular those that can be ascribed to practice and learning.

An analogy from sport may be a useful starting point. Running 5 000 metres without stopping may well be beyond the capacity of many people, whereas others may be capable of doing it, but they will take their time. However, a group of people who set running 5 000 metres as a goal and start training systematically will probably achieve the goal if they are relatively young and do not suffer from physical conditions that make the task impossible. If our imaginary runners persist with their training programme, they will not only develop the ability to run 5 000 meters without a break, but they will also improve their performance, so they run faster and faster, at least up to a point. Yet, within the group, individual performance will vary even if all members follow the same training programme and make roughly the same effort. The world record for 5 000 metres in track and field is under 13 minutes, but no one in our group is likely to run anywhere near this fast. Performance will depend not only on the physical condition of each person, but also on how well they learn running techniques and other "tricks of the trade".

If we imagine that the task is not to run 5 000 metres, but to skate that distance, the importance of learning the right technique will be even more apparent. The reward of learning may also be greater: the world record for 5 000 metres in speed skating is below 7 minutes. In other words, a top skater can cover 5 000 metres almost twice as fast as a top runner, but someone who does not know how to skate is likely to find it much harder to complete the distance at all, regardless of time, than someone who is trying to run the distance without much training. Running, after all, comes more naturally to humans than skating. Whether they are runners or skaters, if the members of our group persist in their endeavours over 10 or 20 years, at some point they will find that not only does their performance not improve, but it actually grows worse, no matter how many hours of practice they put in and no matter how hard they try. This has to do with the effects of ageing on physical performance, which are fairly individual and which can be retarded by physical exercise. Luckily, the effects of ageing on our intellectual performance are not quite as brutal.

Let us then move to the world of learning and imagine the same group of people exchange their running shoes or skates for books, classrooms, discussion groups, laboratories and whatever else makes up a higher education programme. Let us imagine that they enrol in a first degree programme specialising in a foreign language they have not studied before. In other words, they are starting from scratch, much as they started running or skating from scratch. In the first weeks of their studies, they will spend a lot of time and effort mastering the basics of their chosen language. In the beginning, they will have a hard time identifying individual words in a spoken sentence, and their passive competence will be greater than their active one. If we refer back to the European Language Portfolio, they will be able to recognise and understand more complicated language much sooner than they will be able to produce even simple statements or engage in interaction with other speakers.

If our imaginary group is as persistent in language learning as they were in running and skating, they will make progress and soon – which is a relative and imprecise expression of time – be able to understand the language when spoken, to speak it themselves, and to read and write it. Again, not all members of the group will do so equally well. For the sake of argument, let us imagine that all members of the group are native English-speakers and that their knowledge of foreign languages (other than the one they are taking up together) varies considerably. If they are studying Russian, members of the group who have some knowledge of another Slavic language such as Bulgarian, Czech or Serbian will have a considerable advantage over those in the group who speak languages from the Germanic or Romance families. These latter will in turn have a marked advantage over those members of the group who speak only their native language. Granted, the danger of interference from another foreign language is also greater for those with knowledge of another Slavic language. The group member who knows some Serbian may construct a Russian word for 40 based on the Serbian *četrdeset* (literally four-ten), since Russian constructs numerals according to the same pattern. However, there is one exception to this rule in Russian: 40 is *sorok*. The advantages of knowing a related language, however, far outweigh the inconveniences of interference.

Where does this leave us in terms of academic workload? At the start, the group members who know another Slavic language, even if they make special efforts to avoid interference, are likely to need less effort to reach what the European Language Portfolio labels level A1 and level A2 in Russian, compared to group members who know other languages; they in turn are likely to need less effort than those who know only their native language. Any attempt to estimate the time and effort needed will be entirely arbitrary, but the point can be illustrated by the claim made in an introduction to Esperanto: "A trained linguist will probably acquire a reasonable command of Esperanto after no more than a dozen hours of study. Those who are not specially trained will need perhaps a hundred hours."[30] I will not vouch for the claim, which may underestimate the effort needed even if we take into consideration that Esperanto is a constructed language aiming for simplicity, but the claim illustrates our basic point: that the workload needed to complete a given learning task depends on our experience, prior knowledge and abilities. As our group progresses in learning Russian and hopefully reaches the levels that correspond to B and C in the European Language Portfolio, the members will find that the time and effort they needed at the start to read two pages of simple text is now enough for them to read a chapter or more of much more complex text. The effort it took to write a short letter will now perhaps allow them to write an article on a topic of their choice.

If we move from language learning to learning in general at higher education level, the points made remain valid. Within their academic disciplines, average second degree students will be able to learn more in terms of volume and/or complexity than average first degree students. Therefore, if we want to indicate the workload needed to earn a given qualification, we may well find that indicating just the number of credits is unsatisfactory. We would also want to say something about the level at which these credits should be earned.

At US universities, requirements for graduation are generally expressed not only in terms of the number of credits that students should earn, but also the progression expected in terms of level. These are generally described by the number of a course, as in 100, 200 or 300 courses, where the higher the first digit, the higher the level of the course. Hence, "101" is often used as a euphemism for "basic", as in Woody Allen's quip about taking "Truth 101". Students who stayed with 100-level courses might earn a sufficient numbers of credits, but they would not graduate because they would not have sufficient credits at a higher level.

In Europe, there is increasing awareness of the need to take level into account in describing workload. Within the Tuning Project, a report of an ECTS national counsellors' working group in 2003 raised the issue of linking credits and different levels of study.[31] This report, in what it termed "tentative proposals", suggested that credits be designated at one of eight levels, four of which would be at first degree, two at second degree and two at third degree. As at most US institutions, the level would be indicated by the first digit of the credit or course number, so that a 1 would indicate credits at the lowest and 8 at the highest level. In my view, devising a link between level and credit would be a major development of ECTS, as I find simply recording credits without indicating the level at which they were earned is deeply unsatisfactory. The development of an overarching qualifications framework for the European Higher

30. John Cresswell and John Hartley, *Teach Yourself Esperanto*, 3rd edn (London 1973: Teach Yourself Books), p. 13.

31. "Report of ECTS National Counsellors Group, Antwerp, 7/8 February 2003".

Education Area[32] with level indicators through the cycles of the qualifications framework should make this task much less complicated.

Within the Bologna Process, the Finnish authorities organised conferences on the description of first and second degrees, in 2001 and 2003 respectively. The conference on second degrees adopted a recommendation that makes explicit reference to level in the description of the workload required for a second degree. It stated:

> While master degree programmes normally carry 90–120 ECTS credits, the minimum requirements should amount to 60 ECTS credits at master level. As the length and the content of bachelor degrees vary, there is a need to have similar flexibility at the master level. Credits awarded should be of the appropriate profile.[33]

What the Helsinki conference essentially said was that a second degree should carry a prescribed workload, that most of this should come from courses at second degree level, but some courses at lower level could form part of a second degree, for example where students needed a basic knowledge of a supporting discipline. That leads us to consider the profile of qualifications. We will return to this after considering the issue of quality in the next chapter.

While we may have an intuitive understanding of workload, actually measuring it in terms of education is exceedingly difficult, and it may be even more difficult to measure at more advanced levels of education than at lower levels. The time it takes to carry out a task gives a rough indication, but we need to take account of the fact that, in education as in other walks of life, some people work faster and/or more intensively than others. Besides, as we have seen, cumulative measures of time, such as hours, weeks, months and years, are less straightforward concepts in the world of education than they are as measures of chronological time, because practices vary from one country or even institution to another. While the differences within the world of education are probably no greater than they are in the world of work, they are sufficient to justify looking for alternative measures of workload.

Credits are the least problematic measures of workload so far. They were originally developed to facilitate mobility, but their utility as measures of workload has been clearly established, even for those students who complete their entire degree at one institution. Yet, credits are not an unproblematic measure of workload, since some of the problems related to time in this sense also apply to credits. Time is in fact an element of credits, but in addition credits stipulate an amount of work that will normally be achieved to a satisfactory standard within a given time. At the risk of oversimplification, credits describe not only for how many hours an individual is expected to read, but also how many pages he or she is supposed to read during this time. If the concept

---

32. See Chapter 10.
33. See http://www.bologna-berlin2003.de/pdf/Results.pdf (accessed on 2 February 2006).

of level is associated with credits, we may also get an indication of the intellectual challenge involved in reading those pages.

Yet, it should be clear from our exploration of levels and credits that while they are highly useful elements in describing qualifications, they are still insufficient, and we have hinted that the profile of a qualification may play a role. Before we turn to the concept of profile, however, we will consider quality.

6 Quality

If we want to assess a qualification, we need to know the level of the qualification and the workload required to earn it; but we also need to know whether the qualification is any good at all. In other words, we need to know something about the quality of the qualification. This in turn means we need to know something about the quality of the institution where the qualification was earned and the quality of the education system to which it belongs.[34] To assess the quality of institutions and systems, we need information on their quality assurance systems, for internal quality development at institutions and for external quality assurance of institutions and/or programmes. In brief, we need to be reassured that the institution and higher education system we are interested in are trustworthy, and that we can trust their quality assurance system and use its outcomes.

The quest for quality is not new, nor limited to education. If we go back to our prehistoric examples in Chapter 1, the individuals who were highly appreciated for their specialised knowledge and abilities were valued because they had reached a high level of skill and knowledge, but also because these were of good quality in the sense of fitness for purpose: a highly qualified hunter brought more food home than a less qualified one; a highly qualified medical practitioner – if that is the appropriate term – showed a greater ability to cure illness. Often the quest for quality has been expressed as a desire to reach certain standards. A well-known contemporary example is the ISO standards.[35] Yet the concept of European standards is not new, and it is not always very precise, now or in the past. In the late eighteenth century, Ottoman military officials realised that the locally produced gunpowder was both scarce and of bad quality – not an ideal combination, but perhaps preferable to an abundance of low quality – and took measures to raise the quality to what they called "European standards" (or sometimes "English standards"),[36] though almost certainly without having precise industrial standards in mind.

Quality can be assessed at two levels, which we might call individual and collective levels. If we adopt this terminology, the individual level would be the quality of the qualification in question, whereas the collective level would mean the quality of education provision, normally the quality of the programme or institution in which the qualification was earned.

In current higher education debate, quality is a key issue, and much of the debate focuses on how quality can be assured – and quality assurance means focusing on the collective level. If we return to our imaginary street survey of attitudes

---

34. The particular issue of institutions and programmes that belong to no national education system, or for which it is difficult to decide whether they belong to a particular national system, is addressed in Chapter 12.

35. International Standards Organisation, see http://www.iso.org/iso/en/ISOOnline.frontpage.

36. Philip Mansel, *Constantinople: City of the World's Desire, 1453–1924* (London 1997: Penguin), p. 254.

to qualifications and people's ideas of them, there is a fair chance that many of our fictitious respondents would think of the individual level. In this case, the answer to the question "What do we mean by the quality of a degree?" might well be a counter-question: "How good grades did they get?" Let us therefore first look at individual quality before we move to quality of provision.

Individual quality: grading

If the group of people from the previous chapter – whom we first met running and skating, and who then turned to academic studies – were all to obtain medical degrees, they would presumably all be fit to treat patients. Yet, if we needed medical attention, we might be more eager to consult some members of the group rather than others, and some group members might find they had better opportunities than others to pursue a given career in medicine. Our preference for one or another medical doctor might of course have nothing to do with the grades they obtained in their final exams – we might be more interested in how they relate to their patients, whether they take the time to listen and whether they charge reasonable fees or not. Whether they practise general medicine, pursue a specialisation or go into research and teaching may also have to do with their individual preferences, but chances are that – barring financial impediments and/or social discrimination – those who earned the best grades would be more likely to go into research, or study to qualify as specialists in, say, surgery, gynaecology or ophthalmology, than those who got close to passing grades.

We need only open a newspaper or turn on the television to be reminded that a bare pass is often not sufficient. Advertising is generally not about convincing potential customers that a product meets minimum standards, but rather about persuading them that it is the best on the market and preferably making them believe it is so good that it is worth paying more for it. If we turn to the sports pages, Monday newspapers will not focus on how many competitors finished a race within a given time, but who ran, swam, skied or skated the fastest. In many contexts, holders of qualifications too may need to persuade – or try to persuade – people that their qualifications are better than those held by their peers. Graduates competing for jobs are often in this position, as is someone applying for a scholarship or a place on an over-subscribed course.

Assessing educational achievement is therefore not only about setting minimum standards and judging whether they have been met, but also about assessing relative merit. In education, relative merit tends to find formal expression in grades, and comparison is made possible by grading scales. But comparison of educational achievement across programmes, institutions and countries is made difficult by the use of different grading scales as well as by different use of similar – or even the same – grading scales.

Grading scales

Educational achievement should be assessed in relation to determined objectives, so that a given grade corresponds to a defined achievement. The description would then for example stipulate that in order to get grade X, the learners must demonstrate a good understanding of the subject and demonstrate some ability to apply the knowledge to a specified situation but with scope for considerable errors in form and content, whereas for grade Y learners must demonstrate more than basic understanding and be able to apply their knowledge with only minor errors of content and some more scope for errors of form. If we refer back to the European Language Portfolio, levels A1, A2, B1 and so forth describe levels of competence, but levels of competence can also be described in terms of grades. Therefore, the description of the different levels could also be used to describe the achievements associated with a given set of grades in a language. If adequate descriptions of achievement are associated with the grades, these may be thought of as shorthand for these description. If we accept the description of the requirements for obtaining grade X given in this paragraph, and if this description is well known, we know that someone obtaining grade X has achieved this competence. The description of grade X would relate to how well a learner has achieved knowledge, understanding and skills at a given level.

Often, however, grades measure achievement in relation to other learners, for example all members of a school class, as much as achievements in relation to defined standards – or there is a combination of the two. Grading individual achievement in relation to other learners can be meaningful, but only if the distribution of grades is related to a sufficiently large population. The so-called Gauss curve gives the "normal distribution" of characteristics in a large population and it is often used for the distribution of grades. It may give a reasonable indication if applied to a population of, say, 1 000 learners, but applying it to a class of 20, so that no more than one or two learners can get the highest grade no matter how well numbers three and four do, makes little sense. A humorous example of the same question appears in Garrison Keillor's description of Lake Wobegon, the imaginary Minnesota community founded by Germans and Norwegians, as a place where "all the children are above average".

Stipulating a grade distribution can be justified for large populations of learners, in particular where grades in several education or grading systems need to be compared. The guidelines for grading within ECTS use a combination of standards and statistical distribution, by indicating that, among the students who pass (those who satisfy the minimum standards for obtaining credits for a given course), grades would normally be distributed as follows:

A should be given to the best 10% of students

B should be given to the next 25% of students

C should be given to the next 30% of students

D should be given to the next 25% of students

E should be given to the next (bottom) 10% of students

This indication of how ECTS grades would normally be distributed has a function beyond that of guiding teachers in their grading. It is even more useful in guiding the conversion of grades from different systems into ECTS grades. If, in an institution using four passing grades, the best grade is obtained by 10 or 12 per cent of all students, this would be a strong indication that it is roughly equivalent to an A grade in the ECTS system; if, however, 20–25 per cent of students obtain the best grade, the institution would need to give closer consideration to how it would translate this into the ECTS system, since, on the basis of experience, it would seem unlikely that 20 or 25 per cent of a large student population would achieve an A grade. On the other hand, some students clearly would, so it would also be unfair to assume that the top grade in this imaginary system corresponds only to a B, the second-best grade in the ECTS system. In this case, the institution would probably need to re-examine its grading practice.

The ECTS grading scale also makes a distinction between the grades FX and F that are used for unsuccessful students. FX means: "fail – some more work required to pass" and F means: "fail – considerable further work required".[37] In these cases, the guidelines do not specify what percentage of failing students should receive grade FX and what percentage grade F, nor what percentage of students should fail. These grades are entirely performance-based.

The point should also be made that the ECTS scale was devised as a translation mechanism between grading scales used in different countries and different institutions. It was not devised as a freestanding grading scale, and therefore the different levels of achievement were not defined on the basis of learning outcomes. As the ECTS scale is now being adopted as the national grading scale by some countries, there is every reason to encourage research on whether the adoption of the ECTS scale as a grading scale proper – rather than as a translation mechanism – has been preceded by work linking the grades to achievements and learning outcomes, and also on the extent to which these considerations are comparable in the countries concerned. If they are not, we could end up with a similar-looking grading scale being used very differently in European countries. A seemingly similar European grading scale could in this case come to mask very different practices and considerations of the relationships between a given grade and the learning outcome it certifies.

How accurately can educational achievement be measured?

The example of the Gauss (normal distribution) curve points to another dimension of grades: how accurately they measure achievements. Grading is not an exact science, and systems vary in how accurately they try to measure achievements. The ECTS grading scale distinguishes five levels of achievement at or above the minimum score needed to pass the course, and 80 per cent of learners who pass are expected to obtain

---

37. See http://europa.eu.int/comm/education/programmes/socrates/ects/index_en.html (accessed on 3 February 2006).

one of the three middle-range grades; of the rest, 10 per cent are top learners, and 10 per cent score in the lowest pass category.

In a sizeable student population, the ECTS system will give us an indication of relative performance, but it will hardly enable us to establish fine distinctions between the results obtained. However, other grading systems use more categories. The Netherlands uses a system of 1 to 10, where grades are described as follows:[38]

10 outstanding

9 very good

8 good

7 very satisfactory

6 satisfactory

5 fail

4 unsatisfactory

3 very unsatisfactory

2 poor

1 very poor

Five of the ten grades in the Dutch system are passing grades and five are failing grades. Therefore, while the system at first sight seems to allow finer distinctions of grading than the ECTS system, it in fact has the same number of passing grades, but a broader range of failing grades. The system also indicates a level of achievement associated with each grade but, at least as described above, these descriptions are less than self-explanatory. Although terms like outstanding, very good and good, as well as unsatisfactory and poor with their accompanying qualifiers, are readily comprehensible, it is not clear why "very satisfactory" should be – well, less satisfactory – than "good". The description from which this sketch is taken also notes that grades 9 and 10 are rarely given, so that most students who succeed receive one of three grades, ranging from "satisfactory" through "very satisfactory" to "good". The distinction between "fail" and "unsatisfactory" is also not immediately apparent. Perhaps the ambiguity arises from an attempt at describing degrees of achievement by one word only, so that the text is less an explanation of the grading scale and more an attempt to replace a number by a word.

The French grading system expresses finer distinctions still, as it runs from 1 to 20, with 10 as the lowest passing grade. As in the Dutch system, half the grades are failing grades, and the very best grades are rarely given. From observing the French school system from the vantage point of a parent, I found that typical passing grades ran

---

38. See http://www.utwente.nl/en/education/grading_system.doc/ (accessed on 3 February 2006).

from 11 to 14, or perhaps 15. Even though the grading system theoretically makes fine distinctions, the majority of students seem to fall into one of four or five, rather than one of twenty, categories.

Quite apart from the question of why a grading system would find merit in making fine distinctions among performances that were too poor to reach the pass level, the Dutch and French examples raise the question: How precisely can educational achievement be measured in meaningful ways? Let us illustrate this question with an example from Norway. The current grading system in Norwegian higher education – introduced as part of the comprehensive reforms furthering the Bologna Process – uses the ECTS grading scale. The previous system was more finely tuned. For humanities, social sciences and natural sciences, the scale ran from 1.0 (the best possible performance) to 6.0, with 4.0 as the lowest passing grade.

Therefore, though at first there would seem to be four passing grades, the use of decimal points made the system (potentially) ten times as precise. For example, in some disciplines a grade of 2.7 was required for access to the second degree programme. Now it can be argued that any cut-off point is to some extent arbitrary, but one might well ask whether the distinction between a grade of 2.7 and one of 2.8 was significant in terms of learning outcomes. It clearly was in terms of effect, since the first grade could be sufficient for access to the second degree programme while the second often was not. It is easier to intuitively grasp the difference between grades A, B, C, D and E in the ECTS system. In law and economics, a grading system of 1.0–4.0 was used, with 3.15 as the lowest passing grade. This system gave rise to the expression of a "pi (π) lawyer" to denote an unreliable lawyer who had barely passed his exams, since in mathematics π equals 3.14. While it is easy to see that a lawyer who obtains a grade of 2.55 has achieved significantly better results than his colleague the π lawyer, it is considerably less easy to persuade oneself that the difference between 2.55 and 2.56 is meaningful.

The Norwegian example also illustrates how the same grading scale could be used very differently. On the face of it, one would assume that second degree students with grade 2.0 in mathematics, political science and Italian had achieved roughly equal results. However, the distribution of grades was entirely different in some disciplines and faculties, though they all used the same 1.0–6.0 scale. Broadly speaking, grades in the 1.7–2.0 range were not uncommon in natural sciences, but they were excellent grades in humanities and quite outstanding in social sciences. Employers faced with applicants from different disciplines therefore needed intimate knowledge of grading practice to avoid making potentially serious mistakes. The situation was particularly challenging in geography because natural geography was part of the Faculty of Natural Sciences, cultural geography was in the Faculty of Humanities and the two branches of geography adhered to the grading practices of their respective faculties. A cultural geographer competing with a natural geographer had to hope that those assessing the applications were well informed about the practice of grading.

Consistent use of grades?

Some people would question whether grading is useful, fair or even possible, and hence they question whether it is useful or relevant to try to assess how much better than the minimum standard a given educational achievement is, but we need not go into this discussion here. For our purposes, we may take as a given that most higher education systems use grading. There are also clear indications that employers[39] as well as admissions officers consider grades an important, though far from the only, criterion for selection. I personally take the view that it is possible, useful and fair to distinguish outstanding educational achievement from that which goes only a little beyond the minimum acceptable.

However, the examples above give reasons to be sceptical of the utility of trying to make very fine distinctions of grading. It would be difficult to argue that any education system has identified the perfect grading system, but the ECTS grading scale, which distinguishes five levels of acceptable performance, seems to be a reasonable solution. It also has the merit of indicating only two degrees of failure.

Ideally, then, we should see grades as indicating a broad spread of achievement, but we should avoid trying to make fine distinctions between achievements at roughly the same level. Ideally, grades should be based on established standards rather than on average distribution of achievement, but in practice they are based on a combination of described standards and average distribution in a sizeable group. Trying to apply this average distribution to a small group could easily give rise to distortions that would undermine the basic assumption that grades express individual levels of achievement. For instance, if 12 students in a group of 20 obtain an ECTS grade of B, this does not necessarily mean that the grading system was used badly. It could mean that the group has a high proportion of academically proficient students.

Ultimately, just as some learners progress faster than others and some degrees are more advanced than others, so we should be willing and able to discriminate between various levels of achievement beyond the minimum requirement. However, this should be done within reason, and we should not read more into a grading system than it can actually tell us. With this caveat, individual performance should be an integral part of the concept of qualifications.

Quality of provision: institutions and programmes

So far in this chapter we have dealt with the commonly accepted assumption that, provided with equal conditions, individual learners will perform differently and reach various degrees of achievement. However, we also recognise that the conditions and characteristics of the study programmes and institutions at which they pursue their learning are of great importance to the results obtained by learners. In other words,

---

39. As an example, see http://forbruker.no/jobbogstudier/studier/article1217508.ece (accessed on 8 February 2006).

the quality of institutions and programmes will influence what we may term individual quality.

This is one of the major issues in current higher education debate in Europe, and the debate is conducted under the heading "quality assurance". The topic and the debate around it are far too vast to be adequately summarised in a book on qualifications, yet we cannot entirely ignore the quality debate. Without pretending to be exhaustive or original, we will therefore look at some elements of the quality debate that are particularly relevant to qualifications.

The first point to be made is perhaps that, even though much of the higher education debate focuses on quality assurance, the first consideration should be quality itself. Quality assurance should be a methodology of assessing quality, so it presupposes that there is quality to assess and assure in the first place. Secondly, the term "assurance" may be understood as referring to a steady state, but quality is not static. In one sense, quality is like natural languages: if they cease to develop, they eventually cease to exist. We will refer to "quality assurance", but with these caveats in mind, and we will use the term in a broad sense.

We may also wish to give consideration to what is meant by quality. A dictionary definition of quality is "excellence, superiority" or "degree or grade of excellence".[40] The same dictionary also defines quality as "a characteristic or attribute of something; property; a feature" and "the natural or essential character of something".

Quality in education is closely related to the concept of excellence, and we would hope that quality would also be an essential characteristic of education. However, it has proved difficult to reach agreement on what this actually means in practice. The Tuning Project maintains that "the general objective of the entire higher education sector must be to create, enhance and guarantee the best and most appropriate experience of higher education possible for the student".[41] Tuning further underlines that any higher education programme "should be of relevance for society, lead to employment, prepare for citizenship, be recognized by academia and sufficiently transparent and comparible [sic] to facilitate mobility and recognition".[42]

It is also quite common to refer to quality as encompassing both fitness *for* purpose and fitness *of* purpose. The first describes whether a given arrangement or mechanism is likely to achieve its stated goals, while the second describes whether those goals are in fact appropriate. If the stated goal of a study programme is to enable native speakers of French to analyse eighteenth-century English literature – and only that – the pro-

---

40. *The Illustrated Heritage Dictionary and Information Book,* op. cit., pp. 1067–8.
41. Julia González and Robert Wagenaar (eds), *TUNING Educational Structures in Europe: Universities' Contribution to the Bologna Process. Final Report Pilot Project Phase 2* (Bilbao and Groningen 2005: Publicaciones de la Universidad de Deusto), p. 271.
42. Ibid., p. 272.

gramme will be fit *for* purpose if its graduates are able to write good analyses of eighteenth-century English literature, even if they have to do so in French because their English language competence is entirely limited to reading skills. Whether the programme has achieved fitness *of* purpose is another matter, and such a study programme is unlikely to be considered relevant nowadays unless we consider active speaking and writing skills as immaterial to graduates of any English language study programme. The example is not entirely far-fetched, since many university programmes in foreign languages until a couple of generations ago strongly focused on the study of the literature of the target language and considered students' ability to use the language in practice at best as incidental, at worst as irrelevant to academic study. Luckily, times are changing and the definition of fitness of purpose with them.

Internal and external quality assurance

Much of the current discussion on quality assurance focuses on the responsibility of public authorities to ensure that public funds for higher education go only to institutions of sufficient quality and that students, employers and other users of qualifications have reliable information about the quality of a given institution or programme. The authorities also have a responsibility to provide foreign partners with reliable information about the quality of the institutions and programmes that make up their higher education system. For example, the Slovenian authorities should provide information to the competent authorities of other countries on the quality of the institutions and programmes that are a part of the Slovenian higher education system.

Yet, there is also agreement that the main responsibility for developing and ensuring the quality of study programmes – and of research – lies with the higher education institutions themselves. Within the Bologna Process, this was recognised explicitly by the ministers of education, who in their Berlin Communiqué of 2003 stated that:

> consistent with the principle of institutional autonomy, the primary responsibility for quality assurance in higher education lies with each institution itself and this provides the basis for real accountability of the academic system within the national quality framework.

In many contexts, we distinguish between internal and external quality assurance. As shown above, quality development tends to be seen as more prominent in internal quality assurance and accountability (including justifying the use of public funds) as a more important characteristic of external quality assurance. Nevertheless, both accountability and quality development are goals for both kinds of quality assurance.

Internal quality assurance refers to the work of each higher education institution – or its components, such as faculties and departments – in order to ensure that its teaching and research are of high or at least sufficient quality. In fact, quality assurance is only a part of this work, for which quality improvement and quality culture are equally important concepts.

External quality assurance refers to the responsibility of public authorities for ensuring the overall quality of higher education systems and the institutions that make up the systems. There are, as indicated above, two rationales for external quality assurance: ensuring that public funds (an essential part of higher education finance in most European countries) are put to good use, and ensuring that qualifications are considered of sufficient quality.

An alternative view would be to distinguish between summative and formative quality assurance, where the former focuses on controlling the results of higher education – and hence the quality of provision – whereas the latter focuses on developing quality culture and quality management at institutional level.

The emphasis on quality assurance – especially in its external aspect – is not new, but it has increased greatly since the end of the twentieth century. As late as 1997, when the Council of Europe/UNESCO Recognition Convention was adopted, there was discussion on whether or not formal arrangements for quality assurance were needed. Some countries already had such arrangements; others resisted the idea. Thus the convention does not refer explicitly to quality assurance, but states that all parties should be able to provide information on the institutions and programmes that make up their higher education systems.[43] It also noted that countries with a formalised quality assurance system should provide information on the methods and results of this assessment. Now the discussion is no longer about whether a formal quality assurance system is needed, but about how this system should be designed or should operate. Today, it is difficult to see how a party to the convention could fulfil its obligation to provide information on the institutions and programmes of its higher education system without referring to the outcomes of formal quality assurance.

Quality assurance became an important part of European higher education debate at a time when the provision of higher education was diversifying, in particular through a rapid increase of private higher education in many countries. Traditionally, there seems to have been an assumption that public higher education was of adequate quality, and that this quality was guaranteed by the fact that higher education was primarily financed through public budgets. The argument that publicly financed provision must be of good quality because public funds would never be used for sub-standard provision is hardly the norm in newspaper debates about health provision or public services, but it seems to have been an underlying if unstated assumption in the case of higher education. When the quality debate was launched on a broader scale, much of the initial focus was on private higher education.[44] While there was reason for scepticism about many new providers, the debate relatively soon came to include public institutions. From a quality perspective, the important element is not whether provi-

---

43. Cf. Section VIII of the convention.
44. For one example, see the Council of Europe's Recommendation No. R (97) 1 on the recognition and quality assessment of private institutions of higher education.

sion is public or private, but whether it is of sufficient quality, and the quality criteria should be the same regardless of the ownership of the means of education provision.

Learning about the quality of an institution or a programme

Those who try to select a study programme, appoint a qualified employee, assess applications to a course or make any use of qualifications, need information on the quality of institutions and programmes. How can this best be provided? The obvious answer is to look at the results of the quality assessment of the institution or programme. This solution is not quite as obvious as it seems, and maybe not as obvious as it should be. The outcomes of quality evaluations are not always public; and, even if they are, they may be difficult to read. Also, quality assurance agencies in different countries may use different standards, methods and terminology.

In this context, it may also be useful to distinguish between "quantitative" and "qualitative" approaches to quality assurance. Both rely on factual information, but the use of the factual information differs considerably. In one approach – which may be termed "quantitative" – the emphasis is on statistical information, aiming to achieve a high degree of objectivity by measuring a large number of factors – such as the number of books in the library, computer access, student/teacher ratio, the number of academic staff and their qualifications, research and teaching experience, the infrastructure and so on. In another approach – which may be called "qualitative" – there is less emphasis on statistical information and a more explicit attempt to assess what is seen as the reality behind the facts. This does perhaps imply a higher degree of explicit evaluation – which could be seen as subjectivity – but does perhaps give a more realistic impression of the quality that is to be assessed. However one views these two approaches – or the many possibilities in between the two "pure" models – we can assume that there will be no agreement on mutual acceptance of the outcome of quality assessment unless there is at least broad agreement on standards, procedures and methodology.

Within the European Higher Education Area, it is an important goal that all participants carry out external quality assurance, that the results be made public and that the results in one country will be accepted in the other countries of the area. This requires trust among members of the area, but trust is built up through actions and cannot be decreed. Just as the Bologna Process does not aim at establishing a single European higher education system, so too it recognises that there are different approaches to quality assurance.

The aim, therefore, is to arrive at quality assurance practices and methods that are sufficiently similar for trust to be established and maintained, so that no agency will ever feel a need to reassess an institution or a programme that has been assessed by a recognised quality assurance agency in another member of the process. As in the recognition of qualifications, this means accepting a measure of diversity within common guidelines and principles. With this aim, the ministers of the Bologna Process adopted a set of European Quality Assurance Standards at their meeting in Bergen in May 2005:

A. European standards for internal quality assurance within higher education institutions

1 Policy and procedures for quality assurance:

Institutions should have a policy and associated procedures for the assurance of the quality and standards of their programmes and awards. They should also commit themselves explicitly to the development of a culture which recognises the importance of quality, and quality assurance, in their work. To achieve this, institutions should develop and implement a strategy for the continuous enhancement of quality. The strategy, policy and procedures should have a formal status and be publicly available. They should also include a role for students and other stakeholders.

2 Approval, monitoring and periodic review of programmes and awards:

Institutions should have formal mechanisms for the approval, periodic review and monitoring of their programmes and awards.

3 Assessment of students:

Students should be assessed using published criteria, regulations and procedures which are applied consistently.

4 Quality assurance of teaching staff:

Institutions should have ways of satisfying themselves that staff involved in the teaching of students are qualified and competent with regard to teaching. The methods and procedures for ensuring that this is the case should be available to those undertaking external reviews, and commented upon in reports.

5 Learning resources and student support:

Institutions should ensure that the resources available for the support of student learning are adequate and appropriate for each programme offered.

6 Information systems:

Institutions should ensure that they collect, analyse and use relevant information for the effective management of their programmes of study and other activities.

7 Public information:

Institutions should regularly publish up-to-date, impartial and objective information, both quantitative and qualitative, about the programmes and awards they are offering.

B. European standards for the external quality assurance of higher education

1 Use of internal quality assurance procedures:

External quality assurance procedures should take into account the effectiveness of the internal quality assurance processes described in Part A above.

2 Development of external quality assurance processes:

The aims and objectives of quality assurance processes should be determined before the processes themselves are developed, by all those responsible (including higher education institutions) and should be published with a description of the procedures to be used.

3 Criteria for decisions:

Any formal decisions made as a result of an external quality assurance activity should be based on explicit published criteria that are applied consistently.

4 Processes fit for purpose:

All external quality assurance processes should be designed specifically to ensure their fitness to achieve the aims and objectives set for them.

5 Reporting:

Reports should be published and should be written in a style which is clear and readily accessible to their intended readership. Any decisions, commendations or recommendations contained in reports should be easy for a reader to find.

6 Follow-up procedures:

Quality assurance processes which contain recommendations for action or which require a subsequent action plan, should have a predetermined follow-up procedure which is implemented consistently.

7 Periodic reviews:

External quality assurance of institutions and/or programmes should be undertaken on a cyclical basis. The length of the cycle and the review procedures to be used should be clearly defined and published in advance.

8 System-wide analyses:

Quality assurance agencies should produce from time to time summary reports describing and analysing the general findings of their reviews, evaluations, assessments etc.

C. European standards for external quality assurance agencies

1 Use of external quality assurance procedures for higher education:

The external quality assurance of agencies should take into account the presence and effectiveness of the external quality assurance processes described in Part B above.

2 Official status:

Agencies should be formally recognised by competent public authorities in the European Higher Education Area as agencies with responsibilities for external quality assurance and should have an established legal basis. They should comply with any requirements of the legislative jurisdictions within which they operate.

3 Activities:

Agencies should undertake external quality assurance activities (at institutional or programme level) on a regular basis.

4 Resources:

Agencies should have adequate and proportional resources, both human and financial, to enable them to organise and run their external quality assurance process(es) in an effective and efficient manner, with appropriate provision for the development of their processes and procedures.

5 Mission statement:

Agencies should have clear and explicit goals and objectives for their work, contained in a publicly available statement.

6 Independence:

Agencies should be independent to the extent both that they have autonomous responsibility for their operations and that the conclusions and recommendations made in their reports cannot be influenced by third parties such as higher education institutions, ministries or other stakeholders.

7 External quality assurance criteria and processes used by the agencies:

The processes, criteria and procedures used by agencies should be pre-defined and publicly available. These processes will normally be expected to include:

1 a self-assessment or equivalent procedure by the subject of the quality assurance process;

2 an external assessment by a group of experts, including, as appropriate, (a) student member(s), and site visits as decided by the agency;

3 publication of a report, including any decisions, recommendations or other formal outcomes;

4 a follow-up procedure to review actions taken by the subject of the quality assurance process in the light of any recommendations contained in the report.

8 Accountability procedures:

Agencies should have in place procedures for their own accountability.[45]

Those who assess qualifications or who consider enrolling in a study programme are rarely quality assurance specialists. They need not be able to assess the quality of institutions and study programmes themselves, but they do need to be aware that what we have labelled quality of provision is an important aspect of the concept of qualifications. They also need to be able to make use of quality assessments performed by those competent to do so.

In this, they would of course be much helped if there were agreements on procedures and methods and if the results of institutional quality assessments were made public. The standards adopted by the ministers of the Bologna Process will not put in place a single quality assurance methodology in all of Europe, but they should enable countries and agencies to accept quality assessments carried out by the competent agencies of other countries of the European Higher Education Area.

We must hope that increased awareness of quality assurance will also increase pressure for all institutional assessments to be made public in a form that makes them comprehensible to non-specialists. This is already happening, and it will benefit students, employers and others who need to assess qualifications, but also institutions that offer programmes of good quality.

Level and quality

It is important to distinguish between level and quality. A second degree may well be better than a first degree, but not because it is of a higher level. First and second degrees serve different purposes, and their quality should be assessed in relation to their purpose. This is no different from considerations of quality in other areas of activity. We would not look for the same characteristics in a car intended for family use as in one needed for transporting goods, nor would we look for the same abilities in a sprinter as in a long-distance runner. The quality of athletes is normally assessed on the basis of their relative performance in competition against other athletes in the

---

45. See http://www.bologna-bergen2005.no/ (accessed on 5 February 2006). Go to Adopted by Ministers, then to European Quality Assurance Standards. The background report for the standards may be accessed at http://www.bologna-bergen2005.no/Docs/00-Main_doc/050221_ENQA_report.pdf.

same disciplines. Consequently, votes identifying "the best athlete of the year" are hardly objective indicators of quality.

We may seek to use a qualification for a purpose that is not closely linked to its level; in this case, we may focus on other aspects than level, such as learning outcomes and profile. For example, if our main concern is to find someone whose qualification has developed a generic competence, such as the ability to communicate with a broad, non-specialist target group or perhaps analytical ability, it may well be that someone holding a first degree has obtained better results in this respect than a holder of a second degree. If however we want to find someone with well-developed subject-specific competences in mathematics or linguistics, chances are that we would look for the holder of a second (or even third) degree rather than someone with a first degree in the discipline.

Whether, in both cases, the second degree or the study programme in which it was earned was of higher quality than the first degree would, however, depend on the objectives of the degree and on how well the study programme met these objectives. There might well be cases in which an applicant with a low- or medium-quality degree of higher level would be preferred to someone with a high-quality degree of lower level. If we were assessing applications to a second degree study programme, we might well be reluctant to admit someone with low grades or whose degree was from an institution that had done badly in a quality assessment. However, we would certainly not consider an application from someone holding only a secondary school leaving certificate, even if that individual's grades were excellent and he or she were a graduate of an excellent secondary school.

The example is an extreme one, but it underlines the distinction between level and quality. It leads us to a second and less clear-cut example, that of access to third degree programmes. The normal route is through a second degree qualification, and since third degree programmes tend to be competitive, successful applicants would normally need to have obtained their second degree with good grades at an institution of good quality. However, there may be cases where applicants are admitted to a third degree programme on the basis of less than a completed second degree. We use the term "less than a completed second degree" rather than "first degree" because in some systems, promising second degree students may change track and transfer to a third degree programme without obtaining the second degree. There may also be rare cases where promising students are admitted to a third degree programme on the basis of a first degree, in which case they may well be required to do some extra work as a part of their third degree studies. In both cases, considerations of quality over-ride considerations of level. Specifically, those responsible for admitting students to third degree programmes may consider that the quality of some applicants' first degrees is such that they are likely to do well in a third degree programme even if they need to make up for a lack of level with some extra work. In such cases, their potential (implying potential for level, learning outcomes and quality) is assessed on the basis of past performance – of the individual, but perhaps also of the programme and institution – rather than on an assessment of the level already obtained.

In considering quality, we mentioned the distinction between fitness for purpose and fitness of purpose. This consideration leads us to the fourth element of qualifications: that of profile.

7 Profile

Let us revisit our group of runners and skaters turned students and then degree holders. In the previous chapter we met them as medical doctors, but let us imagine that some of them have pursued different careers. We may imagine a group of 10 people who all hold second degrees, all with good grades – perhaps ECTS grade B – from institutions that have all had favourable assessments by external quality assurance agencies. In other words, the 10 individuals have achieved the same level of education, with roughly the same workload and degrees of approximately equal quality, both individually (expressed by grade) and in the quality of the institution from which they graduated (expressed in quality assurance reviews). Would they all be equally well qualified?

In one sense they would, but let us imagine that they graduated in different disciplines. If the group included a mathematician, a physicist, an anthropologist, a political scientist, an economist, a linguist, a specialist in Spanish literature and a historian of religion, they would clearly not be equally well qualified for all purposes. If the political scientist and the mathematician both applied for a job as a political analyst, one would expect the political scientist to be qualified but not the mathematician. In the same way, if the linguist and the economist applied for access to a doctoral programme in linguistics, it should not be too difficult to establish which of the two was better qualified. However, things would become more complicated if for a foreign language teaching job we had to choose between a holder of a second degree in applied linguistics and a holder of a second degree in language acquisition.

In these examples, we are faced with individuals who have good second degrees, so there is no problem with – or indeed great difference – between their higher education qualifications in general terms. However, the profile of their qualifications decides whether they are qualified for the specific purpose in question, whether that be for a specific position or for access to a doctoral programme.

The overall profile of an institution or programme

As applied to qualifications, "profile" has two meanings, as explained by the working group that elaborated the overarching framework of qualifications of the European Higher Education Area:

> Profile can refer either to the specific (subject) field(s) of learning of a qualification or to the broader aggregation of clusters of qualifications from different fields that share a common emphasis or purpose, for example on applied vocational as opposed to more theoretical academic studies.[46]

---

46. *A Framework for Qualifications of the European Higher Education Area* (Copenhagen 2005: Ministry of Science, Technology and Innovation), chapter 2.4.4, p. 47. The report is also available at http://www.bologna-bergen2005.no/Docs/00-Main_doc/050218_QF_EHEA.pdf.

In the latter sense, the profile of a qualification can be linked to that of an institution or a study programme. This can easily be seen in binary systems, that is, higher education systems that formally distinguish two kinds of institution. Some systems, such as the United Kingdom, have established legal definitions of the term "university", but universities generally offer a broad range of study programmes that qualify for a range of activities without emphasising a very specific professional career[47] and that offer at least first and second degree programmes, often also third degree programmes. The European University Association (EUA) will consider applications for full membership from "universities having full power to award doctorates and that have awarded at least one doctorate every year over the last three years" and application for associate membership from "higher education institutions without doctoral programmes (or [that] have started doctoral programmes but have not yet awarded doctorates for three consecutive years)".[48]

As we see, the EUA criteria for full and associate membership emphasise the research dimension of the institution's activities, and in particular its research training. This is also reflected in the fact that university study programmes tend to emphasise a theoretical approach. Other higher education institutions, for which the German term *Fachhochschulen*[49] has come to be widely used as the generic term in preference to the unwieldy and rather negative term "non-university higher education institution", tend to offer a narrower range of programmes, and these programmes are often more clearly focused on a specific sector of the labour market than university studies. *Fachhochschulen* typically offer first programmes that lead to first degrees or short-cycle degrees, but they may also offer second degree programmes. Such institutions have a variety of names, including *főiskola* (Hungarian), *hogescholen* (Dutch), *statlige* (previously: *regionale*) *høgskoler* (Norwegian) and *ammattikorkeakoulu* (Finnish). The English *polytechnic* was also commonly used as a generic term until the United Kingdom reverted to a unitary system, meaning one that makes no formal distinction between the two major kinds of institution.[50]

In practice, the difference between university qualifications and those of *Fachhochschule* is less clear. In some countries, *Fachhochschulen* can offer a limited number

---

47. Although there is a good number of exceptions, not least programmes that prepare for access to regulated professions such as law, medicine or architecture.
48. See http://www.eua.be/eua/en/member_possibilities.jspx. These criteria are for individual members, i.e. higher education institutions. The EUA also has collective members, typically national rectors' conferences.
49. From *Fach*, which means "subject" but also has the connotation of "trade", as in a carpenter's trade, cf. *fachkunnig*, which denotes someone competent in a *Fach* or trade, and *Hochschule* (plural: *Fachhochschulen*). *Hoch* means "high" and *Schule* means "school", so that the literal translation of *Hochschule* is "high school". That would, however, be a mistranslation, since in English "high school" is generally taken to mean secondary school, which is the established sense of the term in American English. In the German term, and in similar terms in other Germanic languages, *Hochschule* means a school at a "high", i.e. higher education, level.
50. With a very limited number of exceptions, such as the Bolton Institute, which for a long time decided not to seek university status and became the University of Bolton only in January 2005.

of third degree programmes; in other countries, universities may offer the kind of shorter, professionally orientated programmes that are typically associated with *Fach-hochschulen*. In France, special university institutes – the *Instituts Universitaires de Technologie* or IUTs – offer programmes of *Fachhochschule* type. In yet other cases, a university and *Fachhochschule* may co-operate to offer a joint study programme or easy transfer to second degree university programmes for students who obtain their first degree at the partner *Fachhochschule*. In the United States, community colleges are examples of institutions that offer shorter programmes aimed at specific segments of the labour market, typically for the Associate degree, which normally requires two years of study. Some of the programmes found at community colleges would generally not be found at higher education level in Europe, whereas others would.

Some countries, as is now the case with the United Kingdom, make no formal distinction between different kinds of institutions, but specific institutions may nevertheless have their own profiles through the programmes for which they are renowned. A particular case is offered by the Netherlands, which officially translates the "non-university" *hogescholen* into English as Universities of Applied Science. Consequently, those trying to find the study programme and the institution that suit them best may well be forgiven if they find the higher education landscape bewildering.

In terms of profile, then, the distinction may lie as much in the study programme as in the institution that offers it. Graduates from a programme that emphasises applied rather than theoretical studies are more likely than their counterparts graduating from a programme that emphasises theory to seek jobs on the basis of their first degree, and they may be more restricted in their choices if they want to enter second degree study programmes. That, however, is an issue to which we will return when we consider qualifications frameworks.

When used of the character and aim of study programmes, "profile" means a set of traits that distinguish the qualifications gained in certain kinds of institution or programme from those of graduates generally. *Fachhochschule* students may earn qualifications in a good variety of disciplines, ranging from accounting through translation studies to technical disciplines, but the different study programmes have common characteristics that at least in binary systems are perceived as important enough to warrant the existence of and distinction between various kinds of institutions. Movement between the different kinds of institutions is often possible, but less often straightforward.

Individual profile

"Profile" can also refer to the characteristics of individual qualifications or, if one prefers, of the qualifications of individuals. Programmes preparing for access to the regulated professions may serve as a first example, as the functions and qualifications of lawyers, dentists, medical doctors, architects and psychologists are closely related to the study programmes from which they have graduated. There are, however, many more subtle distinctions of profile, as between those specialising in, say, criminal law, civil law or international business law. They all have a good grounding in legal concepts and theory, and will have studied many of the same parts of law, but their specialised competence differs.

To a considerable extent, then, the profile of a qualification, in this sense of the term, has to do with the balance between specialisation or concentration on the one hand and a broader orientation on the other. It would be a rare qualification that entirely rejected the concept of broad orientation, at least within the chosen discipline, and it would be an equally rare qualification that did not include some kind of specialisation. Essentially, three types of courses are seen as legitimate within a given study programme:

- those that contribute directly to the student's specialisation or main area of competence
- those that are in other academic areas, but that underpin this specialisation
- those that are in distinct academic areas and do not contribute to or underpin the student's specialisation, but give his or her qualification an added dimension by broadening the student's horizon or by providing a basic competence in a second academic area.

Admittedly, these may seem like abstract speculations, so let us give some examples, at the risk of falling into some of the many pits such an exercise seems to offer.

A student whose academic specialism is history should earn most of his or her credits from history courses, at a level appropriate to the level of the qualification. However, even first degree history students, who are expected to gain a broad overview of their discipline before specialising, will not necessarily have an equal overview of all periods and geographical areas. History is an all-encompassing subject, and a famous joke has it that the historian's equivalent to the waiter's proverbial "I am sorry, this is not my table" is "I am sorry, this is not my period". Even at first degree level, students often have considerable choice in the history courses they can take and to an extent they develop a personal profile. This could be by period, so they might focus more on ancient history, medieval history or modern history. Their profile could be geographically defined, focusing on their home region, for example, whereas others might take courses on the history of other regions. Thus, Hungarian students might well take courses in Latin American or Asian history, but at first degree level they would probably be required to take some courses also in European history and the history of Hungary and its neighbours.

Other disciplines offer similar examples. In political science, students would probably take introductory courses to the major areas of the discipline, such as political theory, public administration, international relations, electoral systems and behaviour, and political representation. There might also be scope for specialisation through supplementary course work or by focusing on a given region. In a foreign language, students would probably be required to take not only courses developing their practical and theoretical knowledge of their chosen language, but also courses giving an overview of its literature and possibly also the broader cultural and historical background of the country or countries in which the language is spoken. Thus, a student of Portuguese would take courses aiming to develop their ability to understand, speak and write Portuguese, but also courses in Portuguese literature and possibly in the history and broader culture (including music and art, but also political institutions and culture) of the Portuguese-speaking countries.

At more advanced level, students are likely to develop their individual profile further. Second degree students cannot possibly deepen their knowledge and understanding of all parts of their academic discipline, even if their second degree studies may have some points in common, for example in deepening their knowledge and understanding of the theory and methodology of their discipline.

If a given first degree programme in history has provided little opportunity for specialisation, second degree history students will normally specialise, as is made clear by the degree profile elaborated within the Tuning Project:

> In almost all cases the work leading to a second cycle degree [in history] comprises both course work and a relevant piece of research presented in written form. Second cycle degrees may be in a specific chronological or thematic area. In some countries and institutions this is specified in the degree title (e.g. Medieval or Contemporary History; Women's History). In others the usual title is simply History, although the programme of studies depends on the area of particular emphasis. There are often second cycle degrees in such subjects as Economic History, or in History related subjects such as Archival studies, Museology, Archaeology and so forth.[51]

Whatever the degree of specialisation allowed or encouraged in the first degree programme, we would therefore expect a second degree history student to pursue some kind of specialisation. Some examples are mentioned in the Tuning description; others could be Latin American, Asian or African history, Roman or Ancient Greek history or the history of migrations.

Again, it may be useful to supplement these with a few examples from other disciplines. Political science students might focus on one or more of the main areas of the field and also specialise within a major area. Thus, some students might focus on political theory and, within that, focus on the political thought of a certain period or region, or on the development of democratic theory, Marxism or nationalism. Others might specialise in political behaviour and representation, and go further into electoral behaviour in North America, the role of non-governmental organisations or political

---

51. González and Wagenaar, op. cit., p. 100.

representation through labour unions.[52] Yet others might specialise in international relations, possibly with a regional specialisation, such as international relations in the Pacific Rim or Sub-Saharan Africa. Our students of Portuguese might well continue to develop their practical language skills, but they would also probably specialise in either literature or linguistics, and further within one of those. Some literature students might focus on medieval literature and others on nineteenth-century or modern literature, or a genre such as theatre or poetry, or a specific country or region, such as Brazilian literature or the literature of Portuguese-speaking Africa. Those specialising in the linguistic aspects of Portuguese might focus on the historical development of the language, its verbal system, regional or national varieties of Portuguese, or the influence of local languages on the Portuguese of Brazil or Angola.

So far, we have considered the profile of individual qualifications only on the basis of what we termed courses that contribute directly to the student's specialisation or main area of competence. Yet, some of the examples given above hinted at the second element in our list, namely courses in other academic areas, that underpin the main specialisation. We might call these "supporting disciplines".[53] This terminology is also used in the Tuning Project, as in the description of the second degree in European Studies:

> Masters in European Studies (with support and specialisation courses in subject specific areas, for example law, politics, economics, history, business administration, sociology, etc.).[54]

Again, the quite broad discipline of history provides examples. In line with the student's specialisation, these supporting disciplines could be economics, statistics, a foreign language or a whole range of other subjects. Someone studying the economic history of Brazil will need a knowledge of economics and statistics as well as a working – or at least reading – knowledge of Portuguese. Someone focusing on the historical development of Portuguese or on its verbal system will need a good foundation in linguistic theory, and the historical linguist of Portuguese will need knowledge of Latin and comparative Romance linguistics. Somebody studying the influence of other languages on Portuguese will need a structural knowledge of those languages. Those studying international relations in the Pacific Rim area will need to know the history of the area and its main actors, and very possibly have a reading knowledge of some languages of the area.

Our third group of courses that may define the profile of individual qualifications comprises those that broaden students' horizons or add a second area of competence. History students might take some courses in music, geography, mathematics, law or

---

52. Which, in democratic societies, are also NGOs, but which have traditionally played a broader political role than single-issue groups like environmental NGOs or pro- or anti-abortion NGOs.
53. May I be forgiven for calquing this term on the one that has been used in my native language to describe such disciplines: *støttefag* or *redskapsfag*.
54. González and Wagenaar, op. cit., p. 94.

a foreign language. The same list could apply to students of political science or Portuguese, whereas, for a student of mathematics or biology, courses in history might serve the same function.

The distinction between "supporting disciplines" and non-related credits may sometimes be difficult to draw and may depend on the precise specialisation the student chooses. This freedom to choose some credits that do not seem immediately relevant from the strict point of view of the main discipline is also important in averting the danger that the boundaries of academic disciplines become fossilised, by encouraging a measure of transdisciplinarity. Students of Latin American history can hardly do without Spanish and Portuguese whereas, for students of economic history, Spanish and Portuguese may provide an added qualification and broaden their horizon. Typically, a foreign language may not add to the core competence of someone graduating in business studies, but it may provide a crucial supplementary competence. Russian-speaking business graduates will have obvious advantages in the Russian market, yet this added competence may not be relevant in other areas of the world.

Profile, level and workload

In discussing the three categories of courses making up an individual's profile, we made little or no reference to levels and workload. We did make the point, however, that history students are likely to take most of their courses in history. In more formal terms, what we are saying is that within the total workload of a qualification, most work is likely to be in the area that determines the main profile of that qualification. In discussing workload in a previous chapter, we pointed to credits as the best instrument that has so far been developed to measure and indicate workload, even if this instrument is not perfect. What we are then saying is that, within the total number of credits required to obtain a given degree, a high proportion of those credits are likely to be taken in the discipline in which the degree is obtained.

The proportion will vary. Institutions will often have general rules about what proportion of a first and second degree should be taken within the main discipline of the degree as well as about how and to what extent credits from supporting courses and from courses that have little to do with the main profile of the degree can be incorporated. Individual study programmes may also have specific rules on this, in the same way that they may specify which core courses are mandatory for all students or to what extent students may choose courses within their main discipline. Mandatory courses are most likely to be found at first degree level, but they may also be found at other levels, for example in the form of required courses in methodology and the history of the discipline. Certain "support disciplines" may also be mandatory at second or third degree level, as may be the case, for example, with statistics for second degree students of political science.

Credits are relevant to this discussion not only as a measure of workload, but also as an instrument that greatly facilitates the inclusion of courses outside the main discipline in a degree. Before the introduction of the credit system, specific study programmes might have allowed or even required the inclusion of supporting disciplines, but study programmes in many European countries are much more flexible today than they were a couple of decades ago. This is not only a result of the credit system. It has as much or even more to do with changing conceptions of disciplines, interdisciplinarity and competence, and the credit system should be regarded as a technical instrument rather than as a matter of principle. Nevertheless, having an instrument that allows increased emphasis on interdisciplinarity and flexibility to be put into practice has been of considerable importance. It has also been important that the credit system makes it perfectly possible to impose limits on flexibility, so that rules may be established on how many credits need to be in the main discipline and how many may be taken in other categories of courses.

Even if we say that most credits earned will normally be in the main discipline of the degree, so far we have said little about level. At first sight, this may seem unnecessary, as it may seem to go without saying that the level of the courses should be appropriate to the level of the qualification. Second degree students should take courses of second degree level, and first degree students should earn first degree credits, preferably with some progression in level from the first to the final semester of their studies – end of story. If we think of the credits earned in the main discipline of the qualification, we are no doubt close to the end of this part of the story. Second degree students in political science will take second degree political science courses, while doctoral students in history will take third degree courses in history.

However, as we have just seen, not all courses need be in the main discipline of the degree, and then the link between the level of the qualification and the level of an individual course is less obvious. If we refer back to the Helsinki definition of a second degree encountered in Chapter 5, we remember that while the total work load of a second degree in the European Higher Education Area should be 90–120 ECTS credits beyond the first degree, the Helsinki definition also stipulates that at least 60 of these should be of second degree level. In other words, the definition says that some credits may be of another level. It also stipulates that credits awarded should be of appropriate profile.[55]

Let us go back to our students of history, political science and Portuguese. Second degree students in all these disciplines may well need an introduction to statistics,[56] but it will only be an introduction. It would be unreasonable to stipulate that statistics courses offered to – or required of – second degree students in other disciplines be of second degree level, in the same way that it would be unreasonable to offer only second degree courses of Spanish, Russian or Chinese to second degree students of business administration. A basic knowledge and understanding of other disciplines may even

---

55. See http://www.bologna-berlin2003.de/pdf/Results.pdf (accessed on 2 February 2006).
56. The need is perhaps more obvious for political science students, but students working on certain topics in history and linguistics may also need statistics.

be a requirement for students to do appropriate work at second or third degree level in the main discipline. Advanced level political science requires some knowledge of statistics, and serious work on the history or politics of Latin America requires a working knowledge of Spanish and/or Portuguese. Neither, however, requires advanced academic standing in the supporting disciplines.

When I was a student representative in the Academic Senate of a large European university in the early 1980s, the Senate once had a discussion about the distinguishing features of a university as opposed to other higher education institutions, what are now generically referred to as *Fachhochschulen*. Much of the debate was both nuanced and interesting, but some statements were sweeping. When one professor maintained that all university teaching is research-based, one of my fellow student representatives could no longer hold back. He had just suffered through the mandatory introductory course in book-keeping for law students, and his question as to whether the professor's statement also applied to this course drew many laughs but received no clear answer.

Changing profiles

The discipline of history may also serve to show that the boundaries between academic disciplines are neither watertight nor immutable. The reference to economic history in the Tuning description of a second degree in history hinted that few disciplines are "pure" and that history can also be an aspect of other disciplines. Whether we consider economic history to be a part of a history programme or of an economics programme may be a matter of taste and, in more formal terms, of the definition of the study programme. Some study programmes may include mandatory or optional courses on the history of the discipline, such as the history of medicine or of linguistics. These are unlikely to be a part of any study programme in history, unless we consider the social implications of disease, such as the Black Death, as medical history.

Some kinds of history are established disciplines in their own right or integral parts of established disciplines. The history of literature is studied as a part of comparative literature as well as of a given language. The history of Greek and Dutch literature is a part of study programmes in Greek and Dutch as well as in comparative literature. The history of law, or a course with a historical dimension, such as Roman or Napoleonic law, is more likely to be a part of a legal qualification than a qualification in history. At least at some universities, the history of ideas is a study programme in its own right, whereas it is difficult to imagine the history of philosophy or theology as a study programme entirely separate from the disciplines of philosophy and theology.

However, disciplines also change, and there seems to be increasing contact and co-operation between disciplines. Their boundaries change or may be difficult to establish. The disciplines themselves evolve and sometimes merge or split. Where are the exact borders between physics, astronomy and astrophysics? Between sociology and social anthropology, or between sociology, linguistics and sociolinguistics? Is a second degree student working on a Master's thesis on the influence of Guaraní on the

Spanish spoken in Paraguay writing the thesis towards a qualification in Spanish or one in comparative linguistics?[57] Is it even important to know which, other than possibly for administrative reasons within the university? Is it important to know whether the holder of a doctoral degree with a thesis on economic history is an economist or a historian?

In some circumstances, the answer may be that it is. The answer may depend on formal criteria, such as the study programme to which the student was actually admitted, or on whether most of his or her credits were earned in courses defined as economics or as history, as Spanish or as linguistics. The formal definitions may be of importance to the future career of the degree holder, at least if one of the possible affiliations is with a study programme giving access to a regulated profession. The holder of a law degree who has undertaken significant work on the history of law may still practise as a lawyer, whereas the holder of a history degree who has done the same almost certainly will not.

Yet for many purposes, what counts most is not the formal designation of the study programme but the competences the holder of the qualification has developed. The profile of the individual qualification goes beyond the profile of a given study programme, as in the previous example of the business graduates with good knowledge of Russian obtained by taking courses not related to their main discipline. Both competences are part of the individual profile of their qualification and what component of that profile will weigh most heavily will depend on the purpose for which the qualification is used.

By now, we have explored four key components of the concept of qualifications: level, workload, quality and profile. We will now turn to a consideration of how they fit together. This is the topic of the next chapter, on learning outcomes.

---

57. Or, theoretically, a qualification in Guaraní, but study programmes in Guaraní do not abound.

8 Learning outcomes

Learning outcomes should be the key element in describing and assessing qualifications, since they indicate what the holder of a given qualification is expected to know, understand and be able to do. The other four elements discussed in Chapters 4 to 7 converge in the discussion of learning outcomes, since learning outcomes relate to level and profile, and are normally the result of learners completing a given workload in study programmes of adequate quality.

The caveat "normally" is important, since some learners may reach given learning outcomes by other means than traditional study programmes. They may not acquire the necessary knowledge, understanding and ability all in one go, or all in the same way. In practice, the real possibility for learners to acquire the specified learning outcomes by other means, including individual learning, varies from discipline to discipline. It is undoubtedly easier to acquire proficiency in a foreign language by individual study or informal learning – for instance, by living in a country where the language is spoken – than it is to acquire competence in brain surgery in such a way. Besides, formal regulations oblige candidates in brain surgery to follow some organised training for reasons of public protection. Nevertheless, most learning outcomes can in principle be obtained through a variety of learning arrangements.

Measuring or assessing learning outcomes is not new. After all, it is what examinations are all about, and achievements are measured by grades as we saw in Chapter 6. The form, content and objectives of examinations, what is emphasised in them and the details of grading scales have changed considerably over time, but the principle and practice of assessing learning outcomes are old. Yet, the current emphasis on learning outcomes has some new elements, and some learners as well as teachers may feel it is almost entirely new. This has less to do with the reality of learning outcomes than with the increased and explicit emphasis on this concept and with the ways in which learning outcomes are described and assessed.

Stephen Adam traces the origin of the concept of learning outcomes to the work of the nineteenth-century Russian psychologist Ivan Pavlov – the one famous for his experiments on dogs' reactions to real and expected stimuli, where dogs learned to expect food at the appearance of certain signs and reacted accordingly – and the American "behavioural school" represented by Watson and Skinner.[58] While the behaviourist approach in some cases led to excesses, it did emphasise some elements that have become key to the concept of learning outcomes: identifiable and measurable goals and achievements. Learning outcomes, in the way we use the term today, were first developed in Australia, New Zealand, South Africa and the United Kingdom. They

---

58. Stephen Adam: "An introduction to learning outcomes. A consideration of the nature, function and position of learning outcomes in the creation of the European Higher Education Area", article B 2.3-1 in Eric Froment, Jürgen Kohler, Lewis Purser and Lesley Wilson (eds), *EUA Bologna Handbook – Making Bologna Work* (Berlin 2006: Raabe Verlag). The author would like to take this opportunity to express his particular thanks to Stephen Adam for his comments on the present chapter.

are now being developed in other European countries, but the development and even understanding of learning outcomes is still very uneven and many countries still rely on more traditional descriptions of study programmes, where the emphasis is on input rather than output. Thus, programmes may even today be described in terms such as "the programme will include a one semester course in the history of language A" rather than "the successful learner will be able to demonstrate knowledge and understanding of the main stage in the development of language A, to identify the main linguistic markers in texts from different periods, to explain the main developments that have led to the language as spoken and written today and to explain the relationship between language A and other members of the same linguistic family".

At this point, it may be convenient to point out that there is no agreement on a single definition of learning outcomes. Just by perusing a selection of the English-language literature on learning outcomes, Stephen Adam found eight definitions, and these eight definitions are probably only a fraction of those that would be found by conducting a more extensive search. However, more important than underlining the differences between the definitions is to identify what they have in common. In fact, a closer look reveals that all definitions identified by Stephen Adam have their core elements in common. What varies is the way in which these core elements are phrased and not the elements as such. In the words of Stephen Adam:

> It is clear that these definitions of learning outcomes do not differ significantly from each other. A learning outcome is a written statement of what the successful student/learner is expected to be able to do at the end of the module/course unit, or qualification. The key aspect each of the definitions has in common is the desire for more precision and consideration as to what exactly a learner acquires in terms of knowledge and/or skills when they successfully complete a period of learning.[59]

The triple emphasis on "knowing", "understanding" and "being able to do" is an important development compared to the situation a few generations ago, when emphasis often seemed to be squarely on knowledge with less demonstrated concern for its application. The rote learning of facts – or what are perceived as facts – is still important in some systems, whereas others have gone almost to the other extreme. "Encyclopaedic knowledge" may still be a term of honour, but our admiration of someone who possesses this kind of knowledge is likely to increase considerably if he or she is able to put this knowledge into context and use it to explain and not just describe phenomena. An impeccable knowledge of the conjugations of Polish nouns and verbs is not easily acquired by foreign learners and should rightly be admired, but our admiration is all the more deserved if a person uses this knowledge in speaking or writing Polish with fluency rather than just reciting a set of declensions without being able to put them into the context of the living language.

---

59. Ibid., p. 5.

Assessment of learning outcomes relates to what the learner has actually achieved. In more technical terms, they may be called "retrospective learning outcomes". However, learning outcomes are normally assessed in relation to expectations about what learners should know, understand and be able to do. Learning outcomes formulated as goals for learning may be called "prospective learning outcomes".[60]

Approaching learning outcomes

In Chapter 2 we had our first encounter with learning outcomes, and it may be useful to return to some of these for a moment. For students of the language that is now often called Bosnian/Croatian/Serbian, but was referred to as Serbo-Croatian in the 1980s when these descriptions were formulated, two expected or prospective learning outcomes were:

- Good practical knowledge of modern Serbo-Croatian language and practice in using it orally and in writing. Translation skills.
- Theoretical knowledge of the Serbo-Croatian language. The main emphasis will be on modern grammar, in particular syntax. In addition, students should gain an overview of dialects and know the main aspects of the developments of the Serbo-Croatian written language from the past century until today, in order to understand the present language situation. Students should also have an overview of the classification of Slavic languages.[61]

Both descriptions relate to subject-specific competences, since the language is specifically mentioned. However, we could easily replace "Serbo-Croatian" with a generic term like "the target language" or "the language studied", especially if we also replaced the reference to Slavic languages by the generic "language family to which the target language belongs". The learning outcomes would still be subject-specific, since they clearly relate to language learning, but they would also to an extent be generic, since they could apply to any language, at least if we refer to foreign language learning.

The learning outcomes described above are, on the other hand, relatively general since they say little about the level of knowledge, understanding and ability expected. "Good practical knowledge" gives some indication that we are not talking about the ability to utter just a few phrases or about oral or written statements with significant mistakes in grammar or vocabulary. Yet "good knowledge" is a fairly flexible term, and the requirements for translation skills and theoretical knowledge contain no qualifiers at all. As they are phrased above, it is difficult to know what level is required.

---

60. The terminology is taken from Jennifer Moon, "Linking levels, learning outcomes and assessment criteria", presented at the Bologna seminar on "Using learning outcomes", Edinburgh, 1–2 July 2004; Jennifer Moon's paper is a very useful overview of the concept of learning outcomes and related concepts and has been of great help in writing this chapter. See http://www.bologna-bergen2005.no/EN/Bol_sem/ Seminars/040701-02Edinburgh/040701-02Linking_Levels_plus_ass_crit-Moon.pdf (accessed on 5 March 2006).
61. From *Studiehandbok for Det historisk-filosofiske fakultet, Universitetet i Oslo, 1980–81* (Oslo 1980: Universitetsforlaget), pp. 610–611.

A much more serious reservation is one that was already made in Chapter 2. This description is, properly speaking, not a description of learning outcomes but of something considerably vaguer: teaching aims or expectations. Nevertheless, it may be a useful starting point because it may help make the sometimes difficult distinction between intentions and outcomes.

Another example used in Chapter 2 was the European Language Portfolio. Here, we are in little doubt as to the levels, and for each level learning outcomes are specified for five different kinds of language skills (listening, reading, spoken interaction, spoken production, writing). For example, the description for spoken interaction at level B2 is:

> I can interact with a degree of fluency and spontaneity that makes regular interaction with native speakers quite possible. I can take an active part in discussion in familiar contexts, accounting for and sustaining my views.[62]

This description can be applied to any foreign language, and this is the purpose of the European Language Portfolio. It is not intended to be language-specific. We could add that the description applies to a learner's knowledge of German or Russian, but this would add little or nothing to the description.

An important difference between the two descriptions is that the first refers almost exclusively to knowledge, even where it probably also encompasses understanding (as in the theoretical knowledge of the language, especially modern grammar, with an emphasis on syntax) or the ability to use the language, referred to as "practical knowledge". The exception is for translation, where the reference is to skills. The European Language Portfolio, on the other hand, emphasises what the learner is able to do ("I can…") without saying much about knowledge and understanding. Of course, the first is a description of prospective learning outcomes in an academic study programme, or rather a description of teachers' intentions for this programme since, as it is, the actual description is some way from being a description of learning outcomes, whereas the European Language Portfolio aims to describe practical language ability for all foreign language learners regardless of their background or the way in which they have acquired their knowledge.

If we stay with learning outcomes for language learners a little longer, we may ask whether it might not make sense, at least in the context of an academic study programme, to try to specify learning outcomes for a specific language. The answer is that in many situations and for many purposes, it may well. A language (or language group) may have its particularities that are difficult for foreign learners to master, but which are nonetheless an essential feature of it. Prospective learners may be well served if the learning goals – prospective learning outcomes – point to these features; and those who assess whether the learners have reached specific learning outcomes

---

62. See http://culture2.coe.int/portfolio/inc.asp?L=E&M=$t/208-1-0-1/main_pages/welcome.html.

– even if they were described in terms similar to those of the European Language Port-folio – would be likely to ascertain whether the learners had mastered these features.

For example, a learner of Turkish will be expected to demonstrate knowledge and understanding of the principle and rules of vowel harmony, and be able to apply them in practice in writing and speaking Turkish. Vowel harmony – the principle that a given word can contain only back vowels like a, ı, o, u or only front vowels like e, i, ö, ü – is a distinctive and central feature of Turkish and other Turkic languages,[63] and a phenomenon unfamiliar to most speakers of other languages. Learners of Slavic languages, on the other hand, will be expected to demonstrate knowledge and under-standing of the concept of aspect, and be able to use the perfective and imperfective aspects of verbs correctly in speaking and writing their chosen language(s). Aspect indicates whether an action is perceived as having a determined duration or not. Many languages express aspect somehow,[64] but the formal expression of aspect is a particu-larly important feature of the grammar of Slavic languages.

Formulating learning outcomes

The examples so far have been limited to the learning outcomes in learning foreign languages. Learning outcomes can of course be formulated for any subject, and they may be generic as well as subject-specific. Nevertheless, this narrow selection serves to illustrate some valuable points in formulating learning outcomes.

The first point is that they should indicate what the learner knows, understands and can do on completion of the course of learning. As the example from Serbo-Croatian shows, they should be more than pure intentions, and they should give learners as precise information as possible of what they will know, understand and be able to do if they successfully complete the programme or learning experience in question. There-fore, descriptions of learning outcomes normally include verbs that indicate this: "the learner is able to", "the learner will be able to", "the learner is expected to master", "the learner can".[65] They tend to be written in the third person, though the European Language Portfolio uses the first person singular. Typically, the verbs used will be in the active voice.

Since learning outcomes refer to knowledge and understanding in addition to ability, we might expect that they would be described in terms such as "the learner will know …", "the learner will understand …", "the learner will realise …" or "the learner

---

63. With some exceptions, as in certain words borrowed from non-Turkic languages, or in some languages, such as in certain varieties of Uzbek.

64. As in "I speak English" (=in general I speak English or I can speak English) rather than "I am speaking English" (=at this moment English is my medium of communication). Spanish, Portuguese and Catalan express the distinction between perfective and imperfective aspect with two verbs "to be" (*ser/ésser* and *estar*), but not with distinct forms for other verbs. See Bernard Comrie, *Aspect* (Cambridge 1976: Cam-bridge University Press).

65. Especially keeping in mind that in some languages, the verb corresponding to "can" may also mean "to be able to".

will see the connection between ...". In practice, we are unlikely to find such terms in actual descriptions of learning outcomes. The reason has to do with how we can ascertain that knowledge and understanding have been attained. While ability is demonstrated by doing – an ability to sing implies that the ability is demonstrated through actual singing – this is not necessarily the case with knowledge and understanding. Knowledge and understanding have to be demonstrated if we are to assess whether a learner has achieved a learning outcome of this kind, and such learning outcomes will therefore normally be phrased as "the learner will demonstrate knowledge of ..." or "the learner demonstrates an understanding of ...".

A part of the learning outcomes for the European Language Portfolio reads:

> I can interact with a degree of fluency and spontaneity that makes regular interaction with native speakers quite possible,

This expresses ability, and we would in many descriptions find it rephrased as:

> The learner is able to interact with a degree of fluency and spontaneity that makes regular interaction with native speakers quite possible,

or

> The learner will demonstrate ability to interact with a degree of fluency and spontaneity that makes regular interaction with native speakers quite possible.

The older description for Serbo-Croatian is more problematic in the light of current practice,[66] and today we would expect to find descriptions like:

> The learner will demonstrate theoretical knowledge of modern Serbo-Croatian grammar, in particular of syntax,

and

> The learner will demonstrate knowledge and understanding of the main aspects of the development of the Serbo-Croatian written language from the nineteenth century until today.

These are still fairly general descriptions, and they say little about the level of knowledge, understanding and ability that is expected. We can get some kind of indication by referring to the level for which the learning outcome is expected, so that we would expect more advanced theoretical knowledge of modern grammar from a second degree student than from a first degree student.

---

66. This should not be read as criticism of a description over 20 years old, but as indicating how practice has evolved. This description was chosen as being among the best examples of older practice available to the author.

The generality of the descriptions also points to a second important point, namely that learning outcomes are most easily defined for limited units of learning. Devising learning outcomes for "history" or "chemistry" is very difficult. Devising them for a first degree programme in history or in chemistry is somewhat easier, but far more difficult than devising outcomes for a specific course of, say, five or ten ECTS credits. At that level, the learning outcomes would no longer be for history or chemistry, but for a specific area of the discipline, such as the history of the Roman Republic, of migrations in the early modern age, organic chemistry or electrochemistry. If we reduce the unit of learning for which the outcomes are devised, it is also easier to indicate the level of learning expected.

At the risk of taxing the readers patience with linguistics, let us nevertheless return to the example of Bosnian-Croatian-Serbian. With the preceding paragraph in mind, we could devise more precise learning outcomes. We could, for example, imagine three different descriptions that cover the same subject matter but indicate different levels of attainment:

> The learner will demonstrate theoretical knowledge of the main areas of modern Bosnian-Croatian-Serbian grammar and some specialised theoretical knowledge of syntax.

> The learner will demonstrate good theoretical knowledge of all areas of modern Bosnian-Croatian-Serbian grammar and advanced theoretical knowledge of syntax.

> The learner will demonstrate excellent theoretical knowledge of all areas of modern Bosnian-Croatian-Serbian grammar and the ability to carry out independent research within an area of Serbo-Croatian grammar of his or her choice.

Most readers, even without the slightest knowledge of the subject described, would probably be able to make reasonable guesses about the level to which each of these three descriptions corresponds.

Thirdly, learning outcomes describe our expectations of the learner at the end of a given learning experience. In an organised study programme, such a learning experience will normally be a course, a module or any other unit given a precise name within a given education system. Rather than saying "the learner will demonstrate …", the description of a prospective learning outcome may therefore state explicitly that "at the end of the course, the learner will demonstrate …". This formulation is of course less relevant if we are describing a learning outcome an individual has actually achieved without reference to the way in which it was achieved, or a learning outcome achieved outside any organised study programme.

Fourthly, we are still referring to subject-specific learning outcomes, and that is hardly a coincidence. If we say that learning outcomes are more easily devised for limited units of learning, we are in a way also saying that they are more easily devised for subject-specific than for generic learning outcomes. Nevertheless, it is in principle equally possible to devise learning outcomes for generic competences, so let us have a go.

Again, we will go back to an earlier part of the book, in this case to the Dublin Descriptors presented in Chapter 2 and commented on in Chapter 3. The Dublin Descriptors have the virtue of describing generic competences linked to a given cycle or level. One important generic competence is the ability to acquire new knowledge, understanding and skills, commonly referred to as "learning skills". This is what the Dublin Descriptors stipulate for expected learning skills:

At short cycle level:

> [Students] have the learning skills to undertake further studies with some autonomy.

At first degree level:

> [Students] have developed those learning skills that are necessary for them to continue to undertake further study with a high degree of autonomy.

At second degree level:

> [Students] have the learning skills to allow them to continue to study in a manner that may be largely self-directed or autonomous.

There is no specific description of learning skills for the third degree level, but the descriptor for the second degree level would apply and be strengthened by the requirement that:

> [Students] have demonstrated a systematic understanding of a field of study and mastery of the skills and methods of research associated with that field,

and that they

> are capable of critical analysis, evaluation and synthesis of new and complex ideas.

Reformulated as: "The learner will demonstrate the learning skills enabling him/her to continue to study in a largely self-directed or autonomous manner", this part of the Dublin Descriptors may well be used as a description of a generic learning outcome, in this case at second degree level. Other parts of the Dublin Descriptors are more problematic, such as the expectation that holders of short-cycle qualifications "can apply their knowledge and understanding in occupational contexts". The point that the knowledge, understanding and skills needed to obtain a given qualification should be applicable in occupational contexts is a very valid one, but it is difficult to see what distinguishes this requirement for the short-cycle degrees from a similar requirement for other levels of education, unless some indication is given as to factors such as the complexity and nature of the occupational tasks or the degree of autonomy expected. It would indeed seem difficult to think of generic learning outcomes at any level that could not be put to use in some kind of occupational context, so a description that gives no further specification on this point is perhaps not very helpful.

Learning outcomes in different contexts

The discussion so far has focused on descriptions of learning outcomes linked to a specific subject, within each subject to specific parts of the discipline and then as defined by level or profile, and the point has been made that it is for subject-specific competences that learning outcomes are least difficult to devise. The term "least difficult" has been chosen with care, because learning outcomes are among the most difficult elements in the concept of qualifications, and I hesitate to use the term "easy" for anything that has to do with learning outcomes.

Nevertheless, it is possible to express a variety of features as learning outcomes. Stephen Adam provides the following categories:[67]

Module: learning outcomes are employed at the level of the unit or module.

Assessment and grading criteria: at the level of module, learning outcomes may be used to express the criteria that establish the standard of achievement and the relative performance of individuals.

Unique individual qualification descriptors: learning outcomes may be used for describing and expressing individual subject-specific qualifications validated/accredited by a higher education institution.

National qualification descriptors: learning outcomes are used as generic descriptions of types of qualifications.

Cycle descriptors: generic learning outcomes are linked to levels or cycles, most typically the Dublin Descriptors for the three cycles of the overarching framework of qualifications of the European Higher Education Area.

National subject benchmark statements: learning outcomes are used as statements designed to make explicit the general subject-specific academic characteristics and

---

67. Adam, op. cit., pp. 10–11.
What follows builds on Stephen Adam's classification. The descriptions in part paraphrase rather than quote Adam's text.

standards of programmes. This approach is typical of higher education in the United Kingdom and is also being developed in some other countries.

National level descriptors: learning outcomes are used as generic statements that describe the characteristics and contexts of learning, often linked to the national qualifications framework if this has been elaborated.[68]

The previous section of this chapter contained an attempt to phrase the part of the Dublin Descriptors concerning learning skills as learning outcomes, and much of the remaining discussion in this chapter refers to modules and what Stephen Adam calls "unique individual qualifications descriptors", whereas the role of learning outcomes as assessment or grading criteria will be addressed in the following section.

National qualification descriptors are discussed more fully in Chapter 9, which refers to level 8 of the Irish qualifications framework, where the Honours Bachelor degree is one of two qualifications. The description of the Honours Bachelor degree may be expressed as prospective learning outcomes, along these lines:

On completion of the Honours Bachelor program, successful learners will demonstrate

• an understanding of the theory, concepts and methods pertaining to their chosen field (or fields) of learning.
• detailed knowledge and understanding in one or more specialised areas, some of it at the current boundaries of the field(s).
• mastery of a complex and specialised area of skills and tools.
• ability to use and modify advanced skills and tools to conduct closely guided research, professional or advanced technical activity.
• ability to exercise appropriate judgment in a number of complex planning, design, technical and/or management functions related to products, services, operations or processes, including resourcing.
• ability to use advanced skills to conduct research, or advanced technical or professional activity.
• ability to accept accountability for all related decision making.
• ability to transfer and apply diagnostic and creative skills in a range of contexts.
• ability to act effectively under guidance in a peer relationship with qualified practitioners.
• ability to lead multiple, complex and heterogeneous groups.
• ability to learn to act in variable and unfamiliar learning contexts.
• ability to learn to manage learning tasks independently, professionally and ethically.
• articulation of a comprehensive, internalised, personal world view manifesting solidarity with others.[69]

---

68. All countries of the Bologna Process have committed to launching work on their national qualifications frameworks by 2007 and to complete it by 2010.
69. Developed from the description of the Irish Honours Bachelor degree (accessed on 1 August 2006) given at http://www.nfq.ie/nfq/en/TheFramework/DiagramTheNationalFrameworkofQualifications/larger/

In Chapter 3, reference was made to subject benchmarking, and an extensive quotation was provided from the United Kingdom subject benchmark for the Honours degree in history. Without repeating or paraphrasing the quotation here, it may be useful to rephrase part of the description in the form of learning outcomes:

The successful learner will demonstrate:

- command of a substantial body of historical knowledge
- the ability to read, analyse, and reflect critically and contextually upon historical texts;
- an understanding of the varieties of approaches to understanding, constructing, and interpreting the past; and, where relevant, a knowledge of concepts and theories derived from the humanities and social sciences;
- a command of comparative perspectives, which may include the ability to compare the histories of different countries, societies, or cultures;
- awareness of continuity and change over extended time spans;
- the ability to express himself or herself clearly, fluently, and coherently in writing.

A quick look at the original text from which this selection of learning outcomes has been taken[70] will show that the relevant section of this subject benchmark was in fact written as learning outcomes and only very minor adjustments were required for the example given here.

Learning outcomes and assessment of performance

To summarise, the formulation of a learning outcome should include:[71]

- an indication of what the learner is able to do (such as "interact with native speakers");
- an indication of the area in which the learner is expected to acquire knowledge, understanding and abilities (e.g. of the development of the Bosnian-Croatian-Serbian written language from the nineteenth century until today);
- an indication of the level of knowledge, understanding and ability expected (e.g. basic knowledge or good understanding);
- an indication of how persons other than the learner can verify that the learner has achieved the learning outcome, in other words how the learner will give evidence of his or her learning. This is often phrased as "the learner will demonstrate ..." but could also be phrased as "the learner will account for .../outline .../describe .../give proof of ...".

HonoursBachelorDegree/.

70. In http://www.qaa.ac.uk/academicinfrastructure/benchmark/honours/history.pdf (accessed on 24 July 2006).

71. See Moon, op. cit., p. 14. See also p. 26 of Jennifer Moon's paper for useful hints on the vocabulary of learning outcomes.

The latter point naturally leads us to consider the use of learning outcomes in examinations and assessment of learner performance. In more technical terms, we shift our focus from prospective to retrospective learning outcomes, since we are concerned with verifying whether stipulated learning outcomes have in fact been achieved.

Ideally, all learning outcomes should be phrased so that they can be assessed at the end of a learning cycle. In practice, assessment criteria are often phrased differently. Jennifer Moon, one of the foremost authorities on learning outcomes and assessment criteria, suggests that:

> An assessment criterion is a statement that prescribes with greater precision than a learning outcome, the quality of performance that will show that the student has reached a particular standard. The standard may be the threshold that is described by the learning outcome or the standard that is required in order to gain a particular grade.[72]

Admittedly, the distinction between learning outcomes and assessment criteria is not crystal clear. Neither is the distinction between prospective and retrospective learning outcomes, where it is often the use of the learning outcomes rather than the characteristics of the outcomes themselves that determines whether they should be classified as one or the other. The theoretical distinctions described are helpful in understanding the various facets and uses of learning outcomes, but a dogmatic approach requiring a formal distinction between them in every situation would hardly seem fruitful and could lead to increased confusion rather than improved comprehension. The distinctions are often helpful, but they need to be approached with common sense.

Let us nevertheless look somewhat more closely at assessment criteria and let us go back to one of the learning outcomes found in – or rather adapted from – the European Language Portfolio:

> The learner is able to interact with a degree of fluency and spontaneity that makes regular interaction with native speakers quite possible.

Since this learning outcome concerns spoken interaction, the assessment method is likely to be conversation between the examiner and the learner. A written examination would seem an inappropriate method of assessing this particular learning outcome. As the learning outcome is phrased, one would expect the examiner to be a native speaker of the language concerned, but this is not really necessary as long as the examiner is an advanced speaker of the language, what is often described as a "near native" speaker.

The assessment criteria would describe more precisely what is meant by "a degree of fluency and spontaneity" as well as what is meant by "regular interaction". They could for example describe the kind of topics or situations the learner is expected to be able

---

72. Ibid., p. 17.

to cope with, "spontaneously and fluently". Should he or she be able to talk about the weather, about current events, about literature or about food? Some of these topics may require understanding and knowledge of content and form, beyond the linguistic aspects of the subject. A meaningful conversation about the literature of the language in question would require at least some knowledge of literary theory and history as well as knowledge of the body of literature in the language. Such a criterion could for example be formulated as:

> The learner is able to discuss the poetry of Gabriela Mistral competently and flu-
> ently in Spanish, without serious mistakes of grammar and vocabulary, to use tech-
> nical vocabulary in Spanish to support the discussion and to explain terms and
> expressions typical of the poetry of Gabriela Mistral.

The latter is an indication of the fact that many terms used by Gabriela Mistral are not immediately accessible even to fluent speakers of Spanish since much of her poetry contains religious imagery as well as expressions typical of agriculture and the countryside. Besides, since Gabriela Mistral was Chilean, some of the terms she used are typical of the Chilean Spanish of her time (she lived from 1881 to 1957), and they may need to be explained also to native speakers of other varieties of Spanish[73] or even to young contemporary Chileans from the larger cities. Of course, this would be a learning outcome for studies in Spanish literature and not of a common language learning course or experience, and such a highly content-specific outcome would never be included in the European Language Portfolio or any similar exercise. In general, language testing authorities around the world are aware of the distinction and try as much as possible not to test content, world knowledge or the like along with language proficiency.[74]

Threshold level or more?

A learning outcome will often describe a threshold level, that is, the minimum knowledge, understanding and ability required for the learner to successfully complete the stipulated unit of learning. If the prospective learning outcome for a course on Gabriela Mistral is the one described above, someone able to discuss Gabriela Mistral's poetry in those terms will have passed the course, whereas someone unable to carry out this discussion in Spanish, unfamiliar with literary theory and/or unacquainted with key terms in Mistral's poetry will fail.

---

73. National and regional varieties of Spanish are quite easily recognised, so that native speakers with some exposure to different varieties will readily distinguish, say, a Colombian from a Chilean or an Argentinean accent. Yet, the differences are relatively slight and do not in any way make mutual comprehension difficult. Some terms may, however, be used differently or be found in only some varieties of Spanish and may require explanation. A Spaniard inviting you to a *comida* will invite you for lunch, whereas a Chilean using the same term will have the evening meal in mind. See for example Bertil Malmberg, *La América hispanohablante. Unidad y diferenciación del castellano* (Madrid 1970; Ediciones Istmo) and Jacobo Grass, *Diccionario de chilenismos* (Santiago de Chile 1993: Librería Editorial Pax).
74. I am grateful to Athanassia Spyropoulou for pointing out the distinction.

Prospective learning outcomes often specify minimum requirements. They are concerned with describing the requirements for learners to obtain a passing grade or, in a grading system with several passing grades, to obtain the minimum passing grade, such as grade E in the ECTS grading system. Some people allege that formulating learning outcomes contributes to lowering expectations and the much discussed level of education. It is, however, difficult to see why this should be the case. Any formal unit of learning would require some specification of the learning expected of the student. Formulating learning outcomes makes these requirements explicit and also indicates how they should be made verifiable, and thus helps both learners and teachers in reaching the learning outcomes and assessors in verifying whether the outcomes have been reached.

Learning outcomes should in no way be read along the lines of "this is all the learner will ever need to do". Even the most traditionalist higher education teacher will provide students with an indication at least of the books and articles they should read – and preferably understand – in order to pass the course. It would be as unreasonable to see this as a discouragement of students undertaking further independent reading as it would be to take explicitly formulated learning outcomes as a discouragement of pursuing further learning goals.

However, systems that have several passing grades may require further specification of learning outcomes or assessment outcomes for each grade. We have seen that often a given percentage of students is expected to obtain a certain grade, such as the general expectation that about 25 per cent of students will obtain ECTS grade B. These indications apply to large student bodies, but are considerably less meaningful if applied to smaller groups. A group of 30 or 40 students may be particularly strong or particularly weak, and it is very helpful to learners and examiners if there are descriptors of the knowledge, understanding and abilities required for learners to obtain a given grade. It also provides a much better common understanding – and hopefully use – of the scale across an institution, a country or a continent if we provide a more accurate definition of what each grade stands for.

A warning

A good summary of learning outcomes is provided by Jennifer Moon:

> A learning outcome is a statement of what a successful learner is expected to know, understand and be able to do at the end of a period of learning. Learning outcomes are linked to the relevant level and since they should generally be assessable they should be written in terms of how the learning is represented.[75]

---

75. Moon, op. cit., p. 12. Stephen Adam has made the case that the term "successful" should be integrated into the definition, rather than be understood implicitly. He also makes the case that "is expected to know, etc." may be replaced by "will know, etc.".

In theory, this is relatively straightforward and there seems to be broad agreement that ideally learning outcomes should be the basis for assessment and comparison of qualifications. However, this chapter hopefully also illustrates why this desired outcome is far from easy to achieve, and why indicators of level, workload, quality and profile are also necessary components of descriptions of qualifications.

Learning outcomes are a highly useful concept and the current tendency is towards greater emphasis on learning outcomes. This means that there is a healthy tendency to emphasise more the content of a qualification and less the procedures by which the qualification is earned.

As we have seen, the description of learning outcomes also has some formalities and conventions of its own. This is necessary for learning outcomes to be comprehensible, verifiable and comparable. There is, however, a danger. The description of learning outcomes may be made so highly formalised, so technically complex and so jargon-laden that it loses some of its value and at worst may be counter-productive. Learning outcomes need to be specified and they represent a significant step forward in describing and assessing the real content and value of qualifications. However, they do so only if they are described in terms that convey their spirit and principles and do not get lost in formalisms.

While they are not learning-outcomed in formal terms, it may be appropriate to close this chapter with the goals formulated for Australian graduates by the Australian Qualifications Framework Advisory Board:

> University qualifications in Australia have derived in their standing from the degrees of the older universities which in the nineteenth century were modelled upon the British universities. Today, Australian universities, wherever their location and whatever their selected profile, must enable their graduates to operate anywhere, and in any sphere, at a level of 'professionalism' consistent with best international practice, and in ways that embody the highest ethical standards.[76]

---

76. *Australian Qualifications Framework Implementation Handbook, Third Edition* (Carlton, Victoria 2002: Australian Qualifications Framework Advisory Board).

Part III

Making qualifications
fit together

9 National qualifications frameworks

Introduction

If we return for a moment to our imaginary group of athletes turned academics, we can see they have had quite varied careers in higher education. They have studied different subjects with different results, but they have all progressed and earned qualifications in different academic disciplines, and at different levels or cycles. First they entered higher education on the basis of secondary school leaving certificates, or in some cases on the basis of other qualifications, then they took first degrees, and then some of them went on to second and even third degrees. In other words, the different degrees in an education system are not loosely independent entities. Rather, they constitute parts of a whole, and this whole is what we call a degree system, which again is an important feature of any education system.

We are used to thinking of education systems consisting of primary school, secondary school and higher education, all with their appropriate qualifications. We have seen that at higher education level, a three-tier degree system is rapidly becoming the norm within the European Higher Education Area, as it was already in several European countries and other parts of the world, such as the United States and Canada. We are also used to assuming that students who have completed a first degree can enrol for a second degree, at least if they have obtained good results. Similarly, second degree holders may apply for access to doctoral programmes.

Yet, most European higher education systems have not been very explicit in describing how their various qualifications fit together. This kind of description, called a "qualifications framework" is becoming a characteristic feature of the European Higher Education Area.

In one sense, all education systems have a qualifications framework, since they do need to describe the different degrees that make up the system and also stipulate access requirements for the various study programmes and levels. Saying that access to higher education normally requires a secondary school leaving qualification, and that access to a second degree programme normally requires completion of a first degree, possibly with more than barely passing grades, in effect implies that there is a qualifications framework. However, the term qualifications framework has come to be used in a sense that is sometimes also called "new-style" qualifications framework, and it is this concept we explore in this chapter.

Put simply, a new-style qualifications framework makes explicit how the qualifications that make up an education system interact and how learners may move among qualifications. Often this movement will be from a lower to a higher qualification, but it does not need to be. It can also be sideways or even downwards. In the first case, someone who holds a first degree in one area, for example mathematics, may decide this is not the discipline that really interests him or her and take another first degree, for example in history. In the second case, someone holding a second degree, for example in engineering, may decide he or she would be well served by also taking a first degree in a different discipline, for example in business administration.

The second important characteristic of a new-style qualifications framework is that, as far as possible, it describes qualifications in terms of learning outcomes. One obtains a second degree because one has achieved certain stipulated (prospective) learning outcomes, in other words because one knows, understands and is able to do things in accordance with pre-established requirements. This is also a new development because, as the working group that elaborated the Danish qualifications framework for higher education stated, educational qualifications have traditionally been described in terms of access requirements, stipulated study time and subject content, and only to a very limited extent in terms of the competences acquired through a given study programme.[1]

Qualifications frameworks bring together all or most of the elements we have considered so far in this book. They include level, workload, quality and learning outcomes. They may also include profile, even if not all qualifications frameworks do so, and they will often specify typical access requirements for each qualification. In so doing, they in fact outline typical learning paths, which we shall consider in more detail in Chapter 11. Qualifications frameworks are general rather than subject-specific, that is, they are valid for all qualifications of a given kind rather than just for a given qualification in a given subject area. Therefore, the learning outcomes associated with qualifications in the framework tend to be generic rather than subject-specific, but the description of individual qualifications within the framework, such as a first degree in electrical engineering in the Irish qualifications framework, will also refer to subject-specific learning outcomes. It is possible that, in some countries, examples of subject-specific learning outcomes may be included once the national frameworks have been elaborated and adopted. The Danish qualifications framework refers to intellectual competences, professional and academic competences, and practical competences.[2]

Qualifications frameworks may be at the level of education systems or at a higher level. Most commonly, they are found at system level, and they are then referred to as national qualifications frameworks even if, strictly speaking, they are system frameworks rather than national frameworks. Most countries in Europe have a single higher education system, but a country like Belgium has two, so it will probably develop two frameworks. In the case of the United Kingdom, there is one framework for England, Wales and Northern Ireland and one for Scotland. While reference in this book will mostly be to qualifications frameworks in European countries, we should not lose

---

1. "Mod en dansk kvalifikationsnøgle for videregående uddannelser", report (dated 15 January 2003) from the Danish Bologna working group on qualifications frameworks, p. 5. The report on the Danish qualifications framework is provided in both Danish and English, whereas the appendices to the report are given in Danish only. See http://www.udiverden.dk/Default.aspx?ID=3555 (accessed on 5 May 2006).
2. Ibid., p. 14.

sight of the fact that they were first developed in Australia, New Zealand and South Africa.

The only qualifications frameworks at a higher level than that of individual education systems known to the author are the one developed for the European Higher Education Area, adopted by the Ministers of the Bologna Process in May 2005, and the European Qualifications Framework developed by the European Commission in 2005–6. We will consider overarching frameworks in the next chapter, whereas this chapter focuses on national frameworks.

Ideally, qualifications frameworks should cover not just the qualifications in a certain part of the system, such as higher education, but all qualifications within a given education system. This is in fact the case for all national frameworks that have been developed so far, at least the ones of which I am aware, with the exception of the Danish framework, which is specified as being for higher education.[3] The framework of the European Higher Education Area, an overarching framework within which countries develop their national frameworks, covers higher education qualifications only since this is the remit of the Bologna Process. The European Qualifications Framework (EQF) of the European Commission has a wider range and covers all levels of education, though its starting point was a desire to incorporate vocational qualifications in an overall qualifications framework at European Union level.

Definition

The working group that elaborated the proposal for an overarching framework of qualifications for the European Higher Education Area defined a national qualifications framework in the following terms, with specific reference to higher education:

> the single description, at national level or level of an education system, which is internationally understood and through which all qualifications and other learning achievements in higher education may be described and related to each other in a coherent way and which defines the relationship between higher education qualifications.[4]

Background and purposes

National qualifications frameworks are more operational than overarching frameworks, and the development of qualifications frameworks began at national level first. In Europe, national frameworks existed in Denmark, Ireland and the United Kingdom

---

3. Ibid.
4. *A Framework for Qualifications of the European Higher Education Area* (Copenhagen 2005: Ministry of Science, Technology and Innovation), Chapter 2.1, p. 30. The report is also available at http://www.bologna-bergen2005.no/Docs/00-Main_doc/050218_QF_EHEA.pdf.

– the latter, as we saw, with two frameworks[5] – before work started in 2003 on the overarching framework for the European Higher Education Area. We therefore begin by considerating national frameworks.

To start from the beginning, however, we must travel outside Europe. New Zealand launched its framework[6] in 1990–1. Development took two years, including wide public consultation. The South African Framework[7] was established in 1995, and the Australian Framework[8] was introduced in 1995 and fully implemented over a five-year period. In each case, the competent authorities felt that their education system needed to be reformed and that the competences they conveyed needed to be adapted to new requirements in society. In the case of New Zealand:

> During the 1980s, a series of reports identified a need to reform education and training in New Zealand to improve competitiveness in global markets, to create a modern education system that would encourage lifelong learning, and to increase skill levels in the labour force. Successive governments have accepted that invest-ment in education and training is of critical importance for the future wellbeing of New Zealand and its citizens. The NQF was seen as a key initiative to respond to New Zealand's need to develop its human resources.[9]

The New Zealand framework has special provision for Māori learners and learning; this part of the framework seems to put greater emphasis on non-traditional learning than other parts.

The South African framework was developed in the light of the need to specify the competence of Black workers from the 1970s onwards, to support their demand for higher wages. The description of competences was important because under the apartheid regime employers repeatedly refused claims for higher wages by maintain-ing that workers were unskilled and wage increases were therefore unwarranted. The Congress of South African Trade Unions (COSATU) played an important role in fur-thering demands for training and definition of competences, and from the mid-1970s in arguing for overall education reform.

The first qualifications frameworks were therefore developed on a background of social and societal demand for qualifications better adapted to changing needs. It is worth noting that all three frameworks place great emphasis on vocational qualifica-tions, since this was the sector of the labour market where the need was felt more

---

5. For practical reasons and without prejudice to the constitutional arrangements of the United Kingdom, the UK frameworks are referred to here as the EWNI (England, Wales, Northern Ireland) and Scottish frameworks.

6. See http://www.nzqa.govt.nz/framework/index.html (accessed on 4 May 2006).

7. See http://www.logos-net.net/ilo/195_base/en/init/sa_16.htm (accessed on 4 May 2006).

8. See http://www.aqf.edu.au/aboutaqf.htm (accessed on 4 May 2006).

9. *The New Zealand National Qualifications Framework* (Wellington 2005: New Zealand Qualifications Authority), p. 3.

acutely. All three frameworks, however, encompass qualifications at all levels: primary, secondary, vocational and higher education.

This holistic approach was also characteristic of the development of the earliest qualifications frameworks in Europe – those of Ireland, the United Kingdom and Denmark. The first national frameworks in Europe were developed for the same reasons as the frameworks just referred to – to make learners more competitive and attractive in the labour market, to enable them to better describe and make full use of their qualifications, and to make it easier for them to alternate work and formal learning. In the words of the Irish Qualifications Authority:

> The need for a more flexible and integrated system of qualifications arises in the main from the national objective of moving towards a "lifelong learning society", in which learners will avail of learning opportunities at various stages throughout their lives.[10]

The Irish Qualifications Authority also emphasises the benefits for learners:

> The Framework is designed to meet the qualifications needs of a more diverse learner group, and many new awards will be developed and made available as lifelong learning gradually becomes the norm in Ireland.[11]

The Danish framework emphasises that for higher education institutions, a qualifications framework provides great help in setting clear goals for curriculum planning.[12] The general aims of the Scottish framework are to:

> • help people of all ages and circumstances to access appropriate education and training over their lifetime to fulfil their personal, social and economic potential;
> • enable employers, learners and the public in general to understand the full range of Scottish qualifications, how the qualifications relate to each other, and how different types of qualifications can contribute to improving the skills of the workforce.

The SCQF will provide a national vocabulary for describing learning opportunities and make the relationships between qualifications clearer. It will also clarify entry and exit points, and routes for progression within and across education and training sectors and increase the opportunities for credit transfer. In these ways it will assist learners to plan their progress and minimise duplication of learning.[13]

---

10. See http://www.nfq.ie/nfq/en/TheFramework/Aframeworkofqualifications-whatandwhy/ (accessed 5 May 2006).
11. See http://www.nfq.ie/nfq/en/TheFramework/Benefitsforlearners/ (accessed 5 May 2006).
12. "Mod en dansk kvalifikationsnøgle for videregående uddannelser", op. cit., p. 6.
13. An Introduction to the Scottish Credit and Qualifications Framework (September 2001), Executive summary, p. vii.

One of the main purposes of qualifications frameworks, then, is to promote flexibility and to make good use of people's real competences regardless of how these have been earned and how they are expressed in educational terms. This is reflected in the key objectives of the Australian Qualifications Framework, which should:

- provide nationally consistent recognition of outcomes achieved in post compulsory education;
- help with developing flexible pathways which assist people to move more easily between education and training sectors and between those sectors and the labour market by providing the basis for recognition of prior learning, including credit transfer and work and life experience;
- integrate and streamline the requirements of participating providers, employers and employees, individuals and interested organisations;
- offer flexibility to suit the diversity of purposes of education and training;
- encourage individuals to progress through the levels of education and training by improving access to qualifications, clearly defining avenues for achievement, and generally contributing to lifelong learning;
- encourage the provision of more and higher quality vocational education and training through qualifications that normally meet workplace requirements and vocational needs, thus contributing to national economic performance; and
- promote national and international recognition of qualifications offered in Australia.[14]

The quotation from the Australian framework also refers to another important purpose: that qualifications frameworks should function as frameworks. In other words, they constitute references and frames within which qualifications find their place, and the frameworks make it easier to compare individual qualifications. A first degree in physics and a first degree in Arabic have very different subject-specific learning outcomes, but they will probably have many generic outcomes in common. For access to a second degree programme, the subject-specific learning outcomes and the profile of a qualification are likely to be very important. As we saw in Chapter 7, if a political scientist and a mathematician both apply for a job as a political analyst, one would expect the political scientist to be qualified, but not the mathematician. Yet, in some contexts, generic learning outcomes may be at least as important as subject-specific ones, and a qualifications framework helps emphasise what qualifications have in common. In a way, it helps make sense of diversity. As we shall see later in this chapter, this is a particularly important function of overarching qualifications frameworks.

Stephen Adam has provided an excellent summary of the rationales behind the development of qualifications frameworks:

Existing national qualifications frameworks are complex structures designed to achieve specific economic, social and political objectives. Many countries are reexamining their qualification structures for the same reasons they signed the Bolo-

---

14. http://www.aqf.edu.au/aboutaqf.htm#why (accessed 4 May 2006).

gna Declaration, which is to modernise their education systems, in order to face the challenges of globalisation. National qualifications structures differ greatly in their detail, articulation and approach. The development of any over-arching European model must be flexible enough to encompass such variations. Qualifications frameworks can accomplish, any or all, of the following:

• Make explicit purposes and aims of qualifications
• Nationally and internationally raise the awareness of citizens and employers in relation to qualifications
• Improve access and social inclusion
• Delineate points of integration and overlap
• Facilitate national and international recognition and mobility
• Identify alternative routes
• Position qualifications in relation to one another
• Show routes for progression as well as barriers
• Facilitate and support learners and clarify opportunities.15

The Bologna Working Group on qualifications frameworks also provides a good summary of various purposes of qualifications frameworks:

• Information to employers and the general public, e.g. about award structure and graduates' competencies
• Guidance to learners, e.g. about pathways and progression in the educational system
• Recognition of former learning, e.g. in connection with credit transfer and Life Long Learning
• Tool for educational institutions, e.g. in curriculum planning and programme development
• International comparability and mobility, e.g. in recognition of qualifications from foreign HEI
• Quality assurance, e.g. as points of reference in evaluations[16].

In 2003, there were only four operational national qualifications frameworks in Europe, but this changed rapidly. In May 2005, the ministers of education of the 45 countries participating in the Bologna Process committed themselves to starting work on their national frameworks by 2007 and to complete this work by 2010. Some countries, like Finland and Hungary, had started work before the ministers met in Bergen in May 2005 and may well complete their frameworks before this book is published. Other countries are just starting work or are still considering how best to launch the process. By 2010, however, all or almost all countries in the European Higher Educa-

---

15. Stephen Adam: "To consider alternative approaches for clarifying cycles and levels in European higher education qualifications", background report for the Danish Bologna seminar on "Qualifications Structures in European Higher Education", Copenhagen, 27–28 March 2003, available at http://www.bologna-bergen2005.no/EN/Bol_sem/Old/030327-28København/030327-28S_Adam.pdf (accessed on 9 May 2005).
16. *A Framework for Qualifications of the European Higher Education Area*, op. cit., p. 142.

tion Area should have completed their national frameworks, so that Europe will have more than 45 national frameworks. For example, Albania has launched work on its national qualifications framework as a part of its Master Plan for higher education. In its turn, the Master Plan is a key element of the implementation of the Bologna Process in Albania. This shows the importance of the overarching framework, as all national frameworks will have to be compatible with the overarching framework for the European Higher Education Area, also adopted in May 2005. Before we turn to the overarching framework, however, we will explore the existing national frameworks in greater detail.

Structure

Qualifications frameworks define the relationships between the qualifications included in the framework, and they do so in large part by specifying the level of each qualification. In all the national frameworks that have been elaborated so far, qualifications span from basic to higher education, but there is no fixed number of levels. Even so, the number of levels in national frameworks does not vary enormously. For example, the Scottish framework has twelve levels, the Irish and New Zealand frameworks have ten, the EWNI framework has nine and the South African framework eight levels. However, of these, the Scottish level 1 corresponds to learning achievements by learners with severe learning disabilities, a level that is not found in any of the other frameworks, even if the New Zealand one states that level 1 is "open-ended downward to capture all learning".[17] The first level of the EWNI framework is labelled "entry level". The New Zealand framework was originally established with eight levels but was extended to ten levels in 2001.

Within this overall structure, three or four levels are typically within higher education. The classical structure is the first, second and third degree that we also find in the Bologna Process, while the fourth level typically is either a variation of the first degree, as the "honours" first degree (Bachelor), or an intermediate degree.

The Danish framework is limited to higher education qualifications and is not specific on levels; but, of the nine degrees it lists, it would be reasonable to consider at least the first – the *erhvervsakademigrad* – as a short-cycle degree; that is, an intermediate degree within the first cycle. This framework also has two Bachelor degrees, one labelled as professional and the other as general. While the first has a more vocational orientation, it would be reasonable to consider both as first degrees.

The full range of a national qualifications framework is illustrated in Table 9.1 by the outline of the Scottish framework, the one encompassing the highest number of levels.[18] The importance of offering a comprehensive framework is seen in the fact that several qualifications may be assigned to the same level, such as level 8 in the Scottish

---

17. *The New Zealand National Qualifications Framework*, op. cit., p. 7.
18. From http://www.scqf.org.uk/table.htm (accessed on 6 May 2006).

Table 9.1: Scottish Qualifications Framework (SCQF)

SCQF level	SQA National Units, Courses and Group Awards	Higher education	Scottish Vocational Qualifica-tions
12		Doctorates	
11		Masters	SVQ 5
10		Honours Degree Graduate Diploma Certificate*	
9		Ordinary Degree Graduate Diploma Certificate*	
8		Higher National Diploma Diploma in Higher Education	SVQ 4
7	Advanced Higher	Higher National Certificate Certificate in Higher Education	
6	Higher		SVQ 3
5	Intermediate 2 Credit Standard Grade		SVQ 2
4	Intermediate 1 General Standard Grade		SVQ 1
3	Access 3 Foundation Standard Grade		
2	Access 2		
1	Access 1		

* These qualifications are differentiated by volume of outcomes and may be offered at either level.

framework, at which we find two higher education qualifications and one vocational qualification. This also implies that while higher education and vocational qualifications may have very different profiles, specific learning outcomes and functions, they may be of the same level, as shown by the Scottish framework.

Describing qualifications within a framework

While the structure is an essential piece of information in a national framework, a simple outline of the qualifications structure does not make a framework. The truly distinctive feature of a framework is the description of the levels and qualifications within the framework, and these should focus on learning outcomes rather than merely on formal aspects of the structure such as length of study. Let us look at some descriptions in existing national frameworks.

The New Zealand framework describes each level in terms of three main elements: process, learning demand and responsibility. Table 9.2 shows the descriptors for three different levels 2, 5 and 9; note that the descriptions for levels 8, 9 and 10 follow a different format.[19] If we compare the three elements of these descriptors with the Dublin Descriptors for generic competences (see Chapter 3) and the learning outcomes we considered in Chapter 8, we see that they have much in common. Essentially, the New Zealand descriptors outline expectations of what complexity of tasks the holders of qualifications of a given level are able to handle, how sophisticated they are in doing so (for example, recall knowledge acquired or analysis of a complex situation) and what kind of leadership and responsibility they are able to exercise. As these examples show, expectations range from very limited to quite heavy.

Table 9.2: New Zealand Qualifications Framework (levels 2, 5 and 9)

Level	Process	Learning demand	Responsibility
2	Carry out processes that: - are limited in range - are repetitive and familiar - are employed within closely defined contexts	Employing: - recall - a narrow range of knowledge and cognitive skills - no generation of new ideas	Applied: - in directed activity - under close supervision - with no responsibility for the work or learning of others
5	Carry out processes that: - require a wide range of specialised technical or scholastic skills - involve a wide choice of standard and non-standard procedures - are employed in a variety of routine and non-routine contexts	Employing: - a broad knowledge base with substantial depth in some areas - analytical interpretation of a wide range of data - the determination of appropriate methods and procedures in response to a range of concrete problems with some theoretical elements	Applied: - in self-directed and sometimes directive activity - within broad general guidelines or functions - with full responsibility for the nature, quantity and quality of outcomes - with possible responsibility for the achievement of group outcome
9	Involves skills and knowledge that enable a learner to: - demonstrate mastery of a subject area; and - plan and carry out – to internationally recognised standards – an original scholarship or research project. Demonstrated by: - the completion of a substantial research paper, dissertation or in some cases a series of papers.		

19. From *The New Zealand National Qualifications Framework*, op. cit., pp. 12–13. The document provides the descriptors for all three levels and is accessible at http://www.nzqa.govt.nz/news/featuresandspeeches/docs/nqf-background.pdf (accessed on 6 May 2006).

The Irish framework also describes levels in terms of what learners are expected to know, understand and be able to do. In the Irish framework, the Honours Bachelor degree is one of two level 8 qualifications, and it is described as follows:

> Innovation is a key feature of learning outcomes at this level. Learning outcomes at this level relate to being at the forefront of a field of learning in terms of knowledge and understanding. The outcomes include an awareness of the boundaries of the learning in the field and the preparation required to push back those boundaries through further learning. The outcomes relate to adaptability, flexibility, ability to cope with change and ability to exercise initiative and solve problems within their field of study. In a number of applied fields the outcomes are those linked with the independent, knowledge-based professional. In other fields the outcomes are linked with those of a generalist and would normally be appropriate to management positions.[20]

The Irish framework also specifies that the Honours Bachelor is a "multi-purpose award-type. The knowledge, skill and competence acquired are relevant to personal development, participation in society and community, employment, and access to additional education and training"[21] and that learners are expected to demonstrate an understanding of the theory, concepts and methods pertaining to a field or fields of learning as well as detailed knowledge and understanding in one or more specialised areas, with the specification that some of it be at the current boundaries of the field. Learners are further expected to "demonstrate mastery of a complex and specialised area of skills and tools; use and modify advanced skills and tools to conduct closely guided research, professional or advanced technical activity" as well as to "exercise appropriate judgement in a number of complex planning, design, technical and/or management functions related to products, services, operations or processes, including resourcing" and to "use advanced skills to conduct research, or advanced technical or professional activity, accepting accountability for all related decision making; transfer and apply diagnostic and creative skills in a range of contexts". Finally, the Irish framework also specifies three kinds of competence for this qualification:

Competence – role: Act effectively under guidance in a peer relationship with qualified practitioners; lead multiple, complex and heterogeneous groups.

Competence – learning to learn: Learn to act in variable and unfamiliar learning contexts; learn to manage learning tasks independently, professionally and ethically.

Competence – insight: Express a comprehensive, internalised, personal world view manifesting solidarity with others.

---

20. See http://www.nfq.ie/nfq/en/TheFramework/DiagramTheNationalFrameworkofQualifications/larger/HonoursBachelorDegree/ (accessed 6 May 2006).
21. Ibid., for this and other elements related to the Irish Honours Bachelor degree.

In the Danish framework, qualifications are described in terms of competency profile, competency goals and formal aspects. The competency goals are specified for intellectual competencies, professional and academic competencies and practical competencies. For the Danish ordinary (as opposed to professional) Bachelor degree, it gives this description:

1. Competency profile:

A Bachelor will have competencies that have been acquired via a course of study that has taken place in a research environment.

A Bachelor should have basic knowledge of and insight into his or her discipline's methods and scholarly foundation. These attributes should qualify a Bachelor for further education at a relevant graduate programme as well as for employment on the basis of his or her academic discipline.

2. Competency goals:

Intellectual competencies

A Bachelor should be able to:

• Describe, formulate and communicate complex issues and results
• Conduct analyses using scientific methods
• Structure own learning

Professional and academic competencies

A Bachelor should be able to:

• Evaluate methods within his or her own academic discipline
• Demonstrate insight into central disciplines, theories and concepts

Practical competencies

A Bachelor should be able to:

• Analyse practical complex issues in a professional context
• Make and justify decisions on the basis of his or her academic discipline

3. Formal aspects:

• Admittance requirements: Upper-secondary education (possibly with certain specific admittance requirements)
• Length: Three years, full-time (180 ECTS credits)
• Further education options: Candidatus and Master programmes[22]

---

22. From the English version of "Mod en dansk kvalifikationsnøgle for videregående uddannelser" – "Towards a Danish 'Qualifications Framework' for higher education", pp. 22–3. In the Danish original, it is on pp. 19–20.

Similar examples, with variations, could be given from other national frameworks, but there is little point in providing the descriptors for all levels of all qualifications from all national frameworks. The examples here suffice to identify some common points among descriptors.

Most importantly, a qualifications framework should describe levels in terms of expected learning outcomes. Several qualifications may be situated at the same level within a framework, and in this case they should have comparable generic learning outcomes. What learners will know, understand and be able to do need not be identical, but should be roughly similar in terms of complexity and sophistication.

A further point is that even if not all frameworks have the same number of levels, a framework should be neither too simple nor too complex. In the frameworks we have referred to, spanning the whole range of qualifications in a system, we find between eight and twelve levels, and this would seem reasonable if we include the very lowest levels (like the Scottish level for learners with severe learning impediments) as well as the highest level (doctoral qualifications). Of these, three to five typically relate to higher education, and some vocational qualifications may be of the same level as some higher education qualifications. Again, the framework is a help to making sense of diversity, and that requires that there be enough levels to make the framework accurate, yet few enough to make it comprehensible.

Another important point is that while levels and qualifications should primarily be described in terms of learning outcomes, those developing frameworks have found it difficult to dispense entirely with more formal considerations. As pointed out earlier in this chapter, frameworks draw on all components of qualifications discussed in this book, with the exception of profile in the case of some frameworks. This leads us to a considerations of pathways within the framework.

Pathways

In the next chapter, we will consider learning paths in greater detail, but at this stage we need to remind ourselves that one of the main functions of a qualifications framework is to make it easier for learners to move among qualifications in a system. While the levels within a system are generally progressive, so that, for instance, level 9 is more advanced than level 7, this does not necessarily mean that someone aiming for the highest level of qualifications needs to pass through every other level on his or her way to the doctorate. It also does not mean that movement can be only from a lower to a higher level; as already pointed out, movement can also be sideways or downwards.

To help learners navigate, as well as to help education institutions define access criteria, frameworks should therefore specify general access requirements. Often they will do so by stating which level of qualification or which degree is required for access to a given study programme. For example, the Danish framework specifies that access to programmes leading to the Candidate degree, which is a second degree in the Danish system, requires a relevant Bachelor's (first) degree.[23]

However, there may be more ways than one of gaining access to a study programme at a given level, and in many cases previous qualifications and experience may count towards a qualification and reduce the time an individual needs to spend in a formal education programme. The webpage for the Scottish framework outlines 13 case studies[24] that show how people have taken less traditional paths toward qualifications, have had their work experience assessed for access to a higher level than their formal education qualifications would imply and in some cases have been given educational credits towards the qualification they wanted to pursue, on the basis of their experience. One such case is that of "Ann", who used credits from her Diploma in Social Sciences to transfer to a degree programme in a related field at a Scottish university. She was given 240 credits at level 8, and started an Honours degree in a related subject halfway through the programme.[25]

The Australian framework outlines a number of alternative paths for each qualification, and we shall look at some of these in more detail in Chapter 10. However, the general point is important: a qualifications framework should specify access conditions for a given level of qualifications and outline some typical pathways. In addition to the formal regulations of a framework, however, it is very helpful to learners when the authorities responsible for a framework illustrate these regulations with specific cases, as the Scottish authority has done. Whether the cases are actual or fictitious matters less than whether they illustrate the range of options that the framework makes available to learners.

Elaborating frameworks

Regardless of the differences that exist between frameworks, there is one feature they all have in common: it takes time to elaborate national qualifications frameworks. It took two years for the pioneering New Zealand framework, and it did not take less time for the other frameworks that have been elaborated so far. As more countries develop frameworks and perhaps learn from each other, it is natural to expect that the time required will be reduced, but that is not necessarily a sound assumption.

The reason is that the process is not purely technical; it is also political. The technical process is complicated enough, as no country can simply copy the framework elaborated by another. No country or education system is a carbon copy of another, however much it has learned from their experience. A qualifications framework must be devised to suit the requirements of each country and not just the current situation, but also its projected future needs. Existing degrees must be accommodated within the framework or new ones must be defined and introduced. In many cases,

---

23. "Mod en dansk kvalifikationsnøgle for videregående uddannelser", op. cit., Appendix, p. 5 (Danish version).
24. See http://www.scqf.org.uk/case_studies.asp (accessed on 7 May 2006).
25. See http://www.scqf.org.uk/cs03.asp (accessed 7 May 2006).

countries do a bit of both: they keep some existing qualifications and introduce some new ones. In the case of qualifications frameworks in European countries, the parts covering higher education qualifications should accord with the overarching framework of qualifications for the European Higher Education Area, which we will consider below; but, within this overarching framework, choices and adaptations still need to be made.

The political process focuses on winning approval for and commitment to the national framework, because a framework will only work in practice if institutions, learners and employers know about it, approve of it, find it helpful and actually use it. Therefore, while it may be theoretically possible to elaborate a national qualifications framework in the seclusion of a ministry office, this is hardly a recipe for success.

The national qualifications framework is ultimately the responsibility of the political authority responsible for education. In most countries, this is the minister of education, even if some countries use a different terminology (such as the Swiss Federal Councillor) or the minister may combine the education portfolio with other portfolios. However, all the frameworks that have been elaborated so far have benefited from the advice given by a wide range of stakeholders, including government agencies (for example the one responsible for employment policy), education institutions and organisations, employers and their organisations, student organisations and not least specialised bodies for recognition and quality assurance. At least at higher education level, the importance of involving student organisations cannot be overemphasised, not simply to avoid protests later, but above all because students usually have well-reflected and helpful views on higher education policy issues. Consultation of stakeholders takes time, but it normally produces a better framework and it is indispensable in producing a framework that is seen as legitimate and is widely used.

Since most European countries have recently completed, are in the process of elaborating or have yet to launch work on the first generation of their new-style qualifications frameworks, it may be thought premature to consider updating frameworks. Nevertheless, this is an important point: both academic disciplines and the broader society evolve, and our understanding of qualifications and their function will, we hope, also continue to evolve. Periodic reviews of national qualifications frameworks will therefore be needed to ensure they continue to serve their purpose in helping define the qualifications that the academic world and society at large need.

National qualifications frameworks, then, help define the qualifications that make up a national higher education system and help learners move within this system. They help ensure coherence within the system. This is important, since substantially different qualifications systems in different parts of a country could hinder the free mobility of its citizens, even within the country itself. Increasingly, coherence and mobility between education systems is also an important concern, and here we turn to overarching qualifications frameworks.

10 Overarching qualifications frameworks

Overarching qualifications frameworks ensure coherence between systems, whereas national frameworks do so within a single system. They have many of the same functions, but some of their features differ, and overarching frameworks are less operational. Learners have their most direct contact with national frameworks, but if they decide to move their qualifications from one system to another, they will benefit from the overarching frameworks.

The Overarching Framework of Qualifications for the European Higher Education Area

In this chapter, we take a closer look at the two overarching frameworks that exist in Europe, and we start with the overarching framework for the European Higher Education Area, since work on this started first. To avoid repetition, we will refer to it as the EHEA Framework.

Definition

The working group that elaborated the proposal for the EHEA Framework defined it as:

> an overarching framework that makes transparent the relationship between European national higher education frameworks of qualifications and the qualifications they contain. It is an articulation mechanism between national frameworks.[26]

Background

One of the over-riding purposes of the European Higher Education Area is to make it easier for learners to move between countries or, in more technical terms, education systems. This requires that they can have the value of their qualifications recognised in other education systems, so they can enter study programmes in other countries without having to repeat courses they have already taken and find employment to suit their real qualifications.

This does not require European education systems to be identical – the term "harmonisation" will not be found in any text adopted by the ministers responsible for the Bologna Process[27] – but it does require a transparent way of describing qualifications

---

26. *A Framework for Qualifications of the European Higher Education Area,* op. cit., Chapter 2.1, p. 29. The report is also available at http://www.bologna-bergen2005.no/Docs/00-Main_doc/050218_QF_EHEA.pdf.
27. The term "harmonisation" was used in the Sorbonne Declaration adopted by the ministers of education of France, Germany, Italy and the United Kingdom in 1998, a year before the Bologna Declaration. The Sorbonne Declaration played an important role in launching the Bologna Process; the declaration speaks of "harmonisation of the architecture of the European higher education system". But the notions of harmonisation and of working towards a single European higher education system have not been made a part of the Bologna Process. Rather, the Bologna Process strives towards establishing a European Higher Education

from different systems, and it helps if the qualifications structures are not radically different from one country to another within the European Higher Education Area.

This is part of the reason why ministers in the Bologna Declaration committed themselves to "the adoption of a system of easily readable and comparable degrees" and of "a system essentially based on two main cycles, undergraduate and graduate. Access to the second cycle shall require successful completion of first cycle studies, lasting a minimum of three years". At the ministerial meeting in Berlin in 2003, research and research training were brought fully into the Bologna Process, so that we now refer to three rather than two cycles. Making the recognition of qualifications easier was not the only reason for this decision. Another important reason was that ministers were concerned that European students took too long to complete their degrees, and that too many abandoned their studies without obtaining a qualification. They hoped that a first degree based on a minimum of three years' full-time study would allow more students to earn a degree that would enable them either to obtain employment or to continue their studies. This is reflected in the stipulation, also in the Bologna Declaration, that "[t]he degree awarded after the first cycle shall also be relevant to the European labour market as an appropriate level of qualification".

Stipulating that all countries in the European Higher Education Area should introduce a three-cycle system for higher education was a major step to take, as many countries had a long tradition of a "long-cycle" degree, often requiring a minimum of five years' full-time study, as their only university degree.[28] Many members of the academic community as well as of the general public were sceptical of the new first degree, and it is something of a success that by early 2005, all except one of the then 40 countries of the Bologna Process had at least started the introduction of the three-cycle system.[29]

Simply introducing a three-cycle system does not by itself ensure greater transparency, compatibility and mobility. Stipulating a minimum time of study for a given level does not amount to introducing a qualifications framework, and there was a sense among those most involved in the Bologna Process that one needed to do at European level what some countries had started doing at national level: elaborate what was then called a new-style qualifications framework.

Denmark, which was just completing its own national framework, took the lead on this issue within the Bologna Follow-Up Group and organised a conference on Qualifications Structures in Higher Education in Europe in Copenhagen on 27 and 28 March

---

Area made up of a good number of (national) higher education systems that are sufficiently compatible to make the EHEA work.

28. The doctoral degree is often referred to as a "research" rather than a "university" degree.

29. *Bologna Process Stocktaking. Report from a working group appointed by the Bologna Follow-Up Group to the Conference of European Ministers Responsible for Higher Education,* p. 33. See http://www.bologna-bergen2005.no/Bergen/050509_Stocktaking.pdf (accessed on 7 May 2006).

2003.[30] For many members of the Bologna Follow-Up Group, this was their first introduction to qualifications frameworks. The conference adopted a set of recommendations, the first of which was:

> The Ministers meeting in Berlin in September 2003 should encourage the competent public authorities responsible for higher education to elaborate national qualifications frameworks for their respective higher education systems with due consideration to the qualifications framework to be elaborated for the European Higher Education Area.

This recommendation was taken up by the ministers responsible for the Bologna Process when they met in Berlin in September 2003. In the Berlin Communiqué, the ministers said:

> Ministers encourage the member States to elaborate a framework of comparable and compatible qualifications for their higher education systems, which should seek to describe qualifications in terms of workload, level, learning outcomes, competences and profile. They also undertake to elaborate an overarching framework of qualifications for the European Higher Education Area.

> Within such frameworks, degrees should have different defined outcomes. First and second cycle degrees should have different orientations and various profiles in order to accommodate a diversity of individual, academic and labour market needs. First cycle degrees should give access, in the sense of the Lisbon Recognition Convention, to second cycle programmes. Second cycle degrees should give access to doctoral studies.

> Ministers invite the Follow-up Group to explore whether and how shorter higher education may be linked to the first cycle of a qualifications framework for the European Higher Education Area.

In other words, the ministers referred to national frameworks as well as an overarching EHEA Framework, to the variety of purposes of the qualifications within the frameworks, and to the issues of access to further study and employment, and they specifically mentioned short-cycle qualifications.

In March 2004, the Bologna Follow-Up Group appointed a working group to elaborate a proposal for an overarching EHEA Framework. The group, with six members, was chaired by Mogens Berg of the Danish Ministry of Science, Technology and Innova-

---

30. Stephen Adam's background report to this conference is available at http://www.bologna-bergen2005. no/EN/Bol_sem/Old/030327-28København/030327-28S_Adam.pdf and the report from the conference, by Sjur Bergan, is available at http://www.bologna-bergen2005.no/EN/Bol_sem/Old/030327-28København/030327-28Report_General_Rapporteur.pdf. The recommendations adopted by the conference may be found at http://www.bologna-bergen2005.no/EN/Bol_sem/Old/030327-28København/030327-28CPH_ Recommendations.pdf (all accessed on 7 May 2006).

tion, and it was authorised to co-opt experts to help with its work. The group met six times and submitted its draft report, including a draft EHEA Framework, to a new conference in Copenhagen, this time called "The Framework for Qualifications of the European Higher Education Area" and held on 13 and 14 January 2005.[31]

The conference supported the proposed EHEA Framework, and when the ministers of the Bologna Process met in Bergen in May 2005, they adopted the overarching framework of qualifications for the European Higher Education Area, with one modification as we shall see.

Purposes

For national qualifications frameworks, a major purpose is to provide a single, transparent description of all qualifications within the national system covered by the framework. The purpose of the EHEA Framework is slightly different since there is no authority responsible for a European education system. Its purpose is not to provide a description of a European system to be used for all qualifications of the nearly 50 education systems found in the 45 countries working to establish the European Higher Education Area, but rather to describe the framework within which these countries should elaborate their national frameworks. This means that the EHEA Framework is less operational than a national framework, since it will not directly determine and describe the degrees students can earn in the respective system. The EHEA Framework is also less detailed than national frameworks, since it is in a sense one step removed from the qualifications that learners will earn.

The EHEA Framework is not less important than national frameworks. It complements them and serves as a reference point for those creating national frameworks. It sets the outer limits within which the national qualifications frameworks must be elaborated to be compatible with the overarching framework and hence for the national frameworks within the European Higher Education Area to be compatible with each other. For example, in purely technical terms, it is entirely possible to elaborate a national qualifications framework consisting of seven different levels of higher education qualifications each requiring 75 ECTS credits or, alternatively, a framework consisting of just one higher education qualification requiring a workload of 700 ECTS credits,[32] but neither would be compatible with the overarching European frameworks we will consider here.

The main purpose of the EHEA Framework, therefore, is to make sense of diversity – or rather to ensure a balance between diversity and unity. Europe is characterised by a diversity of education systems and traditions, but also by a certain unity in diversity.

---

31. Recommendations adopted are at: http://www.bologna-bergen2005.no/EN/Bol_sem/Seminars/050113-14København/050113-14_Recommendations.pdf – the conference report is at http://www.bologna-bergen2005.no/EN/Bol_sem/Seminars/050113-14København/050113-14_General_report.pdf (both accessed on 7 May 2006).

32. For the sake of simplicity, reference is made only to workload in these imagined examples, but there are of course other considerations in elaborating national qualifications frameworks.

The EHEA Framework is intended to help ensure that the various national frameworks have enough in common to make mobility between them relatively easy and painless for learners, yet to allow institutions and systems to safeguard and develop their respective traditions and strengths. The unity between frameworks will hopefully make mobility between systems easy, while the diversity between them will make mobility interesting and worthwhile. We will look again at the relationship between national and overarching frameworks near the end of this chapter.

Structure

The structure of the EHEA Framework was adopted by the ministers of the Bologna Process in Bergen, and it may be worth quoting their decision in the Bergen Communiqué:

> We adopt the overarching framework for qualifications in the EHEA, comprising three cycles (including, within national contexts, the possibility of intermediate qualifications), generic descriptors for each cycle based on learning outcomes and competences, and credit ranges in the first and second cycles. We commit ourselves to elaborating national frameworks for qualifications compatible with the overarching framework for qualifications in the EHEA by 2010, and to having started work on this by 2007.

The last sentence of the ministers' decision relates to national frameworks, but it illustrates the role and function of the EHEA Framework.

The EHEA Framework, then, consists of three cycles, and they are described as follows:[33]

First cycle

> Qualifications that signify completion of the first cycle are awarded to students who:
>
> • have demonstrated knowledge and understanding in a field of study that builds upon their general secondary education, and is typically at a level that, whilst supported by advanced textbooks, includes some aspects that will be informed by knowledge of the forefront of their field of study;
> • can apply their knowledge and understanding in a manner that indicates a professional approach to their work or vocation, and have competences typically demonstrated through devising and sustaining arguments and solving problems within their field of study;

---

33. Description taken from the website of the Bologna Process 2003–5 at http://www.bologna-bergen2005. no/ (accessed on 7 May 2006). It was elaborated by the Bologna Secretariat on the basis of the ministers' decision and the report of the working group (Appendix 8) and approved by the Bologna Board on 15 June 2005.

• have the ability to gather and interpret relevant data (usually within their field of study) to inform judgments that include reflection on relevant social, scientific or ethical issues;

• can communicate information, ideas, problems and solutions to both specialist and non-specialist audiences;

• have developed those learning skills that are necessary for them to continue to undertake further study with a high degree of autonomy.

First cycle qualifications typically include 180–240 ECTS credits.

Second cycle

Qualifications that signify completion of the second cycle are awarded to students who:

• have demonstrated knowledge and understanding that is founded upon and extends and/or enhances that typically associated with the first cycle, and that provides a basis or opportunity for originality in developing and/or applying ideas, often within a research context;

• can apply their knowledge and understanding, and problem-solving abilities in new or unfamiliar environments within broader (or multidisciplinary) contexts related to their field of study;

• have the ability to integrate knowledge and handle complexity, and formulate judgments with incomplete or limited information, but that include reflecting on social and ethical responsibilities linked to the application of their knowledge and judgments;

• can communicate their conclusions, and the knowledge and rationale underpinning these, to specialist and non-specialist audiences clearly and unambiguously;

• have the learning skills to allow them to continue to study in a manner that may be largely self-directed or autonomous.

Second cycle qualifications typically build on first cycle qualifications and include an additional 90–120 ECTS credits, with a minimum of 60 credits at the level of the second cycle.

Third cycle

Qualifications that signify completion of the third cycle are awarded to students who:

• have demonstrated a systematic understanding of a field of study and mastery of the skills and methods of research associated with that field;

• have demonstrated the ability to conceive, design, implement and adapt a substantial process of research with scholarly integrity;

• have made a contribution through original research that extends the frontier of knowledge by developing a substantial body of work, some of which merits national or international refereed publication;

• are capable of critical analysis, evaluation and synthesis of new and complex ideas;

• can communicate with their peers, the larger scholarly community and with society in general about their areas of expertise;

• can be expected to be able to promote, within academic and professional contexts, technological, social or cultural advancement in a knowledge based society.

There is no stipulation of workload for third cycle qualifications, as there has so far been no agreement within the Bologna Process on how or even whether this should be done. Personally, I take the view that even if there may be factors making such stipulation difficult, it should by no means be impossible to stipulate workload for doctoral qualifications, and there may be considerable merit in doing so. It may be worth recalling that where doctoral candidates work on the basis of scholarships or temporary positions as researchers and research assistants, they are normally required to complete their degree within the time stipulated for the scholarship or temporary position.

As mentioned, the ministers did not follow the working group on one point: the inclusion of short-cycle qualifications within the first degree of the EHEA Framework. Instead, ministers allowed for the possibility of "intermediate qualifications" within national contexts, even if the concept of intermediate qualifications was not part of the recommendation of the working group and was not defined in the Bergen Communiqué.

In suggesting the inclusion of short-cycle qualifications within the EHEA Framework, the working group recognised that these qualifications were not found in all national systems, and it did not suggest that all national frameworks should include such qualifications.[34] Nevertheless, many countries have short-cycle qualifications, and at least a million students in Europe follow short-cycle study programmes. The term "short-cycle qualifications" definitely has scope for improvement, but it is unfortunate that this reality of higher education in many countries was not recognised in the EHEA Framework. It could be covered by the term "intermediate qualifications", but this term is much less clear, as it has not been defined in any of the key documents or reports of the Bologna Process, and it could in principle relate to any of the three cycles.

In spite of not making explicit provision for short-cycle qualifications, the EHEA Framework is a very important achievement, since it provides an overarching framework for the higher education qualifications of 45 European countries. By 2010, all Bologna countries should, as we have seen, have completed their own national frameworks, and these should be compatible with the EHEA Framework.

The European Qualifications Framework

When work started on the EHEA Framework in 2003–04, it was clear that this overarching framework would cover only higher education, since this was the remit of the

---

34. *A Framework for Qualifications of the European Higher Education Area*, op. cit., p. 62.

Bologna Process. At the same time, many people felt a need for a similar framework for vocational education and training (VET). In this sector, co-operation at European level is largely organised in the framework of the European Union and is often referred to as the Copenhagen Process. Progress on the EHEA Framework led to increased interest in a similar framework for VET qualifications, and a meeting in Maastricht in December 2004 of the ministers responsible for vocational education and training called for the development of "an open and flexible European qualifications framework, founded on transparency and mutual trust".

The framework will provide a common reference to facilitate the recognition and transferability of qualifications covering both VET and general (secondary and higher) education, based mainly on competences and learning outcomes".[35] The European Commission appointed an expert group to give advice, and this work led to a proposal for a European Qualifications Framework covering the full range of qualifications. The Commission launched a consultation on the European Qualifications Framework (EQF) in July 2005, with a deadline for comments by late December 2005. The consultation process included two large conferences: one in Glasgow in September 2005 and one in Budapest in February 2006.[36] This consultation process led to a revised draft EQF, which was adopted by the European Commission on 5 September 2006 and is to be submitted to the European Parliament and Council for adoption, probably by the end of 2007.

At the time of writing, the EQF has therefore not yet been adopted. The discussion here is based on the outline of the EQF submitted for consultation, a Staff Working Document dated 8 July 2005, which was the basis for the consultation, [37] and the latest, revised proposal available at the time of writing: the Proposal for a Recommendation of the European Parliament and of the Council on the Establishment of the European Qualifications Framework for Lifelong Learning of 5 September 2006.[38]

While the EQF covers a fuller range of qualifications than the EHEA Framework, it is much narrower in geographical scope. All 25 members of the European Union are also in the Bologna Process, as are the three additional member countries of the European Economic Area, while the Bologna Process currently (2006) has 45 members.[39]

Purpose

The purpose of the European Qualifications Framework is much the same as for the EHEA Framework: to provide a framework for national frameworks and to ensure suf-

---

35. For the Maastricht Communiqué, see http://www.eu2004.nl/default.asp?CMS_ITEM=9D72E2AC57E 84C3BB74CAE002CEC4BD7X1X63053X71&CMS_NOCOOKIES=YES (accessed on 9 May 2006).

36. See http://europa.eu.int/comm/education/policies/educ/eqf/index_en.html (accessed on 8 May 2006).

37. Sec (2005) 957, available at http://europa.eu.int/comm/education/policies/2010/doc/consultation_eqf_ en.pdf (accessed on 8 May 2005).

38. COM(2006) 479 final, available at http://ec.europa.eu/education/policies/educ/eqf/com_2006_0479_ en.pdf (accessed on 8 September 2006).

39. Montenegro acceded to the Bologna Process, becoming its 46th member, at the ministerial conference in London on 17-18 May 2007, after the manuscript of this book was completed.

ficient consistency between national qualifications frameworks at all levels to facilitate mobility, with comparison and recognition of qualifications at all levels of education, not only higher education. In the words of the Commission proposal:

> The main purpose of the EQF is to act as a translation device and neutral reference point for comparing qualifications across different education and training systems and to strengthen co-operation and mutual trust between the relevant stakeholders. This will increase transparency, facilitate the transfer and use of qualifications across different education and training systems and levels.[40]

One important stated objective of the EQF is to support lifelong learning by making it easier for learners to alternate between learning and work, and to obtain recognition – in their home country or in other EU countries – of the qualifications earned through a variety of learning experiences. The EQF takes an inclusive view of learning:

> Learning is a cumulative process where individuals gradually assimilate increasingly complex and abstract entities (concepts, categories, and patterns of behaviour or models) and/or acquire skills and wider competences. This process takes place informally, for example through leisure activities, and in formal learning settings which include the workplace.[41]

Structure

The EQF is to consist of three main elements:

- The core would be a set of common reference points – referring to learning outcomes located in a structure of eight levels.
- These reference levels would be supported by a range of tools and instruments addressing the need of individual citizens (an integrated European credit transfer and accumulation system for lifelong learning, the Europass instrument, the Ploteus database on learning opportunities).
- An EQF would also include a set of common principles and procedures providing guidelines for co-operation between stakeholders at different levels – in particular focusing on quality assurance, validation, guidance and key competences.[42]

In other words, the EQF has fewer levels than the number normally included in national frameworks. This seems reasonable for an overarching framework, because several qualifications can be of the same level and the overarching framework would gain little in transparency and usefulness if many of its levels were not relevant to most national frameworks. Having too many levels, into each of which few national qualifications would actually fit, could create rather than reduce obstacles to mobility and recognition. On the other hand, the overarching framework should contain a suffi-

---

40. Ibid., pp. 2–3.
41. Sec (2005) 957, p. 10.
42. Ibid., p. 4.

cient number of levels to cover the major levels common to most national frameworks. From this point of view, eight seems to be a reasonable number of levels to cover the full range of education qualifications.

The EQF does not explicitly attribute levels to primary, secondary and higher education, but it does indicate that higher education qualifications at level 5 are "associated with the 'short cycle' (within the first cycle) of qualifications in the framework developed under the Bologna process", that level 6 qualifications are "associated with" first cycle higher education qualifications, level 7 with second cycle higher education qualifications and level 8 with third cycle higher education qualifications in the framework developed by the Bologna Process.[43]

Descriptors

The 2005 draft of the European Qualifications Framework proposed eight levels, as shown in Table 10.1.[44] The summary descriptors were complemented by more extensive descriptors organised around four dimensions: autonomy and responsibility, learning competence, communication and social competence, and professional and vocational competence.

It may be useful to illustrate the summaries in Table 10.1 by quoting the descriptions for two EQF levels that are quite far apart.[45] The 2005 proposal gave this description for level 3:

Autonomy and responsibility

Take responsibility for completion of tasks and demonstrate some independence in role in work or study where contexts are generally stable but where some factors change.

Learning competence

Take responsibility for own learning.

Communication and social competence

Produce (and respond to) detailed written and oral communication. Take responsibility for self-understanding and behaviour.

Professional and vocational competence

Solve problems using well known information sources taking account of some social issues

---

43. Ibid., pp. 23–4. A similar indication is given in the revised 2006 proposal, see COM(2006) 479 final p. 20.
44. Sec (2005) 957, p. 41.
45. Ibid., pp. 39–40.

Table 10.1: European Qualifications Framework (draft version, 2005)

Level	Brief indicator of level of qualification
1	Qualifications at level 1 recognise basic general knowledge and skills, and the capacity to undertake simple tasks under direct supervision in a structured environment. The development of learning skills requires structured support. These qualifications are not occupation-specific and are often sought by those with no qualification.
2	Qualifications at level 2 recognise a limited range of knowledge, skills and wider competences that are mainly concrete and general in nature. Skills are applied under supervision in a controlled environment. Learners take limited responsibility for their own learning. Some of these qualifications are occupation-specific but most recognise a general preparation for work and study.
3	Qualifications at level 3 recognise broad general knowledge and field-specific practical and basic theoretical knowledge; they also recognise the capacity to carry out tasks under direction. Learners take responsibility for their own learning and have limited experience of practice in a particular aspect of work or study.
4	Qualifications at level 4 recognise significant field-specific practical and theoretical knowledge and skills. They also recognise the capacity to apply specialist knowledge, skills and competences and to solve problems independently and supervise others. Learners show self-direction in learning and have experience of practice in work or study in both common and exceptional situations.
5	Qualifications at level 5 recognise broad theoretical and practical knowledge, including knowledge relevant to a particular field of learning or occupation. They also recognise the capacity to apply knowledge and skill in developing strategic solutions to well-defined abstract and concrete problems. Learning skills provide a basis for autonomous learning and the qualifications draw on experience of operational interaction in work or study including management of people and projects.
6	Qualifications at level 6 recognise detailed theoretical and practical knowledge, skill and competence associated with a field of learning or work, some of which is at the forefront of the field. These qualifications also recognise the application of knowledge in devising and sustaining arguments, in solving problems and in making judgements that take into account social or ethical issues. Qualifications at this level include outcomes appropriate for a professional approach to operating in a complex environment.
7	Qualifications at level 7 recognise self-directed, theoretical and practical learning, some of which is at the forefront of knowledge in a specialised field that provides a basis for originality in developing and/or applying ideas, often within a research context. These qualifications also recognise an ability to integrate knowledge and formulate judgements taking account of social and ethical issues and responsibilities, and also reflect experience of managing change in a complex environment.
8	Qualifications at level 8 recognise systematic mastery of a highly specialised field of knowledge and a capacity for critical analysis, evaluation and synthesis of new and complex ideas. They also recognise an ability to conceive, design, implement and adapt substantial research processes. The qualifications also recognise leadership experience in the development of new and creative approaches that extend or redefine existing knowledge or professional practice.

Level 7, corresponding to second-cycle higher education qualifications, was described thus:

Autonomy and responsibility

Demonstrate leadership and innovation in work and study contexts that are unfamiliar, complex and unpredictable, and that require solving problems involving many interacting factors. Review strategic performance of teams.

Learning competence

Demonstrate autonomy in the direction of learning and a high level understanding of learning processes.

Communication and social competence

Communicate project outcomes, methods and underpinning rationale to specialist and nonspecialist audiences using appropriate techniques. Scrutinise and reflect on social norms and relationships and act to change them.

Professional and vocational competence

Solve problems by integrating complex knowledge sources that are sometimes incomplete and in new and unfamiliar contexts. Demonstrate experience of operational interaction in managing change within a complex environment. Respond to social, scientific and ethical issues that are encountered in work or study.

We see that these descriptions are not radically different from those of national frameworks. Even though the EQF, like the EHEA Framework, is an overarching framework, the descriptors in such a framework need to be precise and extensive enough to make it possible to place national qualifications and their descriptors within the overarching framework.

The 2005 proposal was submitted to a consultation process that is described below, and the consultation led to a revised proposal published in September 2006 that simplified the description. This revised proposal is the Commission's proposal to the European Parliament and the European Council, and at the time of writing it is the most recent version of the proposed European Qualifications Framework. It may, of course, be further modified before it is adopted, but it would be hazardous to try to foresee what any amendments might be. The Commission's proposal of September 2006 still contains eight levels described in terms of learners' knowledge, skills and competences, as described in Table 10.2.[46]

---

46. COM(2006) 479 final, pp. 19–20.

Table 10.2: European Qualifications Framework (revised version, 2006)

Level	Relevant learning outcomes for that level		
	Knowledge	*Skills*	*Competence*
	is described as theoretical and/or factual	*are described as cognitive (use of logical, intuitive and creative thinking) and practical (involving manual dexterity and the use of methods, materials, tools and instruments)*	*is described in terms of responsibility and autonomy*
1	basic general knowledge	basic skills required to carry out simple tasks	work or study under direct supervision in a structured context
2	basic factual knowledge of a field of work or study	basic cognitive and practical skills required to use relevant information in order to carry out tasks and to solve routine problems using simple rules and tools	work or study under supervision with some autonomy
3	knowledge of facts, principles, processes and general concepts, in a field of work or study	a range of cognitive and practical skills required to accomplish tasks and solve problems by selecting and applying basic methods, tools, materials and information	take responsibility for completion of tasks in work or study adapt own behaviour to circumstances in solving problems
4	factual and theoretical knowledge in broad contexts within a field of work or study	a range of cognitive and practical skills required to generate solutions to specific problems in a field of work or study	exercise self-management within the guidelines of work or study contexts that are usually predictable, but are subject to change supervise the routine work of others, taking some responsibility for the evaluation and improvement of work or study activities
5*	comprehensive, specialised, factual and theoretical knowledge within a field of work or study and an awareness of the boundaries of that knowledge	a comprehensive range of cognitive and practical skills required to develop creative solutions to abstract problems	exercise management and supervision in contexts of work or study activities where there is unpredictable change; review and develop performance of self and others

6**	advanced knowledge of a field of work or study, involving a critical understanding of theories and principles	advanced skills, demonstrating mastery and innovation, required to solve complex and unpredictable problems in a specialised field of work or study	manage complex technical or professional activities or projects, taking responsibility for decision-making in unpredictable work or study contexts; take responsibility for managing professional development of individuals and groups
7†	highly specialised knowledge, some of which is at the forefront of knowledge in a field of work or study, as the basis for original thinking; critical awareness of knowledge issues in a field and at the interface between different fields	specialised problem-solving skills required in research and/or innovation in order to develop new knowledge and procedures and to integrate knowledge from different fields	manage and transform work or study in contexts that are complex, unpredictable and require new strategic approaches; take responsibility for contributing to professional knowledge and practice and/or for reviewing the strategic performance of teams
8‡	knowledge at the most advanced frontier of a field of work or study and at the interface between fields	the most advanced and specialised skills and techniques, including synthesis and evaluation, required to solve critical problems in research and/or innovation and to extend and redefine existing knowledge or professional practice	demonstrate substantial authority, innovation, autonomy, scholarly and professional integrity and sustained commitment to the development of new ideas or processes at the forefront of work or study contexts including research

Compatibility with the Framework for Qualifications of the European Higher Education Area
The Framework for Qualifications of the European Higher Education Area provides descriptors for cycles. Each cycle descriptor offers a generic statement of typical expectations of achievements and abilities associated with qualifications that represent the end of that cycle.

* The descriptor for the higher education short cycle (within or linked to the first cycle), developed by the Joint Quality Initiative as part of the Bologna Process, corresponds to the learning outcomes for EQF level 5

** The descriptor for the first cycle in the Framework for Qualifications of the European Higher Education Area corresponds to the learning outcomes for EQF level 6

† The descriptor for the second cycle in the Framework for Qualifications of the European Higher Education Area corresponds to the learning outcomes for EQF level 7

‡ The descriptor for the third cycle in the Framework for Qualifications of the European Higher Education Area corresponds to the learning outcomes for EQF level 8

Elaboration

In discussing national frameworks, we underlined the importance of consulting widely with stakeholders in elaborating the framework. The same is, of course, true for overarching frameworks. Neither the EHEA Framework nor the EQF was elaborated in splendid isolation: in each case, there was a large international conference open to representatives of all competent public authorities involved in the Bologna Process and the European Union/European Economic Area respectively, European organisations of higher education institutions, students and employers, and international organisations. In the case of the EQF, the Commission also invited written comments from any organisation, authority or individual wishing to submit them, whereas the EHEA Framework was discussed on several occasions in the Bologna Follow-Up Group, where many of the main stakeholders were represented.

Ultimately, a qualifications framework is the responsibility of the competent public authorities, and they have to make a decision where opinions expressed in the consultation process differ, or where they themselves hold opinions different from the majority view in the consultation. For the overarching framework, the decision is made by a body involving the competent public authorities of the countries concerned, in our case the ministers of the Bologna Process for the EHEA Framework, and the European Parliament and the European Council for the EQF.

Consultation means all relevant views are likely to be brought to the attention of the decision makers, but it does not mean all opinions are heeded. We can illustrate this by two examples. As we have seen, the ministers decided not to include short-cycle qualifications in the EHEA Framework, even though many ministers, along with the European organisations representing students, higher education institutions and employers in the Bologna Process, and the participating international organisations argued strongly in favour of inclusion. The second example refers to the relationship between the EHEA Framework and the EQF.

The relationship between the two overarching European frameworks

As we have seen, the EHEA Framework encompasses 45 countries, while the EQF applies to countries of the European Union and the European Economic Area. In both cases, the number of countries could increase, since the European Union is likely to admit new members within the next few years. The Bologna Process, on the other hand, is unlikely to be significantly enlarged, though Montenegro is likely to accede in 2007 as it is already *de facto* involved in the process, and it is conceivable that Belarus could join the process some time in the future if and when the country gets a democratic government.

For levels below higher education, there is no overlap between the two frameworks, since only the EQF applies; but, for higher education, there are two overarching frameworks. There are no great divergences between them, though they are not identical. There are, in fact, two points of divergence.

Firstly, EQF level 5 in effect corresponds both to short-cycle higher education qualifications and to vocational qualifications at that level. Therefore, EQF makes provision for short-cycle qualifications whereas the EHEA Framework does not. It is worth recalling that the EHEA Framework admits the possibility of "intermediate qualifications" within national frameworks but makes no provision for such qualifications within the overarching framework. From my point of view, the *de facto* inclusion of short-cycle qualifications in the EQF is positive. However, the opposition to including them in the EHEA Framework did not primarily come from countries outside the European Union/European Economic Area, so that, if the EQF is adopted in its current form, the same public authorities will in fact make different decisions on the same issue in two different frameworks.

More seriously, while the descriptions of levels 6, 7 and 8 in the EQF are not radically different from the description of the first, second and third cycle in the EHEA Framework, they are also not identical. The 2006 proposal is less detailed than the 2005 proposal in this sense, and the differences with the EHEA Framework are therefore less explicit. Nonetheless, if the EQF is adopted as proposed in September 2006 and if the EHEA Framework remains unchanged, there will be two overarching qualifications frameworks for higher education in Europe. One key purpose of the EHEA Framework, and presumably also of the EQF, was to provide a single framework for the description of European qualifications to education institutions, public authorities, students and employers from other parts of the world, but they will now be faced with a situation in which there are two largely compatible, but still different European frameworks. At the very least, this is hardly a brilliant communication strategy.

In the consultation process for the EQF, many respondents from many countries did in fact point out that it would be very unfortunate if the EQF did not incorporate the EHEA Framework, which had already been adopted by the ministers of the Bologna Process, all the more so as all the ministers who would be invited to adopt the EQF had been party to the adoption of the EHEA Framework. These comments were made by many national bodies and authorities, as well as by the Bologna Follow-Up Group, a body in which the member states are represented by civil servants from their ministries responsible for higher education. The Bologna Follow-Up Group held its discussion on the basis of a comparative analysis of the two documents elaborated by the Bologna working group on qualifications frameworks, and its views were transmitted to the Commission by a letter from the (then) United Kingdom Presidency of the Bologna Follow-Up Group in December 2005. The letter states that, while the two frameworks are not inconsistent and incompatible, they do overlap and there is potential for confusion. It also underlines that the added value of a separate European Qualifications Framework would be to relate higher education to other areas of education and training and vice versa. The importance of these comments made in the consultation process was not acknowledged in the Commission's proposal of September 2006, which indicated that the main outcome of the consultation process was a "refinement and simplification of the reference level descriptors".[47]

---

47. COM (2006) 479 final, p. 6.

Two other elements of the 2006 proposal also give rise to concern. One concern is that, while it is hoped the EQF will be adopted in 2007, member states should "relate their national qualifications system to the European Qualifications Framework by 2009".[48] One key measure in this respect is the elaboration of national qualifications frameworks, so European Union countries should complete this process by 2009. Within the Bologna Process, the deadline is 2010, so that – if the proposal is adopted – the EQF rather than the EHEA Framework will be the reference for European Union countries. Similarly, by 2011, "all new qualifications and 'Europass' documents issued by the competent authorities [should] contain a clear reference to the appropriate European Qualifications Framework level".[49] The Diploma Supplement, which was elaborated jointly by the European Commission, the Council of Europe and UNESCO, is also an important transparency instrument of the European Higher Education Area, where ministers committed themselves to issuing the Diploma Supplement automatically, free of charge and in a widely spoken European language by 2005.

It is unfortunate that the Commission so far does not seem to have taken account of the weighty arguments against in effect establishing two largely compatible, yet not identical overarching qualifications frameworks for higher education in Europe. It would be doubly unfortunate if 25 of the 45 ministers who adopted the EHEA Framework in 2005 were to adopt a second framework covering higher education a year or two later. The logic and rationale for proceeding in this way is difficult to discern, and the effect could easily be to create confusion rather than transparency about European higher education qualifications.

Relationship between national and overarching frameworks

If the European frameworks are overarching and the national frameworks more operational, how do the two levels of framework relate to each other? The overarching frameworks are intended to offer assistance and guidance to national frameworks, and to ensure that the national frameworks of countries and education systems that not only coexist, but co-operate within a given European framework – whether the larger one of the Bologna Process or the narrower one of the European Union – are compatible and consistent.

As an illustration, let us consider an admittedly far-fetched example. It would be perfectly possible to elaborate a national qualifications framework that had only one qualification below doctoral level, with the stipulation that learners studying for this qualification – for the sake of argument, let us call it a first degree – must be able to conduct independent research in two fields of knowledge as well as demonstrate creativity and flexibility in the application of knowledge and skills, advanced analytical ability, high-level communication skills in three foreign languages and high aptitude for teamwork

---

48. Ibid., p. 15, point 2.
49. Ibid., p. 15, point 3.

and independent work. The framework might stipulate the workload for this imaginary first degree as 600 ECTS credits. As long as such a national framework described its qualifications in the terms discussed in this chapter, it would qualify as a framework. It would be possible to do this, but it would not be advisable. Such a framework would clearly not be consistent with the policies of the European Higher Education Area, and it would hardly do learners or employers any service or justice.

We have seen that compatibility between two overarching frameworks partly covering the same qualifications levels in the same geographical area has so far not been ensured. So how do we ensure that national frameworks are compatible with the overarching framework(s) to which they relate? How can we ensure compatibility, if there is no supranational authority with the power and competence to approve or reject national frameworks?

The answer is that probably there is no foolproof method. National authorities are responsible for their education systems, with the usual caveat for countries where competence in education matters is at sub-national level, and nobody has so far put forward convincing arguments for transferring this authority to a supranational level. In the European Union, education is one of the most important areas for the application of the subsidiary principle. Therefore, if a country were to insist on introducing a first degree like the imaginary one just described, no international legal authority could prevent it from doing so.

European co-operation in education, including higher education, is voluntary, and it relies on building up trust between participating countries as well as between public authorities, institutions, students, employers and other stakeholders. Therefore, the informal pressure to abide by the overarching qualifications framework is likely to be strong and persuasive, once the overarching framework has been adopted.

Within the European Higher Education Area, countries will certify the compatibility of their own national frameworks with the EHEA Framework. The ENIC and NARIC networks[50] have been asked to maintain a register of these self-certifications, which will therefore be publicly available and hence also available to scrutiny by co-operation partners in the European Higher Education Area. In practice, a country that certifies its national framework as compatible with the EHEA Framework will have to publish information that will convince other countries that the self-certification is justified.

---

50. The European Network of National Information Centres on academic recognition and mobility, served jointly by the Council of Europe and UNESCO; and the Network of National Academic Recognition Information Centres, served by the European Commission. The two networks are largely made up of the same national centres, since all NARICs are also ENICs, though some ENICs – in countries outside the EU – are not NARICs. The two networks co-operate very closely, hold annual joint meetings and maintain a joint website – http://www.enic-naric.net/ – which is where self-certifications of national frameworks are likely to be published.

Although there are no formal guidelines for self-certification so far, it seems reasonable to assume either that such guidelines will be elaborated within the Bologna Process or that, through the first self-certification exercises, a body of good practice will emerge that may not have formal status, but will constitute informal guidelines for countries that wish their national qualifications frameworks to be well considered by their co-operation partners, and hence their qualifications to be easily recognised within the European Higher Education Area. Probably there will be an incentive for countries to invite foreign experts to participate in the self-certification exercise. In 2006, two pilot projects were launched for self-certification of the Irish and Scottish qualifications frameworks, and in both cases the national authorities invited two foreign experts to participate in the exercise.

As is the case with the EHEA Framework, the European Commission Staff Document underlines that the EQF is not a regulatory instrument, and that it is up to national authorities to determine how their national qualifications link to the EQF. It also calls for self-certification procedures to be developed along with agreement on procedures and criteria. For self-certification, the Commission staff document stipulates that:

> The competent national body or bodies should oversee this process. While the process should mainly be a national one it must be ensured that international experts are involved. It is important that the evidence supporting the self-certification process should identify each of the criteria which are to be developed and that this should all be published. It is envisaged that the evidence would involve addressing in turn each of the criteria which are to be developed and that there would be a formal record of the decisions and arrangements that are put in place in relation to the systems or framework.

> A further key element would be that the relevant networks involved in the transparency of qualifications maintain a public listing of states that have confirmed that they have completed the self-certification process.[51]

Now that the overarching European framework has been adopted (in the case of the EHEA Framework) or is about to be adopted (in the case of the EQF), much of the focus will be on the relationship between national and overarching frameworks. As a part of this discussion, formal or informal guidelines and guides to good practice are likely to emerge that will ensure not only that national frameworks function in their respective national contexts, but also that they help facilitate the mobility of learners and the recognition of their qualifications internationally. This process will have to balance the need for a measure of common criteria, procedures and agreement on the content of qualifications frameworks with the need for each country to develop its education system and qualifications frameworks with due regard to its own traditions and situation.

---

51. European Commission Staff Document Sec (2005) 957, p. 33.

Like Europe itself, this endeavour will need to balance unity and diversity. Our education systems will not and should not become carbon copies of one another. On the other hand, the concern for protecting national traditions and specificities, while healthy and legitimate, should not serve as an excuse not to undertake profound reforms that adapt the form of higher education, including its qualifications, to the reality of modern European society while preserving the core values of higher education.

Qualifications frameworks help learners move between qualifications within the education system, in the case of national frameworks, or between systems, in the case of overarching frameworks. It is to the paths that learners may take to navigate within an education system that we now turn our attention.

11 Obtaining qualifications: learning paths

The term "learning paths" is not exactly on everyone's lips, and some may consider it an over-complicated way to describe going to school and progressing from one class to another, or from one qualification to another. In a system where students' paths were fixed, so they had little choice other than to follow the standard route or drop out, that might be a valid criticism. But few countries can afford not to offer choices within their education systems or to force learners to choose at an early age with no chance to change their mind. That would be unfair to individuals, and it would be unwise to waste society's human potential. Human beings develop at different speeds: what interests us at age 25 might have bored us stiff at age 10, and what we found most interesting at 25 might bore us a decade or two later.

Learning paths, then, designate the routes along which learners may move within an education system. In a broader sense, they designate any route along which knowledge, understanding and ability may be picked up and assimilated, formally or informally. However, since this is a book on qualifications, and it deals with the reality behind a formal aspect of education, we will use the term "learning paths" in its more common sense: the routes that lead to education qualifications. We start with a consideration of the most well-trodden paths.

Classic learning paths: school education

I would not blame readers if they were slightly tired of our athletes-turned-academics by now, but let us stay with them a little longer. They eventually earned different higher education qualifications – different in level and in profile. Some earned first degrees and stopped there; others went on to second and even third degrees. Some went into medicine, while others studied natural sciences, humanities or social sciences. Chances are that some of them studied law, architecture or agricultural science, and others earned short-cycle qualifications in more vocational studies. If we let our imagination run, we should soon have a fairly representative sample of people with a higher education background. Or will we?

Chances are we will think of more and more professions and academic disciplines, but not think much about how our friends obtained their qualifications. Chances are, I would guess, that we will imagine they all earned ordinary secondary school leaving certificates and then went on to study at a higher education institution. They may have worked in the summers and, judging by those of them we met in Chapter 5, some of them may have been so busy running and skating that their academic progress suffered. Some may have earned fewer than 60 ECTS credits in an academic year, and so have taken longer than the average student to complete their study programmes. In "old speak", some of them may have completed a four-year degree in five. To paraphrase an astute observer of contemporary life from the perspective of someone well versed in the classics, with his values and priorities well defined (and they emphatically did not include sports): "Happiness today is being 18 and not having had the time to read the great authors because one has been too busy skiing".[52] The most intrepid ones may even have taken a year off to travel around the world, and in the process they may have accomplished a lot of informal and maybe also some formal learning. Yet, when we think of their education, we are likely to think of the study programme in which they enrolled, from which they may have taken a year off, and through which they may have progressed at different speeds, but from which they eventually emerged with a qualification.

In our imagination, did some members of our group earn access to higher education on the basis of qualifications other than from the theoretical strand of secondary education? Did some of them break off their studies, work for some years and then return to complete their degree? Did some of them earn their first degree, work and re-enrol at a higher education institution to earn a second degree? Did some of them combine study and work? Did some of them study in an arrangement involving long-distance, open or distance learning? Did some of them even combine work, family life and study, and maybe even find the time to be active in an association? Did at least one of them serve as a full-time student representative on a university governing body or in the national student union for a year or two and then go back to his or her studies afterwards?

The possibilities are many, and while some readers will certainly have thought of several of them, chances are that most of us will have stuck to the beaten track. That may also be a good place to start exploring learning paths. At first glance, they may seem surprisingly familiar.

The classic learning path toward a higher education qualification is primary school followed by secondary school. Where choices are available, the classic learning path has an emphasis on theoretical rather than practical or vocational studies, preferably without repeating classes along the way. In terms of the qualifications frameworks we explored in the two previous chapters, the classic learning paths lead from level 1:

> basic general knowledge and skills and the capacity to undertake simple tasks under direct supervision in a structured environment. The development of learning skills requires structured support

through level 2:

> limited range of knowledge, skills and wider competences that are mainly concrete and general in nature. Skills are applied under supervision in a controlled environment. Learners take limited responsibility for their own learning

---

52. Paraphrasing Fr Hallvard Rieber-Mohn, OP (1922–1982), a Norwegian Dominican and well-known cultural commentator when the author of this book was growing up.

and level 3, to attain level 4:

> Qualifications at level 4 recognise significant field-specific practical and theoretical knowledge and skills. They also recognise the capacity to apply specialist knowledge, skills and competences and to solve problems independently and supervise others. Learners show self-direction in learning and have experience of practice in work or study in both common and exceptional situations

as a typical description of a secondary school leaving qualification.[53] Then the classic path would follow the standard progression route of higher education, through a first degree:

> detailed theoretical and practical knowledge, skill and competence associated with a field of learning or work, some of which is at the forefront of the field. These qualifications also recognise the application of knowledge in devising and sustaining arguments, in solving problems and in making judgements that take into account social or ethical issues. Qualifications at this level include outcomes appropriate for a professional approach to operating in a complex environment

and possibly end with a second degree:

> detailed theoretical and practical knowledge, skill and competence associated with a field of learning or work, some of which is at the forefront of the field. These qualifications also recognise the application of knowledge in devising and sustaining arguments, in solving problems and in making judgements that take into account social or ethical issues. Qualifications at this level include outcomes appropriate for a professional approach to operating in a complex environment.

Repeating the level descriptors in one of the qualifications frameworks discussed in Chapter 10 serves to underline the link between qualifications frameworks and learning paths, but also to illustrate an important aspect of what we tend to consider the standard learning path: from basic to much more advanced and complex knowledge, understanding and abilities.

The classic learning path, then, follows the structure of the school system and progression is upward: obtaining qualifications at one level opens access to the next level up. Hence, the precise classic learning path depends on the education system of the country concerned. It may be six years of primary school followed by three years of lower secondary and three years of upper secondary school, or it may be seven years of primary school followed by two and three years, or there may be no formal distinction in the system between primary and lower secondary school. The total length of primary and secondary education is usually 11 or 12 years, and for these levels it is still far more common to talk about years of study rather than credits earned. The

---

53. The descriptions are from the European Qualifications Framework described in the previous chapter, but they could equally well have been taken from a national qualifications framework.

total length could be 10 or 13 years, but those would be much rarer cases. Two learn- ers making their way through the same national system might even follow different paths and study for different lengths of time. Since school systems are reformed from time to time, a learner who completed secondary school 30 years ago might not have followed the same learning path and taken the same time as a learner who completed secondary education in the same country last year.

On the basis of their secondary school leaving qualifications, learners then gain admis- sion to higher education, where they follow a similar route. If they are successful at first degree level, they may go on to earn a second degree and maybe even a doctoral degree. If they do, their degrees at different levels will probably be in the same academic dis- cipline, or, if their system allows them to combine different disciplines at first degree level, they will probably choose to specialise in one of them at second degree level and then maybe choose a specialisation within this discipline for their doctorate.

So far, our map of learning paths is easy to follow. It looks more like a highway, and there is little risk of confusion at entry and exit points. Some learners, however, will have problems finding their way onto the highway, while others may have problems finding suitable exit points and may be left by the wayside. If the education system is flexible, perhaps with the help of a well-developed qualifications framework, they may find alternative routes.

Alternative learning paths: school education

Countries start differentiating between tracks within their school systems at various levels and in various ways. At the latest by the time they reach upper secondary school – and in many cases earlier – students have to make choices that to some extent decide how they will continue their formal education. Another way of seeing these choices is to say that students choose different learning paths. Typically, the paths will differ in the relative weight of theoretical and practical subjects, and they may also differ in the emphasis they put on natural sciences, social sciences and humanities. The possibili- ties of variation are numerous.

However, the choices of different learning paths may have consequences for whether learners will have access to higher education later on. In all countries that differentiate between a more theoretical and a more practical strand at secondary level – or that have a variety of such strands – it is the theoretical strands that provide the easiest access route to higher education. Those who choose more practical strands may be aiming primarily at earning vocational qualifications. All this is straightforward as long as learners make the right choices and do not wish to change tracks after a few years. If they do wish to change, however, their possibilities depend on whether their education system is flexible or rigid, on whether the qualifications framework provides for easy movement between qualifications or in effect discourages such movement.

In some countries, the theoretical strands may be the only access route. In this case, those who have secondary school leaving qualifications that do not give access to higher education – or for that matter any other qualifications that do not give such access – will have to enrol in a secondary school programme that does give access and continue from there.

This is of course a possible learning path, but it is not necessarily the most rational one. Even if the profile of different strands of secondary education may be very different, and even if there may also be significant variations in terms of generic learning outcomes, the difference may not be substantial enough for the learner to need to start at the entry level to secondary education. More flexible systems will allow learners to transfer between different strands of secondary education and may make explicit provision for such transfer in their system by indicating points at which the transfer may best be made. What these systems do is to provide for alternative learning paths and show how learners may move from one path to another.

However flexible a system may be, it does not mean that learners may transfer exactly as they like or that there is no cost involved. Where the differences between strands are significant, learners may have to do extra work to bring their knowledge, understanding and abilities into line with the requirements of the strand to which they wish to transfer. Nevertheless, there is a big difference between doing some extra work and starting from entry level.

Let us, for the sake of argument, imagine a system with two strands of secondary education. Let us imagine that strand A is theoretical and leads to a school-leaving qualification giving general access to higher education, while strand B leads to a vocational qualification that does not give general access. Let us imagine that someone who opted for strand B and is halfway through the first year of secondary education now decides that strand B is really not what he wants to do and he would like to take strand A instead. Rather than starting again at entry level in strand A in the next school year, he might complete the first year of strand B, take extra courses during the summer designed to make up for the differences between the two strands in profile and possibly in generic learning outcomes and enter the second year of strand A at the start of the next school year. He will have to do some extra work and sacrifice part of his summer, but he will not have to repeat the first year of secondary school.

A second case could be someone who completes secondary education in strand B, earning the appropriate qualification, and only then decides she would like to enter higher education. In her system, this is not possible with the diploma she has just earned. If the system is rigid, she might have to enter the first year of strand A and invest another three years to obtain the kind of secondary school qualification that will give access to higher education. She would enter higher education at an age when she might have obtained her first degree had she made a different choice when she entered secondary education. By making a choice that seemed right at the time, but subsequently turned out not to satisfy her interests and aspirations, she has lost three years. In a more flexible system, however, other options might be open to her. She might be able to make up for the differences between the two strands by taking a specially designed one-year course or even, if the differences were smaller, by taking a summer or a semester course. In this way, her decision to change tracks would cost only one year of extra work rather than three, or maybe even less. Perhaps she could enrol on a part-time course for one year; that way she could work part-time and might not need to take out study loans.

In either of these scenarios, our new acquaintances would be ready to enter higher education on the basis of a secondary school qualification from a theoretical strand. However, there might also be systems that allowed access on the basis of other strands, such as strand B in our example above. Here we would have an alternative learning path, not within secondary education, but from secondary to higher education. Some education systems provide for such alternative paths, but in others a secondary school leaving qualification from the theoretical strand is the only access route to higher education. In systems that allow access on the basis of "strand B" qualifications, these may either give general access to higher education or they may give access only to certain specified programmes. For example, a vocational secondary school qualification may give the holder access to any higher education programme ranging from humanities through social sciences and law to architecture, or it may give access only to programmes with some relation to the profile of the secondary qualifications, for example certain technical *Fachhochschule* programmes.[54]

Once our friends enter higher education, they may also follow different learning paths. Although we have not used the term "learning path" much until this chapter, we have in fact considered many elements of higher education learning paths earlier in this book, and we do not need to repeat considerations of workload, level, profile and learning outcomes. There may, however, be considerable value in seeing that the different concepts all fit together. There may also be value in realising that various higher education systems and qualifications frameworks may be more or less flexible, that is, provide more or fewer learning paths. Some systems may require that once students have chosen their disciplines, they follow a fairly set programme with few choices available within that, especially at first degree level. That would have been fairly typical a generation or two ago, whereas today the tendency is generally to make more learning paths possible. The development of the credit system has been very helpful in this respect. Within a system, some study programmes may be more flexible than others: programmes leading to qualifications in regulated professions, for example, may be less flexible than study programmes in mathematics or in foreign languages. Within most programmes, however, there is at least a measure of flexibility with regard to elective courses.

---

54. As mentioned earlier, *Fachhochschule* has come to be used as the generic term for what is also referred to as "non-university" higher education, which typically has a more vocational profile than classic university programmes and may also lead to short-cycle qualifications, as a way into the labour market or as a step towards a first cycle qualification. *Fachhochschule* study programmes can also lead directly to a first degree.

There may be different provisions for transferring from one study programme to another, and perhaps even more so for enrolling in a second degree programme with a profile significantly different from that of one's first degree. Yet, for higher education, the most difficult question is to what extent knowledge, skills and abilities acquired outside formal higher education programmes may be recognised and used as credit towards a higher education qualification.

Alternative learning paths: non-traditional learning and experience

When we talk about school and studies, we tend to think of learning as a formal, organised undertaking. This is not wrong, because much learning is formal and organised, and the formal education system is our most important way of transmitting knowledge and developing understanding after a person's early, formative years. Yet this caveat also illustrates the importance of other forms of learning. Our first learning is informal and experiential, and without it all formal education would be futile. Informal learning does not stop when we start school – it continues in parallel and interacting with our formal learning. We learn from reading books, visiting new places, going to museums, planting a garden, participating in an association, writing a newspaper article, participating in a cooking group or simply trying new recipes and numerous other activities, more often than not without any consideration of having our newly acquired knowledge, understanding and abilities formally recognised within a qualifications framework. Much of the learning we pursue or accidentally acquire in this way would be very difficult to place within a qualifications framework, but some learning could and should be so considered. It can be of great importance to the individual concerned.

In all our examples so far, the different learning paths were made up of formal learning. While most learners gain access to higher education on the basis of a secondary school leaving qualification from the theoretical strand, many (but far from all) systems give access also on the basis of other kinds of formal education. However, there is no reason why the knowledge, understanding and skills needed to successfully undertake higher education must be acquired only through formal education, nor any reason why educational achievements described by learning outcomes at the upper end of the qualifications frameworks should be acquired solely through organised higher education study programmes.

While this statement of principle is almost self-evident, it raises a number of issues that are far from straightforward. For instance, what kind of learning can be accepted as qualifying for access to what kind of education programme or what kind of work? Asking this question may mean asking about the duration and intensity of an activity in which learning is involved, but above all it means asking about its key features. Firstly, what are the learning outcomes, and how can they be described? Secondly, how can they be attested?

In principle, outcomes of informal learning could be described much in the same way as outcomes of formal learning. In principle, informal learning could be measured against the descriptors of a qualifications framework, and descriptors could be developed for various kinds of informal learning that would allow educationists, employers and others to compare the outcomes of a given informal learning experience against the descriptors of a given qualifications framework. Somebody undertaking informal learning in Hungary could in principle have this measured against the descriptions of learning outcomes and levels in the Hungarian qualifications framework.

For foreign language learning, such descriptors do in fact exist, since the descriptions in the European Language Portfolio apply equally well to all language learning, whether this has been acquired formally or informally. For example, the description for level B2 in reading:

> I can read articles and reports concerned with contemporary problems in which the writers adopt particular attitudes or viewpoints. I can understand contemporary literary prose[55]

applies to all learners. Where the learning has been formal, the description as well as the attestation that the learners have indeed achieved this learning outcome can be provided by those who organise or teach the course. Where the learning has been informal, learners can use the description provided by the European Language Portfolio, but they will either have to attest themselves that they have reached the learning outcome or find someone who can provide the attestation for them. This will normally require some kind of test, or sustained observation of their language abilities.

This is often referred to as Assessment of Prior Learning or Assessment of Prior Experiential Learning (APEL), and also as Prior Learning Assessment and Recognition (PLAR).[56] While the term "recognition" is most often used for the assessment of foreign qualifications within a given education system, as we shall see in a later chapter, it may also denote the formal acknowledgement of learning outcomes achieved in non-traditional ways within a qualifications framework.

In practice, of course, learners cannot be expected to provide their own descriptions of learning outcomes for all learning they undertake, nor can one easily expect public authorities responsible for education to provide standard descriptors of all possible learning outcomes of informal learning. One major challenge is therefore to relate informal learning experiences to descriptors in national frameworks, where it is relevant to do so.

This challenge brings us to the second major issue: how can informal learning be attested, and by whom? As we saw with the European Language Portfolio, informal learning can in principle be attested by the learners themselves, but if informal

---

55. See http://culture2.coe.int/portfolio/inc.asp?L=E&M=$t/208-1-0-1/main_pages/welcome.html (accessed on 13 May 2006). The European Language Portfolio was discussed in Chapter 2.
56. See Jindra Divis, "Assessment of non-traditional qualifications" in Sjur Bergan (ed.), *Recognition Issues in the Bologna Process* (Strasbourg 2003: Council of Europe Publishing), pp. 109–17.

learning is to be used to obtain benefits and rights in the education system, such as access to a study programme, those responsible for the programme are likely to require some kind of verification. For example, if the normal learning path giving access to higher education is a theoretical strand of secondary education, but access can also be obtained on the basis of informal learning leading to similar learning outcomes, admissions officers are likely to want to assess the outcomes of these alternative, informal learning paths. This can be done by requiring applicants to take the secondary school leaving examination, but that is not a very flexible solution. Strictly speaking, we would then be considering alternative learning paths to the secondary school leaving qualification and not alternative access to higher education.

Instead, outcomes of informal learning can be assessed on the basis of attestations from someone who has been able to watch the learners' performance, such as an employer or the leader of a voluntary association, through interviews or specially designed examinations, or by admitting a certain number of holders of informal qualifications and in effect assessing them on the basis of their success and failure in the first examinations in the study programme. In the French Community of Belgium, for example, those who do not have the required secondary school leaving certificate may gain access to higher education by taking examinations in a number of specified subjects.[57]

Of course, the assessment may combine a number of such factors, and even rely on these factors in addition to qualifications earned through formal education. For example, many universities in the United States interview candidates for admission and/or require them to undergo various tests that assess other learning outcomes than those attested by the high school diploma.

In fact, relying on informal learning outcomes in addition to the outcomes of formal education is far more common than relying on informal learning alone. In several systems, informal learning can count toward a higher education qualification, but it is very rare that a higher education qualification is granted on the strength of informal learning alone. This may depend on the study programme concerned: it is easier to imagine informal learning making up part of a qualification in a foreign language than in a regulated profession like architecture or medicine. Nevertheless, a foreign language qualification in higher education does not require just practical language skills, but also knowledge and understanding of language structures and linguistics, of literature and the cultural and historical background of the areas in which the language is spoken – in short, all the learning outcomes we described in some detail for Serbo-Croatian in Chapters 2 and 8. These may be obtained through informal learning,

---

57. Arrêté du Gouvernement de la Communauté française relatif au programme de l'examen d'admission aux études universitaires de 1er cycle A.Gt 29-05-1996 M.B. 22-08-1996, err 28-05-1997, available at http://www.cdadoc.cfwb.be/RechDoc/docForm.asp?docid=699&docname=19960529s19828 (accessed on 13 May 2006). I wish to thank Andrzej Bielecki (then) of the Ministry of Education of the French Community of Belgium for having drawn my attention to this text.

but more commonly it is the informal language learning that would give learners a number of credits toward a higher education qualification.

One interesting system that goes very far in recognising informal learning paths for higher education qualifications is found in France. Legal regulations adopted in 2002 have made it possible for those with professional or other experience to gain substantial credits towards a higher education qualification and even to obtain such a qualification on the basis of experience alone.[58] These regulations build on regulations dating back to 1992 and, for some provisions, to 1985. Those who want to obtain such credit must submit to a fairly elaborate procedure in which the applications are assessed by juries, and applicants may be interviewed. The procedure seeks to define the applicants' real competences and to assess these in relation to the learning outcomes required for obtaining a given qualification. By 2004, this provision had become well known and 80 per cent of applications had been favourably assessed.

One advantage of the French system for assessing prior learning is that it allows those who have built up substantial competence through informal learning, including work experience, to have it validated towards formal qualifications without having to go through formal study programmes that might to a large extent repeat what they have already learned. However, the procedure is relatively demanding in terms of resources and can also be time-consuming. Many applicants have unrealistic expectations about what they may gain from the procedure, as it is not a formality leading to something close to automatic recognition, but rather a serious assessment that makes very real demands on applicants.

When asked about their experience with this system, almost all French universities reported that they had assessed at least some applications. While most were for credits towards a qualification, 16 universities had assessed at least one application for a full higher education qualification on the basis of prior learning. The universities were divided on the relative weights of the benefits and disadvantages of the system. While some underlined the benefits to individuals who would otherwise not have been able to obtain higher education qualifications, others stressed the cost and disadvantages of what they saw as a very elaborate system. The French experience leads us to a consideration of lifelong learning.

Lifelong learning

There is no generally accepted definition of lifelong learning, perhaps since this could be seen as trying to state the obvious. As we know, that is an exercise that is often much more difficult than it would seem. The Council of Europe has defined lifelong learning as:

---

58. Jacques-Philippe Saint-Gérand, "La validation de l'expérience. L'expérience française, présentation et évaluation" in *A Framework for Qualifications of the European Higher Education Area*, op. cit., Appendix 4, pp. 117–40. Appendix 4 is in French with a summary in English. Report available at http://www.bologna-bergen2005.no/Docs/00-Main_doc/050218_QF_EHEA.pdf.

a continuous learning process enabling all individuals, from early childhood to old age, to acquire and update knowledge, skills and competencies at different stages of their lives and in a variety of learning environments, both formal and informal, for the purpose of maximising their personal development, employment opportunities and encouraging their active participation in a democratic society[59]

whereas the European Commission sees lifelong learning as:

all learning activity undertaken throughout life, with the aim of improving knowledge, skills and competence, within a personal, civic, social and/or employment-related perspective.[60]

May the present author be forgiven for preferring his own, shorter definition: lifelong learning is the kind of learning about which nobody can speak with the authority of a fully accomplished learner.

Learning should be thought of as something that does not end, at least within the lifespan of an individual human being. Learning should be thought of as an integral part of life, and the day we stop learning, we start withering away. Given the brevity of human life, saying that lifelong learning, unlike the traditional concept of "standard learning", is indefinite and so has no beginning and no end, is perhaps something of an exaggeration. However, within the time frame of the life of an individual, the idea of lifelong learning emphasises that one is never done with absorbing new knowledge, skills and competences. Personally, I cannot conceive of quality of life without an opportunity to learn and broaden horizons, as I fully share the desire that Pavel Zgaga, a signatory of the Bologna Declaration and one of the foremost higher education experts in Europe today, once expressed to "live a long life in learning".[61] I also cannot conceive of a developed society that would not offer its citizens an opportunity to develop their understanding, skills and knowledge. The choice in favour of lifelong learning should not be all that difficult if one contemplates the alternatives – is one of them lifelong ignorance?

Lifelong learning, then, is not a dramatically different experience from traditional learning. Rather, lifelong learning should be thought of as a set of learning paths that are alternatives to the "learning highway" that takes the straight road through the education system. Yet the time perspective is different: traditional study programmes begin and end, preferably within stipulated time frames, whereas lifelong learning in principle has no end other than the end of life itself. In reality, of course, lifelong

---

59. Committee of Ministers Recommendation Rec(2002)6 on higher education policies in lifelong learning, at https://wcd.coe.int/ViewDoc.jsp?Ref=Rec(2002)6&Sector=secCM&Language=lanEnglish&BackColorInternet=9999CC&BackColorIntranet=FFBB55&BackColorLogged=FFAC75 (accessed on 13 May 2006).
60. Quoted by Stephen Adam at the Conference on Recognition and Credit Systems in the Context of Lifelong Learning, organised by the Czech authorities in the framework of the Bologna Process in Prague on 5–7 June 2003. See the conference report by Sjur Bergan, available at http://www.bologna-bergen2005.no/EN/Bol_sem/Old/030605-07Prague/030605-07General_Report.pdf (accessed on 13 May 2006).
61. Ibid., p. 14.

learners aiming for a given qualification are very eager to complete that particular learning experience.

Often we hear references to "lifelong learning qualifications". This could lead us to see the qualifications earned through lifelong learning as a separate set of qualifications from those earned by following traditional learning paths. Those who use the term may not intend to say that lifelong learning leads to different qualifications, but this is the obvious interpretation. But lifelong learning does not and should not lead to separate qualifications. If it did, this could easily lead to a set of qualifications that would be not only different from traditional qualifications, but might also be considered inferior.

One may of course take the view that earning one's qualifications off the beaten track, as it were, constitutes an additional value that should be recognised by a separate qualification. However, the opposite view is equally plausible: that any qualification deviating from the traditional ones may easily be considered second-rate, even if the justification for reaching such a conclusion may be entirely lacking. An additional consideration is that, in the interest of transparency, which is another major concern of the European Higher Education Area, a balance has to be struck between allowing learners to define study programmes that fit their own profiles and interests, and providing a framework for describing the qualifications earned through these programmes in a way that is understandable to informed outsiders. Variety has many advantages, but increased transparency is not one of them.

I would therefore argue that lifelong learning should primarily be thought of as alternative learning paths towards qualifications described in the qualifications framework of a given education system. Not all lifelong learning experiences need to lead to a qualification that fits into a qualifications framework. After all, not all organised or formal learning ends up with such qualifications either. In many countries, it is perfectly possible to follow university courses without aiming for the examinations that would lead to formal recognition of this learning. Drivers' education, which has strong elements of formal learning (and in most European countries, privatised, profit-making formal education at that) even where learners are also allowed to practise with drivers who are not certified instructors, leads to a qualification – the driver's licence – but not one that easily fits into a national qualifications framework. There would, however, be reason for concern if lifelong learning a priori had to lead to a qualification marked "LLL", say a Master of Science LLL. Separate learning paths may be seen as equal, but the chances of gaining equal acceptance for separate but equal lifelong learning qualifications is not something I would put a lot of money on if I were a gambler. There is even historical precedent for considering that "separate but equal" will easily end up as anything but.62

---

62. In 1896, a US Supreme Court decision, known as *Plessy* vs. *Ferguson*, approved segregation in schools by accepting the formula "separate but equal". This decision was not overturned until 1954, when the Supreme Court, in *Brown* vs. *the Board of Education of Topeka, Kansas*, ordered the integration of

The concept of learning paths is important to help make lifelong learning a recognised part of higher education in Europe. Learning paths need to be complemented by financial support for learners, incentive to learn and other factors. They are not a sufficient condition by themselves to make education accessible for all, but they are an essential condition. That leads us to a consideration of how learning paths and qualifications frameworks fit together.

Qualifications frameworks and learning paths

As we discussed in our consideration of qualifications frameworks, they are not merely a set of descriptions of individual qualifications. They should also show how qualifications interact and how learners can move between qualifications. The best way qualifications frameworks can do this is by sketching possible learning paths. It is hardly possible to outline all possible learning paths, but by outlining some typical learning paths, frameworks can help show that qualifications can be earned in different ways, at different ages and with different goals. If qualifications frameworks offer information on typical paths, it is of course important that they be perceived as examples and not as exhaustive description of all possible learning paths. It may be useful to conclude our consideration of learning paths by looking at the way two national frameworks show how different learning paths fit into the framework.

In the Australian qualifications framework, the information on learning paths is contained in the *AQF Implementation Handbook*.[63] For each qualification, the Implementation Handbook describes "pathways to the qualification" as one of seven elements of the guidelines. For the Senior Secondary Certificate of Education, the pathways are described as follows:

Access to the qualification could be through:

• accredited course(s) of study delivered by a recognised provider;

• or

• a combination of an accredited course of study and/or recognition of prior learning, including credit transfer and/or experience.

And it gives the following examples of possible pathways:

• Full-Time School Study

A two-year post Year 10 Senior Secondary School Certificate of Education program.

American schools. The implementation of this decision was a central element of the Civil Rights struggle of the 1950s and early 1960s.

63. See http://www.aqf.edu.au/pdf/handbook.pdf (accessed on 13 May 2006).

- Schools/TAFE Programs

A Senior Secondary School Certificate of Education program incorporating units from a Certificate I course.[64]

For Certificate II, which is a vocational qualification, the handbook gives a number of pathways:

- a training program meeting the requirements of an endorsed Training Package or a training program meeting the requirements of an accredited course(s) delivered by a Registered Training Organisation;

or

- a combination of a training program meeting the requirements of an endorsed Training Package or a training program meeting the requirements of an accredited course delivered by a Registered Training Organisation, plus recognition of prior learning including credit transfer and/or experience;

or

- the recognition of prior learning that provides evidence of the achievement of the competencies for the qualification.

And it gives the following examples:

Work-Based Training and Assessment

- Institution-Based Education and Training and Assessment (including schools)
- Part Institution-Based Education and Training and Assessment (including schools)/Part Work-Based Training and Assessment
- Recognition of Prior Learning
- Recognition of Prior Learning combined with Further Training as required
- Accumulation of a Variety of Short Courses/Training Programs[65]

In both cases, the handbook carefully notes that the examples suggest only some of a wide range of possible pathways, and that the examples chosen are not intended to be prescriptive or limited to the qualification under which they are listed.

As a final example, the handbook describes the following pathways to the Master's degree:

---

64. Ibid., p. 12.
65. Ibid., p. 22.

Candidates typically hold the equivalent of a Bachelor Degree or an Advanced Diploma and are expected to demonstrate potential to undertake work at this level. In some circumstances relevant prior work can be recognised, particularly where relevant professional practice has been undertaken. Although the duration of programs may vary, courses at this level typically require six months of full-time study. Issuance of the qualification follows satisfactory completion of the requirements set by the university or other recognised provider.[66]

In the Scottish Qualifications Framework, the examples of learning paths are not given as a part of the framework but through 13 cases presented on the website of the Scottish Credit and Qualifications Framework.[67] We considered one of the cases – that of "Ann" – in Chapter 9. Let us conclude the present chapter by outlining two more Scottish cases.

"Mary" is presented as someone in a difficult life situation and with no qualifications. With encouragement from friends, she enrolled in a community lifelong learning programme in childcare and earned several credits. In other words, her lifelong learning experience led to credits within the national qualifications framework, expressed in terms of formal learning. The pathway was distinct, but it led to credits that she could have earned through more classic learning paths. She also got involved in managing the programme and became chair of the management committee, which gave her additional valuable learning experience. Her coursework gave her credit when she enrolled at a further education college, so she did not have to start from scratch in this new setting. She eventually earned a qualification that led to a new and fulfilling job.

"Gordon" did not go straight from secondary school to university because his grades were insufficient. Therefore, he went to further education college where he earned a qualification that then enabled him not only to be admitted to a first degree programme at a university, but also to get substantial credit toward that first degree.

Both learners avoided starting from scratch because the Scottish system contained pathways that enabled them to get credit for previous learning. The cases presented on the webpage are of course success stories. Few institutions would illustrate their work by outlining possible shortcomings and failures, any more than hotels attract tourists by showing rainy exteriors and smoky interiors. Learning paths can, of course, lead learners off the road, and ultimate success is no more guaranteed in education than in other walks of life. Yet, success also depends on making use of opportunities and, for this to happen, the opportunities have to exist in the first place. Learning paths increase opportunities for learners to obtain qualifications, and qualifications frameworks help make these learning paths feasible.

---

66. Ibid., p. 51.
67. See http://www.scqf.org.uk/case_studies.asp (accessed on 13 May 2006).

So far, we have considered qualifications with reference to national frameworks. True, the two overarching frameworks in Europe are at a level beyond national education systems, but they help connect national systems. Now it is time to take a closer look at the relationship between qualifications and national systems, and in particular to look at qualifications that do not belong to national systems.

Part IV

Qualifications
and education systems

12   National, European, international and transnational qualifications

Qualifications belonging to an education system

So far in this book, we have stuck to the spoken or unspoken assumption that qualifications belong to one and only one education system. Mostly, the assumption has also been that this is a national system, though we have seen that some countries have more than one education system.[1] In Europe, this is true for Belgium, where the Flemish and French Communities have different systems, there is no national ministry responsible for education and there are two ministers of education, one for each community. This was also the situation in Serbia and Montenegro,[2] where education was the responsibility of the Republics, not the Federation. There was a Minister of Education for Serbia and one for Montenegro. Montenegrin independence therefore added a new state to the European family, but not a new education system.

However, some federal countries have only one education system, with a federal Minister of Education, even if the constituent units of the federation have considerable authority in education matters. Switzerland has a federal Minister of Education (though his or her official title is Federal Councillor) and a single education system, but the cantons also have competence in education matters. Incidentally, Switzerland is a multilingual country with four official languages: German, French, Italian and Romansch. Germany and Spain are other examples of countries where competence in education matters is shared between national and regional authorities – *Länder* in the case of Germany and *Comunidades autónomas* in the case of Spain. Yet, in both countries, there is a national education system.

The United Kingdom is not a federal country, but the Scottish authorities have considerable competences in education, which in Scotland has features not found in England, Northern Ireland or Wales. As we saw in Chapter 9, the United Kingdom has two qualifications frameworks, one for Scotland and one for England, Northern Ireland and Wales.

We also saw, in Chapter 10, that Europe has two overarching qualifications frameworks – the one for the European Higher Education Area and the one that is close to adoption within the European Union, called the European Qualifications Framework. However, they are not properly speaking the frameworks of an education system, but rather provide a framework that may bring different national frameworks and systems closer together. This is the main reason they are called overarching frameworks.

---

1. To this author's knowledge, no country is entirely without an education system, even if questions may be raised about how well national education systems actually function in some countries ravaged by civil strife.
2. Formally, the State Union of Serbia and Montenegro. In a referendum on 21 May 2006, Montenegro voted to leave the State Union and become an independent state. On 3 June it formally declared its independence. It acceded to the Bologna Process on 17 May 2007.

It may be useful to distinguish between an education system and a qualifications framework. The former includes, but is not limited to, the latter. The qualifications framework, or – in an earlier but still much used term – the degree system, is a part of a country's education system. In addition, the education system encompasses other elements, such as the legislation on all aspects of education and the institutions and education programmes that the competent public authorities – normally the Ministry of Education – recognise as being a part of the education system. Thus, an Austrian university is an institution that the competent Austrian public authority – the Federal Ministry of Education, Science and Culture[3] – recognises as a part of the Austrian education system and, since we refer to a university, that it also recognises as having university status.

Now we are aware of the caveats, however, let us stick to the notion of national education systems and qualifications frameworks.[4] If someone has a Hungarian first degree, we immediately have a point of reference. We can look up the Hungarian qualifications framework and find a description that will give us a fairly good insight into the qualification in question. Presumably it will be from a Hungarian university or *föiskola* – the Hungarian equivalent of *Fachhochschule*. In sum, a Hungarian qualification is one that corresponds to a given level within the Hungarian qualifications framework and has been issued by an institution that the Hungarian authorities consider as belonging to the Hungarian education system, and that is therefore subject to Hungarian quality assurance. Therefore, if used correctly, a term like "Hungarian first degree" provides us with a lot of information that we can use in assessing that qualification. The importance of this will become apparent when we discuss the recognition of qualifications in the next chapter.

Normally, a Hungarian qualification would be recognised in Hungary without problems. As we saw in the definition of a national qualifications framework, this is:

> the single description, at national level or level of an education system, which is internationally understood and through which all qualifications and other learning achievements in higher education may be described and related to each other in a coherent way and which defines the relationship between higher education qualifications.[5]

Consequently, the holder of a Hungarian first degree will have access to further studies or to the labour market in Hungary.

---

3. Bundesminsiterium für Bildung, Wissenschaft und Kultur.

4. In the rest of this chapter, we will refer to qualifications frameworks rather than degree systems even if, at the time of writing, most countries of the European Higher Education Area have yet to complete their new-style qualifications frameworks. However, as we saw in previous chapters, ministers have committed themselves to elaborating national qualifications frameworks by 2010.

5. *A Framework for Qualifications of the European Higher Education Area*, op. cit., Chapter 2.1, p. 30. The report is also available at http://www.bologna-bergen2005.no/Docs/00-Main_doc/050218_QF_EHEA.pdf.

Until the 1990s, the overwhelming majority of qualifications were of the kind just described. They had been issued by institutions belonging to a national education system, and they were clearly recognised as belonging to the degree system of that country. As we will see in the next chapter, there might have been issues of recognition if holders of qualifications moved from one country to another, but the vast majority of qualifications belonged to a national system and could be assessed in the framework of that system. This is still true for most qualifications, but since the 1990s there has been a considerable increase in the number of qualifications outside this mould. We shall explore the major categories of such qualifications in this chapter.

Cross-border or borderless education

From the mid-1990s onwards, an increasing number of education providers emerged that could not easily be placed within a given education system. Some belonged to an education system, but not to that of the country in which the institution operated; others did not belong to any system at all. There was also a third category of providers, where it was difficult to ascertain whether they did belong to an education system or not and, if so, which. This kind of provision has increased vastly since the 1990s.[6]

The traditional image of the mobile student needs to be supplemented with the new image of the mobile provider. Like students, providers come in many shapes and sizes, and that is one important reason for using the broader term "provider" as well as the traditional term "institution". All higher education institutions are education providers, but there are also providers that cannot be described as institutions by any stretch of the imagination. Today, providers include international conglomerates, business companies and consortia of public and private institutions, and the forms of provision vary widely from traditional campus-based teaching to provision entirely online, with a range of varieties in between.

At first sight, it may seem unbelievable that there could be doubt about the education system to which an institution belongs. If an institution has a campus in country A, does it not belong to the education system of country A? The answer is that it may, but only if the competent authorities of country A confirm that it does. For that certification, the institution will normally need to comply with all aspects of the higher education legislation of country A, it must grant qualifications within the national framework of country A, and it will have to undergo quality assurance as required by

---

6. See Carolyn Campbell, "Transnational education" in *Cuadernos Europeos de Deusto* (Bilbao: Universidad de Deusto) 29/2003, pp. 63–78; Jane Knight, "The impact of GATS and trade liberalization on higher education" in Stamenka Uvalić-Trumbić (ed.), *Globalization and the Market in Higher Education: Quality, Accreditation and Qualifications* (Paris 2002: UNESCO Publishing and Editions Economica), pp. 191–209; Jane Knight, "Programmes, providers and accreditors on the move: implications for the recognition of qualifications" in Andrejs Rauhvargers and Sjur Bergan (eds), *Recognition in the Bologna Process: Policy Development and the Road to Good Practice* (Strasbourg 2006: Council of Europe Publishing – Council of Europe Higher Education Series No. 4), pp. 139–60. Updated information on borderless education may also be found at the website of the Observatory for Borderless Education, based in the UK, http://www.obhe. ac.uk (accessed on 25 May 2006).

the competent authorities of country A. This is true for the classic public institutions, and it is true for many private institutions.

One should be careful not to assume that private higher education is substandard, nor that it does not belong to any education system. Many private institutions operate within the framework established by public authorities, they undergo quality assurance and they grant degrees within the national framework of the country in which they are located. They are part of that country's education system, and they provide good-quality education. However, this does not apply to all private institutions.

In some countries, satisfying all these requirements may be a precondition for being allowed to operate in the country. In this case, all institutions that operate legally in the country belong to the country's education system.

However, in many countries institutions can operate legally without belonging to the country's education system, and that is the starting point for the situations we explore in this chapter. What happens if the institution operating in country A – where, for the sake of argument, the second degree might be called *Step Two* (an obviously fictitious name, but one that avoids identifying a specific country) – attracts students by offering a "country B Master degree"? In this case, do the institution and its qualifications belong to the education system of country A or country B?

The correct answer to the question is "that depends", but by itself that is not a very helpful answer. The chances that country A will recognise as its own an institution that exclusively issues degrees marketed as being "of country B" seem slim. The more relevant question may be whether the competent authorities of country B recognise the institution as belonging to their system.

Again, they might. If they are satisfied that the institution operates in accordance with their education system, that it undergoes quality assurance as required by their system and that it issues qualifications within their national framework, and if there are no legal regulations saying that only institutions located in the country may belong to the education system of country B, they may well. However, it is not unlikely that the institution may fail to satisfy the requirements of the competent authorities of country B, and that it may fail to do so in subtle ways. To use the language of astronomy, the failures may not be visible to the naked eye.

Two imaginary examples[7]

Imagine that the institution in question is the Altruistic Official Public State University of country B, operating in country A. The fictitious name is meant to avoid lawsuits in an area where providers are keen not to be exposed as less than serious,

---

7. A number of real examples may be found in the articles by Carolyn Campbell and Jane Knight referred to previously. The two imaginary examples have been chosen to provide "ideal type" examples illustrating important issues concerning the relationship between qualifications and education systems.

but we can see this is a public institution in country B. Hence, it is presumably recognised as an institution belonging to that education system, though it might be wise to verify this assumption. Incidentally, a name like this, which seems to imply and at the same time overstate the institution's seriousness, modernity or other qualities through its name, may be a warning signal that evaluators should look more closely into the institution's claim of excellence, but we will dispense with such considerations for the time being. It offers "country B Bachelor and Masters degrees", so we might assume that these degrees belong to the education system of country B. Or is this a reasonable assumption?

Let us further assume that our Altruistic Official Public State University has undergone quality assurance in country B and that the competent authorities of country B recognise it as part of that country's higher education system. However, we still need to know whether the part of the university operating in country A was part of this exercise. In many cases, it will not have been. Such operations are commonly called "branch campuses", and they may or may not operate according to the standards of the mother institution, and they may or may not be subject to quality assurance. In assessing qualifications earned at branch campuses, it is important to know whether the branch campus has been subject to separate quality assurance – and if so whether it was of the same kind/level as that of the mother institution – and whether the degrees granted are linked to a qualifications framework; and, if so, to which one.

Only if the branch campus has been assessed by the quality assurance agency of the country of its home institution and it issues degrees within that country's qualifications framework can it be considered as belonging to the same education system as the home institution. In other words, only if the branch of the Altruistic Official Public State University operating in country A has undergone quality assurance in country B[8] and its degrees are issued within the qualifications framework of country B can its qualifications be considered as "country B Bachelor and Masters degrees". If the branch has been assessed by the quality assurance agency of country A and issues degrees within the qualifications framework of country A, it can be considered as belonging to the higher education system of country A, provided the competent authorities of country A grant it such status. In this case, its qualifications would be assessed like other qualifications from recognised institutions in country A, and the claim of the institution that it issues "country B qualifications" would be difficult to justify.

A more likely possibility is that even if the Altruistic Official Public State University is recognised as part of the higher education system of country B, its branch in country A has not been assessed separately and is not recognised as part of any national system, nor are its degrees recognised by the competent authorities of country B as belonging

---

8. By which is meant quality assurance undertaken by a competent quality assurance agency in country B.

to its qualifications framework and hence its system. Even if the mother institution is public, the branch in country A may in effect be a private institution.

A second imagined case may be that of the International University of Excellence, based in country C (though it may not even have a campus there), operating branch campuses in three other countries, teaching all courses in English and offering "international Bachelor and Masters degrees". It is not recognised by the competent authorities of country C as belonging to the education system of that country, and it might not even claim to be. It may well maintain that, for practical or historical reasons, its headquarters are located in country C, but its profile is that of an international institution offering international qualifications. Therefore, the institution and its qualifications cannot be assessed in relation to any given national system, and that may well be its selling point: it is unrestrained by national systems and traditions, and its graduates will be able to work anywhere.

Towards a typology

These are two of several possible arrangements for transnational, cross-border or borderless education. There are differences between the three terms: both "transnational" and "cross-border" have connotations of education provision physically based in one country and crossing national borders to deliver education in other countries, whereas "borderless" has connotations of provision that is not based in any specific place, or whose geographical base cannot easily be determined, which therefore does not cross national borders but rather dispenses with borders. Internet-based education is an obvious example, or perhaps a set of examples, since there may be various types of internet-based education. Nevertheless, the finer distinctions between the terms are in practice less important than what they have in common, and all three tend to be used as generic terms. Whereas "transnational education" is the oldest term, the trend now is to use "borderless education".[9]

These generic terms comprise a range of provision that is so wide that it may be difficult to provide a comprehensive classification. Jane Knight refers to six kinds of providers:[10]

- *Recognised higher education institutions*, which can be public or private, are usually part of a national education system, and can be either non-profit or profit oriented;[11]
- *Non-recognised higher education institutions*, which are usually private, do not belong to any education system and are normally but not necessarily profit-oriented;

---

9. On terminology, see Jane Knight, "Programmes, providers and accreditors on the move: implications for the recognition of qualifications" in Rauhvargers and Bergan (eds), *Recognition in the Bologna Process*, pp. 140–2.

10. Knight, ibid., p. 145.

11. Higher education institutions run by religious institutions are typically formally private and non-profit, and they often belong to the education system of the country in which they are located.

• *Commercial company higher education provision*,[12] which is typically private and profit oriented and usually not part of an education system. In some cases, companies establish institution-like provision, while in other cases they provide different kinds of non-institution based "education services";

• *Corporate higher education provision*, which is not part of an education system and which is provided within major corporations for the benefit of the corporation which provides the education. The home country of this provision is often difficult to determine, and there may not be much point in doing so;

• *Provision by professional, governmental and non-governmental organisations and networks*, which may be private, public or a combination of the two, which may or may not be a part of an education system, and which are usually profit oriented;

• *Virtual higher education*, which relies entirely on virtual provision, which may or may not belong to an education system, and which is usually profit oriented, at least in the cases where education is delivered across borders.

In addition, different kinds of provision may be mobile in different ways. This is illustrated by another typology offered by Jane Knight, which concerns programme mobility:[13]

• *Franchise*, under which a provider in country A authorises a provider in country B to deliver education in its name in country B or even in country C or D. The qualification is issued by the provider in country A.

• *Twinning*, under which a provider in country A co-operates with a provider in country B to develop an articulation system allowing students to take courses in country B as well as in country A. Only one qualification is issued, and it is issued by the provider in country A.

• *Double or joint degree*, under which providers in different countries co-operate in offering a programme from which students receive a qualification from each provider (double degree) or a joint qualification from the co-operating providers (joint degree);

• *Articulation*, which is a term that covers various kinds of agreements between providers in different countries that allow students to earn credits for courses or programmes offered by the co-operating providers;

• *Validation*, which designates arrangements between providers in different countries that allow a provider in country B to grant the qualification of a provider in country A;

• *Virtual/distance*, under which providers deliver courses or programmes to students in different countries through distance and on line provision, with or without some face-to-face teaching.

---

12. For this, for corporate provision and virtual higher education, Jane Knight uses the term "higher education institution". I have preferred not to include "institution" since provision is not necessarily institution-based.
13. Knight, ibid., p. 147.

Finally, a third typology concerns the mobility not of programmes, but of providers:[14]

> • *Branch campus*, where the provider in country A sets up a campus in country B
> to deliver courses and programmes that primarily target students in country B (but
> may also include students from other countries), and where the qualification is
> granted from the "mother institution" in country A;
> • *Independent institution*, where a provider from country A establishes an institu-
> tion in country B with no ties to any other institution;
> • *Acquisition/merger*, where a foreign provider buys all or part of an institution,
> e.g. a provider from country A buys an institution in country B;
> • *Study centre/teaching site*, where a provider from country A establishes a centre
> or site in country B to support students taking the courses or programmes offered
> by the provider from country A. The study centre or teaching site may be inde-
> pendent or be operated in co-operation with local partners;
> • *Affiliation/networks (collaborative provision)*, where different kinds of providers
> (public, private, traditional, new…) co-operate through different kinds of partner-
> ships to deliver courses and programmes. Provision can be face-to-face, virtual or
> a mix of both;
> • *Virtual provision*,[15] in which a provider delivers credit courses and degree pro-
> grammes to learners in different countries through distance education modes, gen-
> erally without face-to-face teaching.

The purpose of this cursory overview is to illustrate the diversity of higher education
provision that has been developed over the past decade or so and that is likely to continue to develop further in the years to come. A thorough discussion would require a
separate volume, and developments in this area are so rapid that no extensive description is likely to be up to date in all its details by the date of its publication.

Our purpose, however, is not to offer anything like a full overview of the different
kinds of provision, but rather to look at the implications of higher education provision
that is not linked to a national education system in terms of qualifications. Before
doing so, however, we will look in somewhat greater detail at a particularly important kind of provision that is normally linked to two or more national systems: joint
degrees.

Joint degrees

The Recommendation on the Recognition of Joint Degrees,[16] adopted in 2004 as a
subsidiary text to the Council of Europe/UNESCO Convention on the Recognition of

---

14. Knight, ibid., p. 149.
15. Knight uses the term "virtual university", but I prefer the broader term "provision" since provision is
not necessarily institution-based or of university status.
16. See https://wcd.coe.int/com.instranet.InstraServlet?Command=com.instranet.CmdBlobGet&DocId=
822136&SecMode=1&Admin=0&Usage=4&InstranetImage=43872 (accessed on 25 May 2006).

Qualifications concerning Higher Education in the European Region, defines a joint degree as:

> a higher education qualification issued jointly by at least two or more higher education institutions or jointly by one or more higher education institutions and other awarding bodies, on the basis of a study programme developed and/or provided jointly by the higher education institutions, possibly also in co-operation with other institutions. A joint degree may be issued as
>
> a. a joint diploma in addition to one or more national diplomas,
>
> b. a joint diploma issued by the institutions offering the study programme in question without being accompanied by any national diploma,
>
> c. one or more national diplomas issued officially as the only attestation of the joint qualification in question.[17]

The essence of a joint degree is therefore that it is issued by more than one institution, and that elements of the qualification have been earned at two or more institutions. However, the participation of two institutions is only a minimum; where several institutions establish a joint framework, such as a consortium or a network, to offer joint degrees, elements for the joint degree should come from at least two members of this arrangement. Normally, a joint degree is issued by institutions from different countries, but it could also be issued by two institutions in the same country, even if there are few if any examples of such degrees so far. In the Bologna Process, the emphasis is on stimulating co-operation in joint degree programmes as a way of strengthening the European dimension of higher education.

The Recommendation on the Recognition of Joint Degrees established the definition now used within the Bologna Process. The need for a definition was underlined by the fact that while there are a good number of joint degree programmes in Europe and the ministers of education encouraged this development in their Prague and Berlin Communiqués, the authoritative study of joint degrees, by Andrejs Rauhvargers, found no commonly accepted definitions. The study found that a joint degree could be said to have all or some of the following characteristics:

- the programmes are developed and/or approved jointly by several institutions;
- students from each participating institution physically take part in the study programme at other institutions (but they do not necessarily study at all co-operating institutions);
- students' stay at the participating institutions should constitute a substantial part of the programme;
- periods of study and examinations passed at the partner institutions are recognized fully and automatically;

---

17. Ibid., paragraph 5.

• the partner institutions work out the curriculum jointly and co-operate on admission and examinations. In addition, staff of participating institutions should be encouraged to teach at other institutions contributing to the joint degree;
• after completing the full programme, students either obtain the national degree of each participating institution or awarding body or a degree (usually an unofficial "certificate" or "diploma") awarded jointly by the partner institutions.[18]

In many cases, two or more institutions offer a joint degree programme without establishing a separate legal structure for doing so. In some cases, however, separate structures are established, such as the Transnational University of Limburg between the Flemish community of Belgium and the Netherlands, the Öresund University between Sweden and Denmark or the Interuniversity Europe Centre established in Bulgaria and Romania with the assistance of Germany.[19]

Even if the ministers of the Bologna Process encourage the development of joint degree programmes, institutions in some countries still face legal and practical obstacles in doing so, and the regulations and practice of some institutions also pose problems. If, as in some cases, institutional rules stipulate that at least half the credits must be taken at the institution for a degree to be issued in its name, it does not take much imagination to figure out what will happen – or rather not happen – if two or three institutions with similar rules try to set up a joint degree programme.

A joint degree as outlined here, then, is a qualification earned at two or more institutions belonging to two or more separate higher education systems and, hence, qualifications frameworks. The challenge, therefore, is not to obtain reliable information on the education systems concerned, but to ascertain how the joint degree relates to the qualifications frameworks of these systems. That leads us to a consideration of the relationship between education systems and qualifications.

Education systems and qualifications

Transnational, cross-border and borderless education, like joint degree programmes, are fairly new developments, at least on a large scale, and the qualifications they issue cannot easily be described in relation to an established qualifications framework. This may be inconvenient, but in a book exploring the concept of qualifications, the question should rather be whether this inconvenience is important.

The answer is that in principle, it probably is not. The real value of a qualification should not depend on the arrangements by which most learners obtain it. This would be consistent with what we discussed when exploring learning paths. However, as we may surmise from our consideration of learning paths, the practical difficulties are such that we are faced with more than a mere inconvenience. Rather, these arrange-

---

18. Andrejs Rauhvargers, "Joint degree study" in Christian Tauch and Andrejs Rauhvargers, *Survey on Master Degrees and Joint Degrees in Europe* (Brussels 2001: European University Association).
19. The examples are taken from the Explanatory Memorandum to the Recommendation on the Recognition of Joint Degrees, available at the same website, and originate from Rauhvargers' study.

ments raise two fundamental questions: how can such qualifications be described, and how can their quality be assured?

Describing "international qualifications"

Let us return to the fictitious example of the Altruistic Official Public State University, which belongs to the education system of country A and operates a branch campus in country B. The mother institution is a public institution, but the branch may be either public or private. Whether this branch is public or private is not per se an important point in assessing its qualifications; but, if it is private, this decreases the likelihood of the branch campus actually being part of an education system. It may well be that even if the institution claims to issue "country B" qualifications, all or most courses are given in the language of country A. This is not a problem in itself, but it could be problematic if the institution does not specify this basic fact on its diplomas. An employer hiring somebody with "country B qualifications" might reasonably assume that the holder of the qualification is reasonably fluent in the language of country B, whereas the branch campus may not require students to do any work in that language or even demonstrate knowledge of it. If the language of country B is English or another widely spoken language, employers may believe that in hiring someone with a qualification from the branch campus of the Altruistic Official Public State University, they will hire an employee with good knowledge of English as well as of the culture of country B. Unless the description of the qualification offered by the branch campus specifies the language of instruction, employers, admissions officers at other institutions and others assessing the qualifications may therefore make assumptions about the qualification that turn out to be untrue.

In the case of the branch campus of our fictitious public university we are therefore faced with two problems: knowing whether the branch campus actually does issue qualifications within the national framework of country B, and then obtaining a transparent description of the requirements for the qualification, specifying for example the language of instruction. The latter can be an issue also with qualifications belonging to a national education system and it can largely be solved by providing transparent descriptions through the Diploma Supplement elaborated by the Council of Europe, the European Commission and UNESCO.[20] Ministers in the Bologna Process have now committed themselves to issuing the Diploma Supplement automatically, free of charge and in a widely spoken language, so that, at least in principle, all students at institutions belonging to one of the national systems of the European Higher Education Area should now receive the Diploma Supplement. Institutions not belonging to a national system may, however, issue Diploma Supplements less readily since they are not party to any such commitment.

A somewhat similar issue might arise if the Altruistic Official Public State University offered a joint degree programme with the Eminent Public University of Official

---

20. See http://ec.europa.eu/education/policies/rec_qual/recognition/diploma_en.html (accessed on 25 May 2006). The Diploma Supplement will be discussed in more detail in the chapter on recognition. The language of instruction and examination should be specified in point 2.5.

Excellence of country X. Let us assume that in spite of their somewhat suspicious and certainly fictitious names, both universities are in fact part of the education system of their respective countries and that they have been quality-assured. Since both countries are part of the European Higher Education Area and their ministers have conscientiously followed up their own decisions, both countries have established national qualifications frameworks with three cycles at higher education level about which there is sufficient and transparent information in the public domain. Therefore we should know enough about the joint degree to recognise its value, and we should be able to determine its level without further ado. If it is a first degree with elements from two universities, it might not matter much that there are slight differences between the two national qualifications frameworks, for example with regard to workload, profile and generic learning outcomes, even if both have been established with reference to the overarching framework of the European Higher Education Area. A good Diploma Supplement issued jointly by both institutions will provide us with the information we need on workload, profile and learning outcomes.

The example of the International University of Excellence raises issues of a different order. As we remember, this provider is based in country C, operates branch campuses in three other countries, teaches all courses in English and offers "international Bachelor and Masters degrees". It is not, and does not claim to be, part of any national education system, but rather markets itself as an international institution. If the branch campus of the Altruistic Official Public State University operating in country A is not part of the education system of either country A or country B, it will in effect be in the same situation, even if it does not market itself as offering an "international qualification", but rather claims a national affiliation that in this case turns out to be unsupported by evidence. In both cases, rather than "international qualifications", we have qualifications without a country, or at least without a system.

At least two unspoken assumptions about "international qualifications" are problematic. One is that qualifications belonging to a national system are difficult to use in other countries. That, however, is an assumption we will address in the following two chapters, when we discuss recognition of qualifications. For now, let us concentrate on the second unspoken assumption: that there is in fact such a thing as an "international qualification".

An "international qualification" is a doubtful term because there is no international education system against or within which such a qualification may be described. Saying that a given qualification is an "international Bachelor" tells us next to nothing except that it is probably not issued within a national framework and that the provider makes no claim for the qualification to be of more than first degree level. That is something, but it is not much.

The problem with the qualifications issued by our fictitious International University of Excellence is therefore that we cannot instantly place them within a known and accepted framework. The institution may well remedy that by providing good descriptions of the level, workload, quality, profile and learning outcomes of all its qualifications. It may issue a Diploma Supplement and it may, in effect, establish and describe its own institutional qualifications framework. This is theoretically a possible solution, but it is not an unproblematic one.

Firstly, the institution would then not be creating an international qualifications framework, but a very local one, valid for one institution only, even if the institution had branches in several countries. The framework thus created would not be accepted by the competent public authorities of several countries as either a substitute or an overarching framework for their own national framework. There would also be no competent authority for this framework other than the institution itself. It is difficult to see how such qualifications would be international in any meaningful sense of the word.

Secondly, if many providers followed the example of the International University of Excellence, it would not produce one broad international framework but a large number of local, institution-specific frameworks. The resulting ambiguity might be beneficial for less serious providers, since they would presumably have little to gain from transparency, but for the same reason it would not benefit serious providers and it would certainly not be helpful for students, employers and others that might wish to use such qualifications.

Borderless quality assurance?

A third problem is that, in the absence of an international education system, it is not obvious who would be responsible for overseeing "international qualifications" and providers. In current higher education debate, the emphasis on quality assurance reflects a strongly felt need for independent assessment of how education providers carry out their mission. An institution is good not because its leadership claims it is good but because an independent assessment has shown its leadership to be right in claiming it is good.

These reservations should not be interpreted to mean that an "international qualification" is theoretically or practically impossible. In practice, however, it is very rare. Leaving aside the highly unlikely event that the competent authorities of a large number of countries agreed on a joint education system to replace all their national systems, it is at least theoretically possible that a group of providers could form a network that would in effect devise a qualifications framework of its own. In practice, for this framework to be really international and viable, its qualifications would have to be recognised by public authorities, higher education institutions and employers in a large number of countries.

In higher education, joint degrees are a more likely outcome of this kind of co-operation, or at least they have been so far. We will examine joint degrees a little later in this chapter. However, at secondary school level, the International Baccalaureate is a truly international qualification that is recognised in many countries and by many higher education institutions as giving access to higher education on a par with national secondary school leaving qualifications. The International Baccalaureate (IB) is organised by the International Baccalaureate Organization (IBO),[21] a non-governmental organisation, and 1 785 schools in 122 countries offer programmes that prepare for the IB. The IBO has its headquarters in Geneva and has regional offices for Europe/Africa and the Middle East, for Asia and the Pacific, for North America and the Caribbean, and for Latin America. The IBO is governed by an international Council of Foundation and carries out rigorous assessments of participating schools and programmes.

It may not be easy to identify any single factor that has made the IB viable, but transparency of governance with members from a variety of national and cultural backgrounds, rigorous assessment of participating schools, working with governments, seeking local partner schools and providing curricula that enable internationally mobile families to keep their children within the same educational framework throughout their schooling, rather than moving between various national systems, seem to be important factors. Some factors may be specific to primary and secondary education, but others also apply to higher education. They illustrate the challenges facing providers who aim to establish a truly international qualifications framework at higher education level.

At higher education level, two initiatives have so far been taken by international organisations to lay down standards for the quality of non-national education provision. The first was the UNESCO/Council of Europe Code of Good Practice in the Provision of Transnational Education, which was adopted as a subsidiary text to the Council of Europe/UNESCO Recognition Convention in 2001.[22] The code seeks to lay down ground rules for providers of transnational education and emphasises the need for transparent information and quality provision. It underlines that the quality of provision and the qualifications of staff should be at least equal to those of the awarding institution as well as to those of the country in which the institution operates. The institution should provide clear information on its programmes and qualifications in good faith, and the awarding institution (the mother institution in the case of branch campuses) should be responsible for the qualifications. It also emphasises that transnational arrangements "should be so elaborated, enforced and monitored as to widen the access to higher education studies, fully respond to the learners' educational demands, contribute to their cognitive, cultural, social, personal and professional development, and comply with the national legislation regarding higher education in both receiving and sending countries. In the case of collaborative arrangements there should be written and legally binding agreements or contracts setting out the rights and obligations of all partners".[23]

---

21. See http://www.ibo.org/ (accessed on 21 May 2006).
22. See http://www.coe.int/T/DG4/HigherEducation/Recognition/Code%20of%20good%20practice_ EN.asp #TopOfPage (accessed on 26 May 2006).
23. Ibid., Section II.1.

When the code was adopted in 2001, it was quite advanced and it broke important new ground. Even if some countries, like Australia and the United Kingdom, had national guidelines for their transnational providers, this was the first international code. As we saw in the preceding paragraph, it focused on transnational or cross-border, rather than borderless provision. It is a measure of how rapid the developments in this area have been and still are that in late 2005, the OECD and UNESCO adopted a second generation of standards, this time Guidelines for Quality Provision in Cross-border Higher Education.[24] Whereas the 2001 code of good practice was mainly addressed to providers – even if they could also be read as a word of caution to those who might consider earning or using such qualifications – the 2005 guidelines are addressed to a number of target groups: governments, higher education institutions/providers, student bodies, quality assurance and accreditation bodies, academic recognition bodies and professional bodies.

The OECD/UNESCO guidelines are "based on the principle of mutual trust and respect among countries and on the recognition of the importance of international collaboration in higher education. They also recognise the importance of national authority and the diversity of higher education systems".[25] They also state that the "effectiveness of the Guidelines will depend on the capacity of national systems to assure the quality of higher education".[26]

The important role of national public authorities – or perhaps, more properly speaking, the public authorities responsible for education systems – is also underlined by the guidelines directed at governments. Among other things, governments are encouraged to:

(a) Establish, or encourage the establishment of a comprehensive, fair and transparent system of registration or licensing for cross-border higher education providers wishing to operate in their territory;

(b) Establish, or encourage the establishment of a comprehensive capacity for reliable quality assurance and accreditation of cross-border higher education provision, recognizing that quality assurance and accreditation of cross-border higher education provision involves both sending and receiving countries;

...

(d) Provide accurate, reliable and easily accessible information on the criteria and standards for registration, licensure, quality assurance and accreditation of cross-border higher education, their consequences on the funding of students, institutions or programmes, where applicable, and their voluntary or mandatory nature.[27]

---

24. See http://www.unesco.org/education/guidelines_E.indd.pdf (accessed on 26 May 2006).
25. Ibid., p. 10.
26. Ibid., p. 11.
27. Ibid., pp. 13–14.

Institutions and providers are, among other things, encouraged to ensure that programmes they deliver in other countries are of similar quality to the programmes they offer in their country of origin and to develop and maintain internal quality assurance systems. Some of the recommendations to the institutions and providers echo those of the 2001 code of good practice. The recommendations directed to other groups contain similar language adapted to the role of the group in question.

These guidelines are an important document, but like most international higher education agreements, they can only be implemented through voluntary compliance. Implementation may, however, be encouraged through peer pressure, by raising public awareness and by national authorities making compliance advantageous, and noncompliance an unattractive alternative. This will take time, but both the code of good practice and the guidelines are important steps in the right direction. One potential stumbling block is the capacity of quality assurance bodies. Even if they charge providers for undertaking an evaluation, it will be very difficult to strengthen their capacity to the point where they will be able to assess all providers that wish to undergo such an assessment. On the other hand, it is difficult for public authorities to make external quality assurance an important requirement if providers do not have effective access to such assessments.

The importance of the link between national systems and qualifications, therefore, is less one of principle than one of practicality. In principle, a qualification may well be free-standing, without any link to national systems or frameworks. In practice, however, the frameworks offered by education systems, in terms of qualifications frameworks and quality assurance systems, offer points of reference that are nearly indispensable for determining the level, quality and value of qualifications. There may be alternatives to linking qualifications to national frameworks, but they are not obviously practicable and the potential for confusion and lack of transparency is real.

This leads us to a consideration of how we assess qualifications issued within a framework other than our own – in other words, to the recognition of qualifications. That will be the topic of our next chapter.

13 Moving between education systems: the setting and legal framework for the recognition of qualifications

A world of mobility

In the modern world, people are on the move. Many of course travel for pleasure and without any thought of leaving home for longer periods, much less permanently. However, many people do leave their original homes and establish themselves elsewhere, perhaps in a neighbouring country or much further afield. Others go abroad for a period to study or work, and then return home. Others live, study and work in a series of countries. What all these movers, except the short-term tourist, have in common is that they learn in different countries, they earn qualifications and they put them to use in different contexts. Too often, those on the move are frustrated because they feel that their real qualifications are not fully appreciated, and many have to accept jobs at a level considerably lower than they feel qualified for. Often they are also frustrated with the procedures they have to go through to be able to use their qualifications in their new country of residence.

Academically mobile people – those who move for professional purposes or for further study and wish to make use of their qualifications in other countries – experience all these frustrations in spite of the fact that many governments speak in favour of academic mobility – not just the countries of the European Higher Education Area, for which the wish to stimulate academic and professional mobility is one of the *raisons d'être*, but many governments on all continents. Traditionally, the governments most sceptical of academic mobility have been those most threatened by the free movement of ideas: people studying abroad gain not only technical skills but also new ideas and outlooks on life. Totalitarian regimes on the left or the right have rarely been enthusiastic supporters of academic mobility; where they have encouraged it, they have often tried to enhance its "desirable" effects – often technical skills perceived as immediately useful – and limit its "dangers" – the stimulation of intellectual curiosity and a critical spirit.

Yet even democratic governments do not always have straightforward attitudes to academic and professional mobility. While most speak in favour of academic mobility, many at the same time seek to limit mobility in more general terms, and this tendency has grown much stronger in Europe since the 1990s. The general mobility we refer to here is also known as immigration, and many governments have been elected on a platform of limiting it, or they depend on parliamentary support from parties with anti-immigration platforms. Academic mobility, however, cannot be strengthened unless governments introduce appropriate policies, and that requires taking a hard look at issues like visas, work permits, social security and – for staff mobility – transferable pension rights. In the construction of the European Higher Education Area, higher education policies will need to interact with other areas of public policy, and the interaction will sometimes be difficult and lead to unenviable choices.

These are important issues, but they go well beyond the scope of this book. However, the core concern of this book is vital to promoting mobility, since that can only be achieved if people can make adequate use of their qualifications where they want to go. They must, so to say, be able to take their qualifications with them. If there ever was a time when students could afford to be academically mobile for pleasure without any thought of formal recognition of their qualifications, this time is long past. "You can't take it with you when you go" is true of our final destination, what Carl Sandburg called "the Last Great Washday",[28] but sometimes it also seems to be the attitude of those watching over the use of foreign qualifications.

Nevertheless, much has been done, and many academically mobile people are able to use their qualifications in other countries without serious problems. Many higher education teachers and officials, employers and others do their best to make life easier for those who are academically and professionally mobile, and international organisations and institutions – in particular the Council of Europe, UNESCO and the European Commission – as well as national governments have sought to establish laws, regulations and practice that make it easier to move from one country to another without losing one's *de facto* qualifications.

In this and the next chapter, we look more closely at the recognition of qualifications: what it is, what the legal and formal framework is, and how good practice can help fair recognition. We will also look at some of the issues facing the recognition community today, and we will see that a good understanding of recognition can help academic mobility. Such an understanding may also help ease frustrations that are caused by unrealistic expectations, because not all the frustration felt by those who try to move with their qualifications is due to public authorities and higher education institutions being unreasonable. Sometimes those who move have little idea of what the move involves; whereas they accept that buying a house in a foreign country or taking their car along will take them through administrative procedures and cause practical difficulties, they often seem to expect that their qualifications can move without being "checked at the border" and without undergoing any kind of assessment.

In this chapter, which in some ways provides the background for the next one, we look at the setting and the framework for recognition. This framework is legal, but it is also practical, since the legal framework needs to be implemented and instruments have been established to help implementation. In the next chapter, we will look at some issues in the recognition of foreign qualifications. First, however, we will take a look at what we mean by recognition.

Bridging education systems

It is time to meet our group of athletes-turned-academics again, maybe at an airport. The group has grown over the past few chapters, and it would be statistically improb-

---

28. In his 1918 poem "Washerwoman".

able if none of them tried to use their qualifications abroad. Again, in our terms, it is not just a question of going to another country, but in more technical terms of moving from one education system to another and, even more precisely, from one qualifications framework to another.[29]

Therefore, let us imagine some of our friends preparing to move to another country, to work or continue their studies. Let us preferably imagine that some of them move for the purpose of work and some for the purpose of study, and we shall soon see why.

The best image I can think of to describe the recognition of qualifications is that of a bridge. Bridges span gaps and make it possible for people and goods to move across them, whether the gap be a river, a lake, a fjord, a canyon or some other quirk of nature. If there were no gap, we would not need a bridge, we could simply move on. If the gap marks the border between two political entities – most commonly two countries – the facility with which we can cross the gap thanks to the bridge may, however, be partly offset by elaborate immigration and customs procedures on the other side of the bridge. The bridge may make it easy to get to the border, but it does not necessarily make it easier to cross that border.

I tend to think of recognition as a bridge that spans the gap between various education systems and makes it possible for learners to move from one system to another. Like physical borders, however, the borders between education systems may also be marked by customs stations where learners have to leave behind a good part of the value of their luggage, in other words where recognition procedures may make it difficult for them to use their qualifications in another system for what they are really worth, if the procedures are elaborate and unreasonable. The main purpose of the work done internationally and nationally on recognition is to make those procedures as unburdensome and reasonable as possible, so that learners may carry the full value of their qualification from one education system to another. This is often referred to as fair recognition. It is the basic principle of the Council of Europe/UNESCO Convention on the Recognition of Qualifications concerning Higher Education in the European Region, and it is a concept we shall look at in further detail when we consider the legal framework for recognition.

We said that some of our acquaintances went abroad to study and others to work, and that we made this distinction for a purpose. This is because we distinguish between three different kinds of recognition:

- academic recognition

- *de jure* professional recognition

- *de facto* professional recognition.

---

29. With all our usual caveats about qualifications frameworks still being developed in many countries.

Academic recognition is recognition for the purpose of further study. Students may take their first degree at one institution and move to an institution in another country for their second degree, and then move to a third institution for their doctorate. In each case, they will need to have their qualification recognised in order to continue their studies at a new institution rather than start all over again. This is perhaps the most typical older form of academic recognition, where learners complete one qualification at one institution and only then move on.

Thanks in part to the organised mobility programmes run by the European Union, the Nordic Council of Ministers, CEEPUS (Central European Exchange Program for University Studies) and others, another kind of academic recognition has become equally important: the recognition of periods of study at another institution as part of a degree from one's home institution. Organised mobility programmes typically help learners spend one, two or even three semesters at a foreign institution and then return home to continue their studies and eventually obtain a qualification from their own institution. As we saw in the previous chapter, this may give rise to a joint degree, or the credits earned at a foreign institution may be recognised at home and integrated into the qualification granted by the home institution.

In the mid-1990s, there was an attempt to distinguish in formal terms between these two main kinds of academic recognition by calling the first kind "cumulative recognition" and the second "recognition by substitution". The reason for the name "cumulative recognition" was easy to understand, since one qualification cumulated on another. For example, a second degree was put on top of a first degree. The term "recognition by substitution" was perhaps less evident, but it indicated that credits taken at a foreign institution substituted for credits that would otherwise have been taken at the home institution. However, while this distinction offered a nice symmetry in parallel to the two kinds of professional recognition, the distinction brought few if any practical advantages and it did not describe a fundamental difference between the two forms of recognition. Therefore, the distinction has been all but abandoned, and we will refer simply to academic recognition, knowing that this term may denote the recognition of either an entire degree or credits taken as a part of a degree, and that in both cases the purpose of recognition is to facilitate further study.

Professional recognition, on the other hand, facilitates entry into the labour market, and here the distinction between two kinds of recognition serves a real purpose. *De jure* professional recognition denotes recognition of qualifications for the purpose of access to a regulated profession. Exactly which professions are regulated varies from one country to another, but typical examples include medicine, dentistry, architecture, engineering, veterinary medicine and at least some kinds of teaching. The common denominator seems to be that these are occupations in which great and in most cases immediate harm can be done if the occupation is exercised without proper knowledge, understanding and skills. In teaching, the potential harm may be less immediate but not less great. *De jure* professional recognition is treated as a separate category because in just about all countries it is subject to strict legal regulation. These regulations exist to protect citizens from the danger of malpractice, but at least a side effect may also be to protect the profession against undue competition from a large number of foreign holders of the relevant qualification, and often professional organisations have an important voice in recognition regulations and possibly also decisions.

This distinguishes *de jure* from *de facto* professional recognition, which denotes access to the unregulated part of the labour market, to occupations like journalism, administration, many forms of commerce and other occupations that require high levels of knowledge, understanding and skill, but are not regulated by rules specific to the occupation.[30] *De facto* recognition is often carried out by employers in deciding whether to appoint an applicant with foreign qualifications, but employers may seek the advice of specialised information centres. *De facto* professional recognition has much in common with academic recognition, which is also important for *de jure* professional recognition. The difference between the three is mainly one of purpose and partly one of regulative framework, but not one of principle.

Legal framework

The legal framework for recognition is national and international. At national or system level, it includes national laws as well as regulations of lesser status, and it includes regulations at individual higher education institutions as well as those of professional bodies. In this chapter, we will be particularly concerned with the international legal framework, which includes a variety of instruments, five of which are particularly important for our purposes:

• conventions, which are treaties between states and which are legally binding on the countries that have ratified the treaty. In Europe, the main example is the Council of Europe/UNESCO Recognition Convention, which we will consider shortly, and UNESCO has similar conventions for other parts of the world;

• recommendations, which are adopted by governments, for example as subsidiary texts to the Council of Europe/UNESCO Recognition Convention or by the Committee of Ministers of the Council of Europe; they are not legally binding like conventions, but they nevertheless express a strong position by the governments that adopt them. Recommendations may be directed at governments themselves or at other actors, such as higher education institutions;

• policy statements, such as the Bologna Declaration or the communiqués adopted by ministers in the framework of the Bologna Process. Statements may also be adopted by other bodies, such as the Council of Europe's Steering Committee for Higher Education and Research (CDESR), UNESCO regional committees and others. They are not legal instruments, but express the political will manifested by those who adopt them and they can give rise to considerable peer pressure;

---

30. These occupations are of course not "unregulated" in the sense that no rules apply. They are all subject to general laws like those on working time, accounting and libel.

• codes of good practice, which are also not legal instruments, but which outline good and recommendable practice. Like policy statements, codes of good practice can give rise to strong peer pressure. Codes of good practice may perhaps even be considered a particular form of policy statements, and they are often if not always inspired by the successful experience of some countries or actors;

• compendia of good practice are what their compilers consider to be examples worthy of emulation. They are not legal texts, but like codes of good practice they can be sources of inspiration; where they have been approved by international bodies, the strength of the examples outlined can be considerable. Whereas codes of good practice normally stipulate ideal norms, compendia of good practice provide examples of actual practice in countries and institutions.

The Council of Europe/UNESCO Recognition Convention

The council of Europe/UNESCO Convention on the Recognition of Qualifications concerning Higher Education in the European Region was adopted in Lisbon on 11 April 1997 and is therefore also known as the Lisbon Recognition Convention.[31] Since it was elaborated jointly by the Council of Europe and UNESCO, and adopted at a diplomatic conference organised jointly by the two organisations, it is also known as the Council of Europe/UNESCO Recognition Convention.

This convention replaces several older conventions, five of which had been adopted by the Council of Europe, mostly in the 1950s and early 1960s, and one by UNESCO in 1979. The Council of Europe conventions addressed specific aspects of recognition, such as recognition of school leaving qualifications for access to higher education or of periods of study, while the UNESCO convention was very general. None of these conventions were any longer in tune with developments in higher education in Europe, and the two organisations decided to elaborate one new, joint convention rather than try to amend the existing conventions.

The importance of the Council of Europe/UNESCO Recognition Convention is underlined by the fact that, by the end of September 2006, it had been ratified by 42 countries, while a further 8 countries had signed it and were in the process of ratification. Also, this convention is the only legally binding text of the Bologna Process. Its importance was also underlined by the ministers of the Bologna Process who, in their Berlin Communiqué of 2003, committed themselves to ratifying

---

31. The full text of the convention, its explanatory report and a continually updated list of signatures and ratifications may be found at the website maintained by the Council of Europe's Treaty Office: see http://conventions.coe.int/ and search for ETS No. 165. N.B: It is important not to bookmark the table of signatures and ratifications on any given date, because the bookmark will reproduce the overview on the date in question. For an updates overview, it is necessary to follow the more cumbersome procedure of searching for ETS No. 165 and then clicking on the table of signatures and ratifications. The full text of the convention and its explanatory report, as well as the subsidiary texts to the convention and an introductory chapter explaining the convention, may be found in Andrejs Rauhvargers and Sjur Bergan (eds), *Standards for Recognition: the Lisbon Recognition Convention and Its Subsidiary Texts* (Strasbourg 2005: Council of Europe Publishing – the Council of Europe Higher Education Series No. 3).

the convention, repeating their commitment in the Bergen Communiqué in 2005. At the end of August 2006, three members of the Bologna Process had neither signed nor ratified the convention, while five had signed but not ratified the convention. Of the latter, one country had, however, reported that all national ratification procedures had recently been completed and that the instrument of ratification would be deposited shortly.

The instrument of ratification is the formal notification to one of the depositories of the convention – in this case the Secretary General of the Council of Europe and the Director-General of UNESCO – that the country has ratified a convention, and it is only when this instrument has been deposited that the ratification becomes effective.[32] Roughly speaking, the convention is divided into the following parts:

• A preamble that sets out the rationale and precedents for the convention and spells out the so-called *considerata,* that is, the major considerations that have led to the adoption of the convention. One example is that the parties to the convention state that they are conscious of the need to find common solutions to practical recognition problems in the European Region.

• A set of definitions of the main terms used in the convention, given in Section I. This section specifies that the definitions are valid for the convention only, and that they may be used differently in other contexts, for example in national contexts in member states. One example is that the use of "qualifications" as a generic term was relatively new and was used consistently in this sense for the first time in the convention.

• Legal provisions on the competence of authorities, in Section II, which in particular apply to countries where central authorities have limited or no competence in recognition matters.

• The key principles of the convention, which are spelled out in Section III.

• Provisions on the recognition of access qualifications (Section IV), periods of study (Section V) and higher education qualifications (Section VI).

• Provisions on the recognition of qualifications held by refugees, displaced persons and persons in a refugee-like situation (Section VII). This section was included not because persons in these categories hold special kinds of qualifications but because for good reasons they often have problems documenting their qualifications, and the section encourages parties to show flexibility in assessing their qualifications.

• Provisions on the assessment of higher education institutions and programmes (Section VIII).

---

32. In fact, the ratification becomes effective at a given date after the instrument of ratification has been deposited, in the case of the Council of Europe/UNESCO Recognition Convention on "the first day of the month following the expiration of the period of one month after the date of expression of its [the country's] consent to be bound by the ratification" (Article XI.3). If the instrument of ratification is deposited on 10 October, the convention will come into force with respect to the country in question on 1 December.

• Provisions on information on recognition matters and on implementation mechanisms (Sections IX and X), in which among other things parties commit to establish national information centres on recognition (ENICs).

• Final legal provisions on technical matters such as the entry into force of the convention and accession by further countries (Section XI).

The underlying principle of the convention is that everyone has the right to fair recognition of their qualifications. This is expressed as follows in Article III.1 of the convention:

1.   Holders of qualifications issued in one of the Parties shall have adequate access, upon request to the appropriate body, to an assessment of these qualifications.

2.   No discrimination shall be made in this respect on any ground such as the applicant's gender, race, colour, disability, language, religion, political or other opinion, national, ethnic or social origin, association with a national minority, property, birth or other status, or on the grounds of any other circumstance not related to the merits of the qualification for which recognition is sought. In order to assure this right, each Party undertakes to make appropriate arrangements for the assessment of an application for recognition of qualifications solely on the basis of the knowledge and skills achieved.

If our group of now academically mobile friends use the convention, does this basic principle mean they have the right to have their qualifications recognised? Yes, but in the sense of the convention, where in fact the term "recognition" means

A formal acknowledgement by a competent authority of the value of a foreign educational qualification with a view to access to educational and/or employment activities (Section I).

In other words, "recognition" in the sense of the convention means something like "assessment". In writing the convention, one option was in fact to use the term "assessment", but since the term "recognition" was well established and had been used in the previous conventions, it was decided to stick to the established terms. The right to fair recognition means, however, that all holders of qualifications have the right to a fair assessment of their qualifications. Competent authorities may decide not to recognise qualifications, but in this case, they should state their rationale so that their decisions may be appealed against if there is reason to do so. This may also help discern whether some competent authorities in given countries tend to be unduly strict in their recognition practice.

A second key principle of the Council of Europe/UNESCO Recognition Convention, outlined in Sections IV, V and VI, is that qualifications should be recognised unless the competent recognition authority – which is very often a higher education institution, but which can also be a ministry or other public body, depending on national legislation – can demonstrate that there is a substantial difference between the qualification for which recognition is sought and the corresponding qualification in their own education system or qualifications framework. No legal text can provide an exhaustive overview of what may constitute a substantial difference, and this is an issue we shall look at more closely in the next chapter. The principle is formulated as follows in Article IV.1, and similar wording is found in Articles V.1 and VI.1:

> Each Party shall recognize the qualifications issued by other Parties meeting the general requirements for access to higher education in those Parties for the purpose of access to programmes belonging to its higher education system, unless a substantial difference can be shown between the general requirements for access in the Party in which the qualification was obtained and in the Party in which recognition of the qualification is sought.

It is also worth noting that the convention addresses, in Article VI.3, the effects of recognition:

> Recognition in a Party of a higher education qualification issued in another Party shall have one or both of the following consequences:

> a. access to further higher education studies, including relevant examinations, and/ or to preparations for the doctorate, on the same conditions as those applicable to holders of qualifications of the Party in which recognition is sought;

> b. the use of an academic title, subject to the laws and regulations of the Party or a jurisdiction thereof, in which recognition is sought.

> In addition, recognition may facilitate access to the labour market subject to laws and regulations of the Party, or a jurisdiction thereof, in which recognition is sought.

While the language is assertive in terms of access to further studies and the right to use academic titles, it is less so in terms of access to the labour market. The reason is that many countries, as well as the European Union, have specific regulations on *de jure* professional recognition, and some potential parties to the convention were reluctant to include provisions that could be seen as covering this type of recognition. The provisions on academic recognition of the Council of Europe/UNESCO Recognition Convention, however, are also applicable to the part of *de jure* professional recognition that concerns the academic qualifications of applicants. In addition, *de jure* professional recognition may include requirements for professional practice periods and other elements that are not a part of academic recognition.

The convention also addresses a number of issues that we have already considered in this book. For example, it stipulates, in Section VIII, that all countries shall provide information on the higher education institutions and programmes that make up their higher education systems. This provision was drafted in 1996–7, and at the time there was still discussion of whether a formal quality assurance system was needed, or indeed desirable. Therefore, the convention distinguishes between the information to be provided by countries that have formal quality assurance systems and countries that do not. In either case, the minimum requirement, however, is that a country be able to state what institutions and programmes belong to its higher education system.

Less than a decade later, however, the discussion is not whether formal quality assurance is needed, but what form it should take. Almost all countries would therefore fall under the provisions for countries that have a formal quality assurance system, and it is indeed difficult to imagine that a party could fulfil its obligations under this article of the convention without making reference to the outcomes of its quality assurance exercise.

A convention is a difficult legal text not only to read – the language is admittedly not user-friendly in all parts of the text – but also to write. It requires agreement among many countries, and since this particular convention was elaborated jointly by two international organisations, it also required co-ordination between two bodies, each of which has its own institutional framework and regulations. Amending the convention would therefore be a formidable task, and while it may be necessary to do so one day, it is clearly not a prospect relished by those overseeing the convention. However, there is another possibility: adopting subsidiary texts. Such texts may be adopted by the Lisbon Recognition convention Committee, which is the intergovernmental body established, in Article X.2 of the convention, to oversee it. Since the convention is a joint text of the Council of Europe and UNESCO, this role could not be fulfilled by one of the existing bodies of one of the organisations, but a new body had to be created. This committee is, however, what is known as a "light structure", since it meets once every two or three years. It is made up of representatives of the states parties to the convention.

So far the Lisbon Recognition Convention Committee has adopted four subsidiary texts:

• The Recommendation on International Access Qualifications (1999)
• The Recommendation on Criteria and Procedures for the Assessment of Foreign Qualifications and Periods of Study (2001)
• The Code of Good Practice in the Provision of Transnational Education (2001)
• The Recommendation on the Recognition of Joint Degrees (2004)

We have already referred to the Code of Good Practice in the Provision of Transnational Education and the Recommendation on the Recognition of Joint Degrees in the previous chapter, and we will examine the Recommendation on Criteria and Procedures for the Assessment of Foreign Qualifications and Periods of Study in the next chapter. The first of the subsidiary texts, the Recommendation on International Access Qualifications, addresses qualifications earned outside national education systems that give access to higher education. The foremost among these is the International Baccalaureate, which we also considered in the previous chapter, and this recommendation seems to have improved the recognition of the IB in some countries that had been somewhat hesitant for a long period.

It is worth noting that three of the four subsidiary texts adopted so far cover qualifications of the kind we discussed in Chapter 11, that is, qualifications that do not belong to only one education system. The reason for this is both that such qualifications have become much more common since the convention was adopted in 1997 and that since the convention is a legal treaty between states, several potential parties were reluctant to include provisions covering qualifications that did not belong to national education systems, since they felt governments had limited authority over such qualifications. The subsidiary texts may therefore extend the basic principles and values of the convention to new areas, and they afford an opportunity to address issues that arise after the convention was adopted.

The subsidiary texts do not have the same legal value as the convention itself, and they are not legally binding in the way that the convention is. This may be inconvenient, but the inconvenience is limited by the fact that the strength of the convention lies not only in its legal nature, but also in the force of its example. The convention in effect has a double function: as a legal treaty and as a code of good practice.

National Information Centres

As is the case for all legal texts, the real value of the convention is measured by its implementation. This is implicitly recognised in Sections IX and X, which call on all parties to establish national information centres on academic recognition and mobility – often called ENICs and NARICs since they are members of the ENIC and/or NARIC Networks, which we shall discuss shortly. The national centre should be the one address that one can turn to for reliable information either about the education system and qualifications framework of the country for which the centre is competent or about the recognition of foreign qualifications in that country. If the centres cannot answer queries, they should be able to refer enquirers to the appropriate bodies, so that all or at least the vast majority of questions can be answered in "one or two stops" – meaning that enquirers should not be referred from one address to another without receiving a proper answer.

In most cases, the national information centre does not make recognition decisions, since those are normally made by higher education institutions, professional bodies or others, such as employers in the unregulated parts of the labour market. However, national centres should be the foremost resource centres in each country on the recognition of qualifications, and they should be where higher education institutions and others turn when they are faced with qualifications from institutions or systems they do not know well. Even if the national centres do not make recognition decisions, they provide valuable advice and the decision-making bodies often follow this advice.

In principle, all parties to the convention should establish a national information centre, but some countries are still in the process of doing so. On the other hand, a few countries have more than one centre. Thus, Belgium has one centre for the Flemish Community and one for the French Community, in other words, one for each education system in the country. Greece has one education system but two information centres because one centre is responsible for information on university qualifications and one for other kinds of higher education qualifications. The size and workload of national centres vary considerably, and the size of a national centre depends not only on the size and financial situation of the country, since the centre requires resources to operate effectively, but also on the number of holders of foreign qualifications that apply for recognition. Some centres have a staff of 20 or more and have the resources to let some staff specialise in qualifications from certain regions, language areas or academic fields, whereas others have only two or three staff – in a few cases only one – who have to cover the whole range of activities of the centre. Some countries also have separate information bodies – usually called "information points" – for European Union directives on the recognition of qualifications for professional purposes, which cover *de jure* professional recognition. Within the European Union, there are also National Reference Points for vocational qualifications.[33]

The typical activities of national information centres were outlined in the charter[34] adopted by the Lisbon Recognition Convention Committee in 2004 after discussion in the ENIC and NARIC Networks. It is worth quoting the list of tasks and activities for national centres outlined in Section II of this charter *in extenso*:

• Provide adequate, reliable and authenticated information, within reasonable time as prescribed by the Lisbon Recognition Convention, national and EU legislation, on qualifications, education systems, and recognition procedures to individual holders of qualifications, higher education institutions, employers, professional organisations, public authorities, ENIC/NARIC partners and other interested parties;
• Provide information, advice or formal decision on the recognition of qualifications on the basis of their assessment by applying existing criteria and procedures developed by the Networks, as well as new criteria for assessment of qualifications described in terms of workload, level, learning outcomes, competences and profile;
• Provide to citizens information on their rights regarding recognition;
• Serve as the main information point on the recognition of higher education and higher education access qualifications at national level;
• Co-operate in related matters with other information centres, higher education institutions, their networks and other relevant actors in the national context;
• In the EU context, and as far as NARICs have competence in professional recognition matters, co-operate with the National Co-ordinator[35] and the competent authorities for the professional recognition of the regulated professions (EU Directives);
• Contribute to higher education policy development and legislation at regional, national and European level;

---

33. See http://europass.cedefop.europa.eu/europass/home/vernav/Information+and++Support/National+ Reference+Points/navigate.action (accessed on 1 June 2006).
34. For the ENIC/NARIC Charter of Activities and Services, see Rauhvargers and Bergan (eds), *Standards for Recognition*, op. cit., pp. 119–29 and https://wcd.coe.int/com.instranet.InstraServlet?Command= com.instranet.CmdBlob Get&DocId=822012&SecMode=1&Admin=0&Usage=4&InstranetImage=43867 (accessed on 31 May 2006).
35. Each member state shall designate a person responsible for co-ordinating the activities of the authorities empowered to receive the applications and take decisions referred to in these directives. His/her role shall be to promote uniform application of these directives to all the professions concerned.

- Co-operate within the ENIC and NARIC Networks on the development of an overarching framework of qualifications for the European Higher Education Area and accordingly contribute at national level to the further development of the education systems;
- Participate in the elaboration of publications, information and other materials on the home education system and participate in publications, surveys, comparative studies and other research activities undertaken by the European Commission, Council of Europe, UNESCO and other international organisations;
- Collect and regularly update information on: education systems, qualifications awarded in different countries and their comparability to the qualifications in the home country, legislation on recognition, information on officially recognised and accredited institutions, admission requirements;
- Develop co-operation with relevant organisations in countries in other regions of the world working in the field of recognition;
- Create, maintain and regularly up-date the information on the national education system in the format given in the Annex to the present document;
- Where entrusted by the national authority, elaborate and maintain the description of the national education system to be included in the Diploma Supplement;
- Promote the activities of the ENIC and NARIC Networks in countries in other regions of the world;
- Refer to the membership of the ENIC and NARIC Networks in all publications and correspondence and on web-sites and make appropriate use of their logo;
- [Perform] other tasks as decided through national regulations.

This is an ambitious list of tasks, and only the largest and best developed centres can adequately fulfil all of them. Nevertheless, the list illustrates the need for centres of competence that can provide reliable information on their own qualifications frameworks as well as on those of other countries, and that can provide advice on recognition. The charter also sets an ambitious goal for the development of those centres that have been in operation for only a few years or that aim to develop their activities further as well as for the remaining few countries that are only now establishing their centres. Needless to say, the importance of the national information centres increases as academic and professional mobility increases, and their competence is not limited to the education systems of the countries making up the European Higher Education Area.

To fulfil their role as centres of competence, national centres should maintain close contacts with those who work with recognition issues at higher education institutions, in professional bodies and in other competent recognition bodies. Ideally, national centres should also have close contacts with employers and their organisations, but in most countries, such contacts have been more difficult to establish than contacts with others who make recognition decisions. In many countries, the national centres organise national conferences on recognition for the major stakeholders. This is a very important way of improving competence at institutions and other recognition bodies, and also of bringing the issues of principle and policy discussed at international level into the national debate.

An updated list of all national information centres in the European Region with their contact addresses may be found at the website of the ENIC and NARIC Networks.[36] For those who require information about the recognition of foreign qualifications, their first point of contact should in general be the national information centre of the country in which they wish to have their qualifications recognised. If need be, they can also contact the information centre in the country from which their qualifications originate. This also points to another important task of the national information centres: that of representing their countries in international co-operation to develop and improve recognition practice.

The ENIC and NARIC Networks

The national information centres in the European Region co-operate through two networks: the European Network of National Information Centres on academic recognition and mobility (ENIC Network), served by the Council of Europe and UNESCO, and the Network of National Academic Recognition Information Centres (NARIC Network), served by the European Commission.

Paradoxically, the ENIC Network is the older, but also the younger of these. In its current form, it was established in 1994 as a joint Council of Europe/UNESCO network, but it was a merger of previous networks served by the two organisations separately, and these date back to the 1970s and early 1980s. The ENIC Network encompasses not only geographical Europe, but the whole European Region, in the sense of the Council of Europe/UNESCO Recognition Convention, including Canada, the United States and Israel, as well as Australia, all of which are party to this convention. The ENIC Network therefore has just over 50 member states.

The NARIC Network was established in 1984 and encompasses the countries of the European Union, the European Economic Area and the countries that participate in certain European Union higher education programmes (Socrates). For legal and institutional reasons, the two networks are separate, but they co-operate very closely. They hold annual joint meetings, and in addition the NARIC Network meets separately once a year. The ENIC Bureau and the NARIC Advisory Board also hold joint meetings, and the three sponsoring institutions co-operate closely in this area, which is to my knowledge a unique example of co-operation between three international institutions. There is synergy also at national level, since in the countries belonging to the NARIC Network the national centres are also members of the ENIC Network. Put simply, all NARICs are also ENICs, but some ENICs – those in countries that are not eligible for the European Commission programmes in question – are not NARICs.

The ENIC and NARIC Networks do not have decision-making authority, but they play an important role as a platform for the development of recognition policy. The ENIC Network is also a preparatory body for the Lisbon Recognition Convention Commit-

---

36. See http://www.enic-naric.net/ (accessed on 31 May 2006).

tee, which means that it prepares issues put to the committee. Thus, it prepared the four subsidiary texts adopted by the committee. By discussing major recognition topics, they develop common attitudes and common practice; even if they cannot make decisions, the networks exercise considerable peer pressure. In addition to the four subsidiary texts just referred to and the ENIC/NARIC Charter of Activities and Services, the networks have considered issues such as:

• recognition issues in the Bologna Process;

• the provision of information on recognition, leading to a code of good practice;[37]

• cross-border/transnational education;

• electronic information, by a working group that oversees the joint website of the two networks;[38]

• improving the definition and understanding of the concept "substantial differences", which is, as we have seen, a key concept of the Council of Europe/ UNESCO Recognition Convention;

• national action plans for recognition in the Bologna Process;

In the 1990s, the networks also considered recognition of qualifications from given countries or areas, such as the Russian Federation and the United States (through working groups led by UNESCO-CEPES) and the new countries of central and eastern Europe that joined the European Cultural Convention (ETS No. 18) after the political changes around 1990 (through a working group led by the Council of Europe). Since about 2000, attention has focused on overall recognition issues, but the European Commission has led work on what are often called "persistent recognition issues" – issues that have been difficult to solve bilaterally or in contacts between a small group of countries. Sometimes broadening such issues and putting them into a context where it may be easier to discuss the underlying issues of principle may help bring about a solution.

Although it is not part of the two networks, it is worth mentioning the European Association for International Education (EAIE), an NGO based in Amsterdam, which has a professional section for admissions officers and credentials evaluators (ACE). The activities of this professional section, especially its sessions at the annual EAIE conferences, play an important role in involving recognition officers at higher education institutions in discussions of recognition issues and in providing

---

37. See http://www.coe.int/T/DG4/HigherEducation/Recognition/ENIC%20NARIC%20Code%20inform ation%20provision_EN.asp (accessed on 1 June 2006).
38. See http://www.enic-naric.net/ (accessed on 1 June 2006). The Canadian ENIC played an invaluable role in setting up and maintaining this website, probably the best source of online information on recognition issues.

them with information on recognition. The ACE professional section also maintains a very good website.[39]

Transparency instruments

The term "transparency instruments" may sound somewhat Orwellian, but it signifies an important and positive reality. These are instruments that help explain the contents of qualifications and put them in their proper context. They make qualifications more transparent and help improve recognition. The two most important transparency instruments at European level are the European Credit Transfer and Accumulation System (ECTS) and the Diploma Supplement. Since we discussed the ECTS[40] at some length in the chapter on workload, we will here focus on the Diploma Supplement. Suffice to recall that the ECTS was originally developed as a part of the EU Erasmus Programme in 1988–95, that it provides a system for expressing workloads in terms of credits and facilitating the transfer of these credits from one institution to another within a country or across the borders of countries and education systems. The normal full-time student workload for one year is 60 ECTS credits, and the ECTS has a grading scale that helps translate the often very different grading scales of institutions. Some countries have now adopted the ECTS as their official credit system and grading scale, which should further facilitate international recognition and, hence, mobility. Currently, the European Commission is working to improve the ECTS as not only a credit transfer but also a credit accumulation system by enabling the ECTS to include an expression of credits according to their level, as was also discussed in Chapter 5.

The Diploma Supplement was developed jointly by the European Commission, the Council of Europe and UNESCO in the mid-1990s, and this work built on a previous version of the supplement developed by UNESCO in the 1980s.[41] As its name indicates, the Diploma Supplement does not substitute for the diploma or attestation of a qualification. Rather, it is used with the diploma, as a supplementary document that helps explain the content of the qualification in question and put it into its proper context in the education system or qualifications framework within which the qualification was earned.

The Diploma Supplement should be issued by the competent authorities of the institution awarding the qualification, and the ministers of the Bologna Process have committed themselves – in the Berlin Communiqué – to issuing the Diploma Supplement automatically, free of charge and in a widely spoken European language from autumn 2005.

---

39. See http://www.eaie.nl/ace/ (accessed on 1 June 2006). This website was established above all thanks to the work of Andrejs Rauhvargers, former President of ACE and of the ENIC Network, currently (2006) President of the Lisbon Recognition Convention Committee.
40. See also http://www.aic.lv/ace/ace_disk/ECTS/index.htm (accessed on 1 June 2006).
41. A good overview is at http://www.aic.lv/ace/ace_disk/Dipl_Sup/index.htm (accessed on 1 June 2006). The Diploma Supplement template is at http://www.aic.lv/ace/ace_disk/Dipl_Sup/DS_form.doc.

It is particularly important that Diploma Supplements be issued automatically because they describe the qualification in relation to the education system as it was at the time the qualification was awarded. As we know, education systems are reformed from time to time, and the longer the period between the issuing of the diploma and the issuing of the Diploma Supplement, the greater the danger that the supplement will not include the description of the education system as it was at the time the qualification was earned. Issuing the Diploma Supplement automatically should eliminate the danger of such confusion and also rationalise administrative procedures for higher education institutions, since they would not have to reply to a large but unpredictable number of individual requests. The language issue can be sensitive, since many institutions are required to issue the supplement in their own language, but there is no contradiction between issuing it in the national language(s) as well as in one or more widely spoken languages. An innovative example is found in Moldova, where bilingual Diploma Supplements are now issued in Romanian and English.

The Diploma Supplement provides information on the following key elements of the diploma and qualification:

Information identifying the holder of the qualification, that is the name, date of birth of the holder of the qualification as well as his or her identification number where this exists and where national laws allow it to be included.

Information identifying the qualification, which includes the name of the qualification in the original language, the main field(s) of study, the name of the institution awarding the qualification as well as of the institution where the studies have been undertaken, if this is different. In some cases, qualifications may in fact be awarded by bodies other than the higher education institution offering the study programme. Information on the language(s) of instruction should also be included, for the reasons discussed in Chapter 11 on education provisions not linked to national systems where in some cases programmes with English-sounding names or with links to English-speaking institutions may in fact be offered mainly or entirely in the language of the country in which they are located.

Information on the level of the qualification, which in addition to information on its place within the qualifications framework includes information on workload or official length of the study programme and on access requirements.

Information on the study programme and on the results obtained, which includes the mode of study (e.g. classroom teaching, distance education, practice periods), the requirements and details of the programme, the grading scheme and preferably guidance on the distribution of grades and overall classification of the qualification (in the original language). This part of the Diploma Supplement can include course transcripts.

Information on the function of the qualification, in terms of the access it gives to further study and, if possible, professional functions. In some countries, institutions may be barred by law from giving information on the professional function of qualifications.

Any supplementary information on the qualification that the awarding institution might consider useful.

Certification of the Diploma Supplement by the issuing institution.

Information on the education system within which the qualification has been earned. This should be information established by the authorities responsible for the system, so that institutions in the same system provide the same information. As countries develop qualifications frameworks, they should be included in the information provided here.

For some categories, it is specified that the Diploma Supplement should provide names of qualifications and institutions in the original language. The reason is that translating names may easily involve an assessment of content that should properly be carried out by competent recognition bodies. For example, describing a qualification as a Master's degree if the original name is *mester* or *maestro* (both names are intended to be fictitious) implies recognising it as a Master's degree in systems that have degrees by this name. The status of a *mester* or *maestro* as a second degree in the system in which it is issued will be apparent from the Diploma Supplement and is not to be established through translation. Likewise, the name of an institution may give unwanted associations to those who are not familiar with the system in question, and who are therefore in particular need of the information provided by the Diploma Supplement. For example, translating the name of a non-university institution as "University of Applied Sciences" may lead the uninitiated to believe the institution is a university, even if this particular translation is by now relatively well known.

In sum, the Diploma Supplement is a very useful tool for explaining the contents and functions of a qualification as well as its place within a given education system. It is not a document that can replace an actual assessment of the qualification, but it should help the assessment, and it should not be considered unless it is accompanied by the actual diploma. The Diploma Supplement has now been included in the European Union's Europass,[42] which is a collection of tools helping describe qualifications and competences at various levels.

Other legislation on recognition

The Council of Europe/UNESCO Recognition Convention is the most important international legal framework for the recognition of qualifications in the European Region. Space does not allow a closer consideration of other laws and regulations, but it should nevertheless be recalled that at least four other kinds of regulations are also important: UNESCO conventions for other regions, European Union directives on *de jure* professional recognition, regional and bilateral agreements, and national legislation.

---

42. See http://europass.cedefop.europa.eu/ (accessed on 1 June 2006).

As we saw, in the European Region the joint Council of Europe/UNESCO Recognition Convention replaces a previous UNESCO regional convention, as well as a number of Council of Europe conventions.[43] In addition, UNESCO has a set of conventions for other regions of the world, and these are:[44]

• Regional Convention on the Recognition of Studies, Diplomas and Degrees in Higher Education in Latin America and the Caribbean (1974);

• International Convention on the Recognition of Studies, Diplomas and Degrees in Higher Education in the Arab and European States bordering on the Mediterranean (1976);

• Convention on the Recognition of Studies, Diplomas and Degrees concerning Higher Education in the Arab States (1978);

• Regional Convention on the Recognition of Studies, Certificates, Diplomas, Degrees and other Academic Qualifications in Higher Education in the African States (1981);

• Regional Convention on the Recognition of Studies, Diplomas and Degrees in Higher Education in Asia and the Pacific (1983).

Discussions are now under way on revising some of the UNESCO regional conventions, since higher education has undergone important reforms since they were first adopted. Four of these conventions are regional, but the one for the Mediterranean is inter-regional, as it has been ratified by countries of the European Region and the Arab Region.

The European Union directives on recognition for professional purposes cover qualifications giving access to – that is, the right to practise – regulated professions. In other words, the directives apply to *de jure* professional recognition. They are of two kinds. The first kind is the various sectoral directives that each concern one specific regulated profession, such as medical doctor, dentist, pharmacist, lawyer or architect. Each sectoral directive contains provisions specific to the profession it covers, and some directives have gone through a number of amendments. The second kind is the general directives, which cover all or several regulated professions. These are:[45]

• Council[46] Directive of 21 December 1988 on a general system for the recognition of higher education diplomas awarded on completion of professional education and training of at least three years' duration (89/48/EEC);

---

43. In effect, in formal terms, the older conventions are replaced by obligations under the Council of Europe/ UNESCO convention as countries ratify the latter. Because the previous conventions contained no denunciation clauses, parties to the 1997 joint convention undertake to be bound by this rather than by older conventions in their mutual relations, cf. Article XI.4.1 of the Council of Europe/UNESCO convention.

44. Links to all conventions can be found via http://www.enic-naric.net/instruments.asp?display=other_ regions &topic=legal_framework (accessed on 1 June 2006).

45. See http://www.aic.lv/ace/ace_disk/Recognition/dir_prof/GENERAL/index.htm#1.%20augst (accessed on 1 June 2006).

46. Here meaning the European Council, which is the EU body made up of the competent ministers of the member states. The European Council should not be confused with the Council of Europe.

• Council Directive 92/51/EEC of 18 June 1992 on a second general system for the recognition of professional education and training to supplement Directive 89/48/EEC, which applies to professional and education training of less than three years' duration;

• Directive 1999/42/EC of the European Parliament and of the Council establishing a mechanism for the recognition of qualifications in respect of the professional activities covered by the Directives on liberalisation and transitional measures and supplementing the general systems for the recognition of qualifications, which covers professions where recognition is based mainly on professional experience;

• Directive 2001/19/EC of the European Parliament and of the Council, which amends a number of sectoral directives as well as Directives 89/48/EEC and 92/51/EEC. This directive is also referred to as the SLIM Directive.[47]

While the European Union directives are very detailed, their basic principle is the same as that of the Council of Europe/UNESCO Recognition Convention: foreign qualifications shall be recognised unless the competent recognition authorities can demonstrate a substantial difference between the qualification for which recognition is sought and the corresponding qualification of the country in which such recognition is sought. In general terms, the directives apply to countries of the European Union, the European Economic Area and countries in the process of acceding to the European Union.

Many countries have established bilateral agreements on the recognition of each others' qualifications, which may even contain provisions detailing specific recognition, such as "qualification X of country A shall be recognised as equal to qualification Z of country B". Such agreements help facilitate recognition between countries that experience a high rate of exchange of students, or that hope to stimulate mutual student exchange. To the extent that they stipulate specific recognition of given qualifications, they need to be reviewed frequently to ensure that the agreements are brought up to date with any modifications of the education system of the countries concerned.

There may also be regional agreements on recognition between a group of neighbouring states or even universities. For example, the University Confederation of the Upper Rhine (EUCOR), which encompasses the three universities of Strasbourg and that of the Haut-Rhin in France, those of Freiburg and Karlsruhe in Germany and that of Basel in Switzerland have established an agreement that provides for easy recognition of courses taken at any of the participating universities. Such an agreement between institutions cannot be considered a legal text, but it is nonetheless an interesting example of good practice, and qualifications earned in this way should be considered as belonging to the education system of the institution that issues them.

---

47. See Andrejs Rauhvargers' explanatory note on the main implications of this directive, available at http://www.aic.lv/ace/ace_disk/Recognition/exp_text/SLIM%20and%20New%20Proposal.pdf (accessed on 1 June 2006).

Another option for such arrangements would be to issue joint degrees. In the 1970s, the five Nordic countries – Denmark, Finland, Iceland, Norway and Sweden – elaborated the Sigtuna Agreement in the framework of the Nordic Council of Ministers to facilitate recognition between the Nordic countries. However, like the older conventions on recognition in Europe, this agreement did not take account of recent developments in higher education. Once all five Nordic countries had ratified the Council of Europe/UNESCO Recognition Convention, they therefore decided to use this convention also in the Nordic context.

Most countries have national legislation on the recognition of qualifications, either specific laws on recognition, as part of their overall higher education legislation and/or as part of their legislation on regulated professions. National higher education laws vary widely, ranging from brief framework laws to very detailed laws with more than 200 articles.

In the case of both regional and bilateral agreements and national laws, it is important that they not be contradictory to the international agreements to which the countries in question are a party. For example, the laws of the 42 countries that have so far (September 2006) ratified the Council of Europe/UNESCO Recognition Convention should be in line with the obligations these countries have undertaken under this convention, and the same applies to bilateral or regional agreements to which they may be party. However, there is reason to suspect that some inconsistencies remain, since the legislation concerned may be quite complex. This is one reason why the ministers of the Bologna Process undertook, in their Bergen Communiqué, to incorporate the principles of the Lisbon Recognition Convention into their national legislation, which in effect requires a review of all relevant national legislation.

Even if this chapter has been able to offer only a cursory overview of the legal and practical framework for recognition of qualifications, and even if it has focused mainly on the Council of Europe/UNESCO Recognition Convention, the reader is probably left with the impression that this is a rather complicated area. That would not be a wrong impression, but it should also be underlined that, while there are important issues of a technical character, it is important that those implementing the legislation and developing recognition practice not lose sight of the basic values and principles of the legislation. The legislation is there to help applicants obtain a fair assessment of their qualifications, not to prevent them from using their qualifications in another country or education system. Sometimes recognition cannot be granted, but in such cases the decision not to recognise should be justified, and before recognition is rejected, the recognition body should explore whether the foreign qualifications may be given partial recognition.

After this consideration of the settings and the legal and practical framework, it is time to look at some of the major issues in recognition and how an understanding of the concept of qualifications may help facilitate fair recognition.

14 Moving between education systems: recognition procedures and issues

Let us go back to our group of athletes turned academics again, perhaps for the last time. Let us imagine that some of them have decided to study or work in another country, and that they therefore need to transport their qualifications across the bridge we talked about in the previous chapter. In other words, they need to take their qualifications with them without losing the real value of those qualifications in another education system. In the previous chapter, we looked at the legal framework that should help them, and in this chapter we will look at how this might be done in practice, as well as at some of the issues that might arise.

Once our friends apply for recognition of their qualifications, they (and we) will follow the road sketched in the Recommendation on Criteria and Procedures for the Assessment of Foreign Qualifications and Periods of Study[48] adopted by the Lisbon Recognition Convention Committee in 2001. As we move along this road, we will encounter some of the issues that arise when credentials evaluators assess foreign qualifications. For the sake of clarity, these will be considered after we have completed the road and obtained a result.

Before they start wandering across the bridge of recognition, however, our friends who plan to study abroad should try to find out how the qualifications they plan to earn are likely to be recognised once they return home. While they may not be able to get a binding promise of specific recognition, either their home higher education institution or the national information centre on recognition (ENIC/NARIC)[49] that we described in the previous chapter should be able to give them useful information and warn them against possible pitfalls. They could also turn to the national information centre if they have already earned a qualification and now want to use it in another country, for the purpose of work or further study. Normally, they should address their first enquiry to the centre of the country in which they want to use their qualifications, but they might also contact the centre in their home country. If they want to use their qualifications abroad, they should start their enquiries as early as possible, to minimise the risk of unforeseen problems and disappointments.

Applying for recognition

An application for recognition should be submitted in writing to the competent recognition authority in question, which may be a university, a professional body or any

---

48. Printed in Andrejs Rauhvargers and Sjur Bergan (eds), *Standards for Recognition*, op. cit., or http://www.coe.int/T/DG4/HigherEducation/Recognition/Criteria%20and%20procedures_EN.asp#TopOfPage. This recommendation is often referred to, for short, as the Recommendation on Criteria and Procedures.
49. A list of national centres will be found at http://www.enic-naric.net/ (accessed on 9 June 2006).

other body designated by the public authorities responsible for the education system. The national information centre may offer help and advice, but it is rarely – apart from a few countries – the body that actually makes recognition decisions. Ultimately, the responsibility for submitting an application to the right body, in due form and – where applicable – within any deadline the recognition authority may stipulate is the applicant's own, though applicants are of course encouraged to seek advice, and the information centres and other relevant bodies should do their best to provide good, rapid and accurate information.

Let us imagine that some of our acquaintances from the previous chapters have just sent an application for recognition. They will certainly be relieved if they receive confirmation from the recognition body that it has received their applications, and in many countries they would get this confirmation. However, some information centres, higher education institutions and other bodies may not give priority to sending confirmations of receipt, as they may think it is a formality that takes time away from the core of their work. This, however, would be an erroneous view, and there are several reasons for that.

Firstly, for the applicant, it is reassuring to know that one's application has arrived and is being considered. Sending a confirmation of receipt therefore shows respect for applicants, but it means a lot more than that. It is also good public relations for the recognition body, and it may help simplify the recognition procedure, especially if the recognition body does not send a simple acknowledgement that they have received the application and put it in a file, but at the same time sends applicants information on how their applications will be assessed, how long this will normally take and what rights applicants have once the application has been assessed.

Of course, this does not substitute for the real assessment, nor should the recognition body go into great detail, but sending applicants a brief explanation of how applications are assessed, and the main criteria used, may help reassure applicants, who may feel less need to contact the recognition body before the application has been considered. Therefore, spending a little time sending out a standard information pack to applicants may save the recognition body a considerable amount of time, by having to answer fewer phone calls and enquiries from applicants wondering what is happening to their applications. This may be particularly true if the information package also informs applicants how long it normally takes to assess their qualifications. Of course, if recognition bodies give information on this, they should be reasonably sure they do assess most applications within the time they give; otherwise they will simply delay the rush of phone calls by a few weeks. Here we may keep in mind the suggestion in the explanatory report[50] to the Council of Europe/UNESCO Recognition Convention that applications should normally be assessed within four months.

---

50. To Article III.5.

Exactly what information will be provided to applicants may vary from one country to another, but the Recommendation on Criteria and Procedures suggests it should contain "at least the following elements": [51]

(i) the documentation required, including requirements as to the authentication and translation of documents;

(ii) a description of the assessment process, including the role of the national information centre, other assessment agencies and higher education institutions;

(iii) a description of the assessment criteria;

(iv) the status of recognition statements;

(v) the approximate time needed to process an application;

(vi) any fees charged;

(vii) a reference to the national laws and international conventions and agreements which may be relevant to the assessment of foreign qualifications;

(viii) the conditions and procedures for appealing against a recognition decision, according to national legislation.

The final point is important. Applicants should have a right to appeal against a recognition decision[52] with which they are unhappy, and they should be informed about this right. There is no formal requirement about when applicants should be informed of their right to appeal, and there is nothing to prevent recognition bodies from informing applicants at the same time that they issue the recognition decision. However, it may be in the interest of recognition authorities to do so at the outset of the procedure, since linking information on the right to appeal to information on the decision itself may easily be read as an inducement to appeal.

First steps in assessing a recognition application

Once the recognition body has sent the information package to the applicants, the assessment can begin. However, the application cannot be assessed unless it is complete, so the first task of the credentials evaluator is to check that the applicants have sent all the documentation and information they are required to send. If they have not, the recognition body should inform them in writing of what further documentation and information it requires, and it should do so in one go. It is very frustrating for applicants to be told that they need to send document A, and then when they do so to be told that they also need to send document B, and when they send document B, to be

---

51. Explanatory memorandum, paragraph 14.
52. Article III.5 of the convention.

told that incidentally they also need to send document C, and so on. Giving applicants complete information on all the extra documentation and information required gives them the impression of dealing with a serious, efficient and reliable recognition body, whereas asking for additional information piecemeal may easily give the opposite impression. It can also give the impression that the recognition body is trying to delay the case or to avoid making a decision by making additional demands as the case progresses.

The recognition authority is responsible for letting applicants know what documentation and information they are required to submit, but the applicants themselves are responsible for submitting the information and documentation asked for, and it is only from the time when the application is complete that any deadlines for the recognition body to issue a decision are counted. Therefore, if the recognition body is required to make a decision within, say, four months, the four months are counted from the day the recognition body receives the last missing piece of information from the applicant.

In some cases applicants may not have the information requested and may need to ask for it from another body. For example, if our acquaintances have a qualification from a higher education institution and want to continue their studies in another country, they may need to obtain documentation from their first institution to prove that they have indeed obtained a qualification. In this case, their first institution should help them as far as possible by responding quickly to requests for documentation and information. To avoid repetition, we will use the term "information" to cover both documentation and information from now on, but it is worth underlining that there is a difference between them. Documentation means official certification of qualifications earned and results obtained, such as documents that show that Ms AA has obtained a first degree in Physics from University Z with an ECTS grade B. Information may mean something less formal and perhaps also more general, such as information on the grading scale the institution uses (or used at the time the qualification was issued), information about courses and education systems, and so forth. This also illustrates the value of issuing the Diploma Supplement automatically to all students, since in these cases students would presumably not need to contact their home institutions for supplementary information or for documentation of their qualifications. One should of course not preclude the possibility of issuing copies of lost documentation, but issuing the Diploma Supplement automatically would at least considerably reduce the number of later requests to institutions.

Sometimes, it may be easier for the recognition body to request information directly from a higher education institution than to ask the applicant to ask the institution. If the applicant agrees, there is nothing to prevent the recognition body from asking for information directly, but in some countries, privacy laws prevent institutions from providing information on individuals to third parties, so institutions cannot provide personal information to anyone but the person in question. In this case, our acquaintances will have to contact their home institution themselves and then pass on the information to the recognition body.

The next step for the credentials evaluator will be to verify that the documentation provided is authentic. This, in fact, implies responding positively to two different but related questions:

- Is the documentation genuine, that is, not forged or falsified?
- Was it in fact issued to the applicant?

One could argue that if the documentation was not issued to the applicant, it has in fact been forged since the personal information on it has been changed. Forging documents in this way is a criminal offence in most countries, and it should at the very least entail the rejection of the application. Yet, though there is no difference in principle and perhaps in legal consequences between forging the name on a genuine document and forging the document itself, it may be useful to make the point that both questions should be asked.

Forged documents in fact seem to be an increasing problem for recognition bodies, and sophisticated software and other technical possibilities make forgeries more and more difficult to discover. Sometimes one wonders if those who forge qualifications put as much energy into the forgery as they would have put into obtaining a genuine qualification in the first place, and they certainly oblige credentials evaluators to spend much time and energy on verification that could have been better spent on assessing qualifications and on developing recognition policies. There have been cases where credentials evaluators needed to consider seemingly very minor details in order to discover forgeries, such as verifying whether a Dean or Rector whose signature appears on a diploma, and who has in fact been Dean of the Faculty or Rector of the institution in question, held this office at the time indicated on the diploma, or where they have discovered that the personal identification number on the diploma had a structure used only for women whereas the applicant was male.[53]

Any comprehensive description of ways to unmask forgeries would be lengthy, it would be partly out of date by the time this book is published and it would indicate ways of carrying out forgeries. At advanced level, unmasking forgeries is a task for specialists; alas, there seem to be a good number of specialists of a different kind engaged in devising the forgeries.

In our context, we should, however, remind ourselves of the need to find a proper balance between the resources a recognition body puts into unmasking forgeries and the potential benefits this effort can have. If they have reason to believe a qualification has been forged, recognition bodies may well be justified in putting considerable resources into proving the forgery. However, as a general rule, they should be careful not to impose undue burdens on themselves and on applicants by making the general verification of documents too extensive or by assuming that most applicants are trying to cheat.

---

53. Such as identification numbers ending in even digits for women and odd digits for men.

Another question is what to do when a forgery is discovered and can be proved. The obvious answer is that the application is rejected, but often a sense of justice dictates that more should be done, and here practice varies from country to country. In some countries, attempted forgeries are automatically brought to the attention of the police or the judiciary, whereas in other countries, recognition bodies may not be legally required to do so and may in fact hesitate to do so. Applicants may, for example, be in a difficult personal situation and may risk expulsion because of the forgery, and the recognition body may consider that the likely punishment is disproportionate to the offence committed. At the very least, recognition bodies tend to inform other recognition bodies in their country of attempted forgeries.

If the information submitted by the applicants is complete and genuine, the credentials evaluator can proceed to the next step, which is to verify the status of the institution that has issued the qualification. Often, this is a simple step, since many applications concern qualifications from institutions that are well known to the recognition body. There is little need to spend much time on considering the status of the Universidad Complutense de Madrid in relation to the Spanish higher education system or Moscow State University in relation to the Russian system if the recognition bodies are well acquainted with these institutions, both of which are incidentally genuine and well reputed.

However, credentials evaluators may be faced with a qualification from an institution or a system they do not know and they will need to make further enquiries. In these cases, they will often contact the national information centre of the country in which the qualification was issued, for information on the education system or qualifications framework and on the status of the institution or programme. Since quality assurance is normally carried out by quality assurance agencies, national information centres on recognition should be able to provide information on the status of institutions and programmes in their education systems, on the quality assurance system and on the outcomes of quality assessments of institutions and programmes.

Assessing qualifications

If the information on the qualification is complete, the qualification is genuine and the institution that issued it is of sufficient quality, the credentials evaluator can finally get down to the core business of assessing the qualification itself. This is where most issues of principle arise and where an understanding of the concept of qualifications is helpful to recognition. Essentially, what the credentials evaluator will do is seek to establish the value of the foreign qualification in terms of the education system of the country in which recognition is sought. As more countries establish national qualifications frameworks, the main task of the credentials evaluator will be to determine the place of the foreign qualification within the qualifications framework of his or her own country. This, of course, requires intimate knowledge of both one's own education system and qualifications framework, and the foreign qualification in question. However, it also requires understanding of the concept of qualifications and of the international legal framework and setting for recognition.

The approach to recognition has evolved, as it is often described, from "equivalence" to "recognition". This implies that, in the early stages, credentials evaluators sought a very high degree of compatibility between the foreign qualification and the corresponding qualification of the host country. The early international legal texts on recognition, such as the two earliest Council of Europe conventions from the 1950s, were called conventions on equivalence.[54] The caricature of "equivalence" is the credentials evaluator conducting a detailed comparison of reading lists to make sure the applicant has studied more or the less the same books he or she would have studied in the country where recognition is sought, but the "narrow" approach to recognition can also take more subtle forms. Even if attitudes have evolved, the "narrow" approach is not entirely a thing of the past.

Many of the factors credentials evaluators have to assess concern what the Council of Europe/UNESCO Recognition Convention calls "substantial differences". We encountered this term in the previous chapter, where I said that the term was too complex to be fully explored in a legal text, and that we needed to return to it. Now is the time to do so.

We have established that qualifications shall be recognised unless the competent recognition authority can demonstrate a substantial difference between the qualification for which recognition is sought and the corresponding qualification in the country in which recognition is sought. That is an important point in itself. It is up to the recognition authority to demonstrate that there is a substantial difference, if it wishes to withhold recognition, and not up to the applicant to demonstrate that there is no substantial difference. The basic assumption is that foreign qualifications should be recognised, and non-recognition is the exceptional case that needs to be demonstrated and reasoned. In the words of the Explanatory Report:[55]

> this Article states the basic principle that Parties should recognize higher education qualifications earned in the higher education system of any other party unless a substantial difference can be shown between the qualification for which recognition is sought and the corresponding qualification in the country in which recognition is sought. It is underlined that the difference must be both substantial and relevant as defined by the competent recognition authority. Recognition cannot be withheld for reasons immaterial to the qualification or the purpose for which recognition is sought. It is the responsibility of the party or higher education institution wishing to refuse recognition to show that the difference is substantial.

The interpretation of the legal text should take account of developments in education policies and in our understanding of relevant concepts. In the same way that it would be difficult to argue today that parties might provide information on the institutions

---

54. European Convention on the Equivalence of Diplomas leading to Admission to Universities (ETS No. 15 of 1953) and European Convention on the Equivalence of Periods of University Study (ETS No. 21 of 1956).
55. To Article VI.1, which addresses the recognition of higher education qualifications.

and programmes in their higher education system[56] without referring to the outcome of quality assessments, in view of the considerable development in policies and understanding of quality assurance since the convention was adopted in 1997, so too the interpretation of the concept "substantial differences" should take account of recent developments in our understanding of the concept of qualifications, which is the concern of this book. As more countries develop new-style qualifications frameworks, evaluators also need to take account of these in determining whether or not there is a substantial difference between two qualifications.

The ENIC and NARIC Networks are currently (2006) engaged in a discussion of the concept "substantial differences". What follows will draw on that discussion, which is led by a working party for which the Council of Europe provides the secretariat, but the discussion is still in progress and the following paragraphs should not be taken as representing the views of the network or indeed any official views.

Our starting point in considering the concept must be that the term "substantial differences" clearly indicates that minor differences between qualifications are not sufficient reason for non-recognition. After all, there would be little reason to study in a foreign country if learners were to undergo an education calqued on the one in their home country. The concept takes account of the diversity of higher education systems and traditions, and recognises that there are usually differences between corresponding qualifications in different education systems. Therefore, not accepting differences between qualifications would very often make recognition impossible. Thus, the existence of differences between the foreign qualification and that of the host country alone does not provide sufficient reason for non-recognition.

The views on qualifications that have developed over the past few years, in particular within the Bologna Process, emphasise the five elements of qualifications that we have considered at some length in this book:

• level
• workload
• quality
• profile
• learning outcomes.

This work was in particular underpinned by two conferences on qualifications structures (Copenhagen, March 2003)[57] and qualifications frameworks (Copenhagen, January 2005).[58] The Conference on Recognition and Credit Systems in the Context of

---

56. See Section VIII of the Convention.

57. General report available at http://www.bologna-bergen2005.no/EN/Bol_sem/Old/030327-28København/030327-28Report_General_Rapporteur.pdf and the recommendations at http://www.bologna-bergen2005.no/EN/Bol_sem/Old/030327-28København/030327-28CPH_Recommandations.pdf (accessed on 10 June 2006).

58. The general report is available at http://www.bologna-bergen2005.no/EN/Bol_sem/Seminars/050113-14København/050113-14_General_report.pdf and the recommendations at http://www.bologna-bergen2005.no/EN/Bol_sem/Seminars/050113-14København/050113-14_Recommendations.pdf (accessed on 10 June 2006).

Lifelong Learning (Prague, June 2003)[59] may also be of relevance. These five elements should also guide considerations of substantial differences.[60] While learning outcomes should ideally be the ultimate yardstick against which substantial differences should be measured, so far relatively few higher education programmes and qualifications provide descriptions of learning outcomes that would allow credentials evaluators to assess qualifications in relation to expected and obtained learning outcomes alone. While some countries and institutions have come far in describing learning outcomes, others are still at an early stage or have yet to begin. The four other elements discussed in this book also provide valuable guidance for determining whether substantial differences exist, and it should be underlined that all five elements constitute a whole. Seeking to establish substantial differences by referring to one factor alone without taking account of the other factors could lead to distorted results.

For example, emphasising workload alone is insufficient, as we already explored in Chapter 5. On the one hand, workload is a relevant criterion because it normally gives an indication of learning outcomes, on the assumption that from a similar point of departure, most students need to undertake a roughly similar workload to achieve similar learning outcomes. To quote the explanatory memorandum to the Recommendation on Criteria and Procedures:

> In general terms, however, length of study may be taken to give an indication of the level of a qualification. The wider the difference in the length of study normally required to obtain various qualifications, the more likely it would seem that these qualifications are not of the same level.[61]

That most students will need to make a broadly comparable effort to master roughly similar amounts of learning is all the more likely as we refer to workload rather than "time of study", since learners may earn a similar amount of ECTS credits even if they do not take the same time to earn those credits. Some learners may earn 75 ECTS credits in an academic year while others, perhaps because they work part-time, might earn 30 or less. For recognition purposes, workload provides some indication of learning outcomes, but it is not the only indication. Some students will cover the required amount of learning with a significantly lower workload, while others need to work considerably more. Therefore, even if most students invest broadly similar workloads, this may not apply to all students. Think of language students. A learner with a good knowledge of a Slavic language, such as Czech, is likely to acquire a working knowl-

---

59. The general report is available at http://www.bologna-bergen2005.no/EN/Bol_sem/Old/030605-07Prague/030605-07General_Report.pdf and the recommendations at http://www.bologna-bergen2005.no/EN/Bol_sem/Old/030605-07Prague/030605-07Recommendations.pdf (accessed on 10 June 2006).

60. From now on, "[the existence of] substantial differences" and similar expressions should be understood as shorthand for "[the existence of] substantial differences between the qualification for which recognition is sought and the corresponding qualification of the country (or rather, education system) in which recognition is sought".

61. Explanatory memorandum to paragraph 40. It should be noted that at the time when this recommendation was elaborated and adopted, it was still common to refer to length of study rather than workload.

edge of another Slavic language, such as Russian or Serbian, with less effort than a learner studying a Slavic language for the first time. Relying only on workload as an indicator may mean that applications for recognition are assessed too severely, since exceptional learners may achieve the stipulated learning outcomes through a lesser workload than the vast majority of their peers. While workload will probably give a reasonable indication in many cases, disregarding other indicators that may show that a learner has indeed – or is likely to have – achieved the desired learning outcomes may do considerable injustice to the applicant.

On the other hand, even if the applicants undertook a sufficient workload, they may not have achieved the required learning outcomes. If the quality of the programme through which they earned their qualifications was insufficient, the credits they earned may not be worth much, and credentials evaluators may determine this by checking the status of the institution or programme. Even if an institution has not been quality-assessed, it may be of sufficient quality, but credentials evaluators may find it difficult to determine whether it is. At the very least, they may have to investigate further, but there is a limit to the time and resources credentials evaluators can afford to spend on verifying a single case. This is also reflected in the explanatory memorandum to the Recommendation on Criteria and Procedures:

> The paragraph concerns the efforts which competent recognition authorities and other assessment agencies can reasonably be expected to undertake in the assessment of individual cases. They should apply all their professional skills and take account of the relevant literature, but they are not required to conduct in-depth research on the comparability of learning outcomes and/or fitness for further activities. In evaluating a foreign qualification, more emphasis should be given to the outcome of the education process (i.e. the knowledge and skills certified by the qualification and the ability to undertake further activities) than to the process itself (i.e. the education programme through which the qualification was earned).[62]

In the same way, applicants may have earned the required amount of credits, but the credits may not be of the required level. For example, if the application concerns recognition of a second degree, the overarching framework of qualifications for the European Higher Education Area stipulates that at least 60 ECTS credits should be of second degree level. There may also be requirements within the first degree that the credits earned show progression from the early to the later parts of the programme, as we saw in Chapter 5, where we considered the report from an ECTS National Counsellors' Working Group in 2003 that raised the issue of linking credits and different levels of study.[63]

To take an Irish example, it would seem that the difference between the Ordinary Bachelor – which generally does not give access to second degree study programmes (but may do so in exceptional cases) and the Honours Bachelor degree – which

---

62. Explanatory memorandum to paragraph 42.
63. "Report of ECTS National Counsellors Group, Antwerp, 7/8 February 2003".

generally does give access to second cycle programmes – is often one of workload, since the Ordinary Bachelor is normally earned on the basis of 180 ECTS credits and the Honours Bachelor is often earned on the basis of 240 ECTS credits. However, the Honours Bachelor may in some cases also be awarded on the basis of 180 ECTS credits, but a number of those credits would be of a higher level than those taken for an Ordinary Bachelor, even if all the credits in both cases would normally be at first degree level. In other words, there is differentiation in the level of credits within the same cycle. Thus, it is important to look at both level and workload.

A significant difference in profile may also constitute a substantial difference. If, for example, our acquaintance has earned most of his first degree credits in mathematics but applies for access to a second degree programme in linguistics at a foreign institution, it is unlikely that he will be accepted without taking courses to make up for the difference in profile. This is an obvious example of differences in profile that must be considered substantial, since the qualifications have been earned in very different disciplines. However, would the difference necessarily be substantial if an applicant with 60 ECTS credits of the required level in Russian linguistics and 30 credits in Russian literature applied to do a second degree programme at an institution where the first degree in Russian would normally include 80 credits in linguistics and 40 in literature? (In both cases, the remaining credits needed for the first degree would presumably have been earned in other areas, such as Russian history, political theory, statistics or any other area allowed in the degree programme.) A credentials evaluator who wanted to turn down the application for recognition by considering these differences as substantial would at the very least need to make a convincing case by arguing that the difference is substantial in terms of the applicant's chances of successfully undertaking the second degree programme.

These examples point to the importance of taking account of the purpose for which recognition is sought in seeking to determine whether or not there is a substantial difference. It may be objected that applicants rarely state explicitly for what purpose they apply for recognition. This is true, but in some cases the context makes it clear what their main purpose is. Those who apply for access to a study programme on the basis of foreign qualifications may have an interest in a general assessment of their qualifications, but their main concern is having their qualifications recognised so they can have access to the study programme for which they have applied. Similarly, those who apply for access to a regulated profession have a clear purpose in mind for their application. In these cases, the competent recognition authorities would normally be a higher education institution and a professional recognition authority, respectively, and these bodies are likely to receive a good number of applications where it is not difficult to discern the main purpose. In other cases, applicants may want a recognition statement without linking it to an application for access to a given study programme or profession.

Where the purpose of the application is clear, the recognition decision should take account of it, and it may also state the purpose for which the decision has been made, such as "recognise the first degree of Ms A for the purpose of access to the second degree study programme of institution Z in zoology".

Attitudes to recognition

While some of the cases described, and others that most readers will be able to imagine, are fairly obvious, in other cases it is possible to find arguments in favour of different decisions. Often this has to do with underlying attitudes to recognition.[64]

Put simply, some credentials evaluators take a "narrow" view. They seem to emphasise the need to "protect" their own education system and prevent students or holders of qualifications from failing in their further studies or professional activities, by making absolutely sure that the foreign qualifications are at least similar to the qualifications of their own system. Other credentials evaluators will take a "broader" view by seeking to determine whether the broad learning outcomes of the foreign qualification are roughly similar to those of the corresponding qualification of their own system while admitting that there may be considerable differences in emphasis. These evaluators will also be concerned with assessing the likelihood that applicants will succeed in their further studies or professional activities, but they are willing to take some risk that the applicants may in fact fail. To some extent, they may also seek to assess applicants' future potential as well as their past achievements. Again, these are "ideal positions" which in reality will often be more subtle and mixed.

There are other ways of characterising this difference in attitudes. One set of attitudes can be seen as emphasising the needs and interests of individual applicants, which would entail a propensity to recognise applicants' qualifications to the fullest extent possible, whereas the other can be seen as emphasising the need to uphold and protect the education system and standards of the home country, which would entail a propensity not to recognise foreign qualifications unless the credentials evaluator is absolutely convinced they are equal to the corresponding qualifications of the home country. Alternatively, one set of attitudes can be seen as seeking to identify pragmatic solutions within a given legal framework and applying a measure of "common sense", whereas the other emphasises the authority of legal provisions and seeks to apply a relatively rigid interpretation of these provisions.[65]

Of course, these are not radically different ways of looking at the phenomenon. Those who tend to take a "broad" view also tend to emphasise the needs and interests of individual applicants and to identify pragmatic solutions. Conversely, those who tend to take a "narrow" view tend to emphasise the need to protect their education system and to favour a rigid interpretation of legislation.

---

64. For a more in-depth discussion, see Sjur Bergan: "A Tale of Two Cultures in Higher Education Policies: the Rule of Law or an Excess of Legalism?" *Journal of Studies in International Education*, 8/2 (Summer 2004).

65. See also Sjur Bergan and Sandra Ferreira, "Implementation of the Lisbon Recognition Convention and contributions to the Bologna Process" in Sjur Bergan (ed.), *Recognition Issues in the Bologna Process* (Strasbourg 2003: Council of Europe Publishing).

There may be differences in national and cultural traditions about the interpretation of legal provisions, in that some cultures may be seen as more rule-bound than others and indeed to give greater importance to legal provision and legal solution, whereas others would take a more content-based and pragmatic approach. However, it would be inaccurate to reduce the issue to one of national and cultural background. Within the same country or administrative culture, there will also be considerable variation between individuals when it comes to recognition practice. The understanding of the concept of qualification, the ability to reason in terms of abstraction and principles – which should in this book perhaps more appropriately be termed a transversal competence – and also the degree to which one trusts one's own judgement are all likely to increase with experience. If other factors are equal, we would expect an experienced credentials evaluator to have a greater ability to reason in terms of content and learning outcomes, and to take a more pragmatic approach, than a credentials evaluator who is still learning their trade. Yet, there are of course considerable individual variations, and greater broadmindedness is not always an indication of increasing age.

Some of the differences in attitudes and practice may also stem from the double function of recognition. On the one hand, recognition of foreign qualifications is an instrument to ensure fair access policies and to make sure that applicants are admitted to study programmes and occupations in which they have a fair chance of success. In particular in the case of regulated professions, there is also a strong aspect of public protection, since the regulated professions tend to be occupations in which malpractice can have grave and immediate consequences. We might remember our earlier – and too simplified – characterisation of regulated professions as those in which practitioners may do great and mostly immediate harm if they are incompetent. On the other hand, recognition is an instrument for enhancing academic mobility and also mobility in the labour market.

The recognition of qualifications may also be considered as a public service since, regardless of the organisational model and status of individual competent recognition authorities, it is carried out with a public mandate. As such, it is subject to the increasing demands on public service that seem to be a general feature of most of our societies, and which tend to emphasise individual rights and aspirations. Sometimes, these expectations may be unreasonable, as when some applicants give the impression of believing they have an automatic right not only to an assessment of their qualifications, but also to a positive result of the assessment. Yet, increased public expectations of a fair, transparent and efficient assessment are healthy and they are a challenge to which credentials evaluators need to rise again and again – and one to which most credentials evaluators in fact seem to be able to rise quite well.

The outcome of the assessment

When the credentials evaluator has assessed the application, the outcome of the assessment needs to be communicated to the applicant, and possibly to other concerned parties, such as admissions officers or employers. The assessment can lead to three different outcomes:

- a recognition decision;
- advice to another body, such as a higher education institution or a competent recognition authority;
- a recognition statement.

Recognition decisions are, as the name implies, formal or *de facto* decisions on the value and place of foreign qualifications in terms of the education system or qualifications framework of the country in which recognition is sought. Typical recognition decisions are those taken by higher education institutions when students apply for access to a study programme on the basis of foreign qualifications, or by professional recognition bodies when people with foreign qualifications apply for recognition for the purpose of entering a regulated profession. In a few countries, the national information centre (ENIC/NARIC) also makes recognition decisions and may even be the sole recognition centre. In reaching their decisions, the recognition authorities should take due account of the international and national legal framework and of international good practice, as described in the last two chapters.

These are typical examples of formal recognition decisions, and the decisions are normally communicated to applicants in writing. If the applicants were not informed at the time they submitted their application of their right to appeal against the decision, they should be informed of their right at this stage. Especially if the decision is not what the applicant had expected or hoped for, the recognition authorities should also justify their decision, since only a reasoned decision will give applicants a fair chance to assess whether to appeal or not.

In addition to the formal decisions, however, there are many *de facto* recognition decisions, and these are often made by employers. When people with foreign qualifications apply for a post in the non-regulated part of the labour market, employers have to assess whether these applicants are qualified for the position. This applies specifically to non-regulated occupations since, in the case of regulated professions, candidates need a formal recognition decision. Employers will not normally issue a written assessment of applicants' foreign qualifications, so it may be argued that they do not make recognition decisions in the terms of the Council of Europe/UNESCO convention. Nevertheless, their decisions on whether to appoint someone with foreign qualifications or not are of course of great importance to those concerned as well as to policy efforts to increase the mobility of learners and of holders of qualifications.

Whereas formal recognition decisions for the purpose of access to study programmes and to regulated professions concern whether candidates fulfil the minimum requirement for entry, *de facto* decisions of employers are most often concerned with identifying the best-qualified person for a position. Therefore, credentials evaluators at higher education institutions or in professional bodies need to assess whether applicants fulfil the minimum requirements, and they will make a positive recognition decision if they do. If places in a given study programme are limited, admissions officers will then select a limited number among the qualified candidates. In the terms of the Council of

Europe/UNESCO convention, those whose qualifications are recognised have access to a given study programme, but they may in fact not be admitted.[66] Admission is granted to those who are actually offered a place on the study programme; if there is competition for places, a considerable number of those who are granted access may not earn admission. In many countries, study programmes in medicine would be typical examples of programmes where many well-qualified candidates are turned down because the number of places is limited.

Employers, on the other hand, may or may not assess applications with a view to determining whether they meet minimum requirements for the post. Their main concern will be identifying the best-suited candidate, and one or more candidates may stand out. Employers may decide to focus their attention on these candidates rather than carry out a full assessment of the qualifications of all applicants. Larger employers with activities in several countries are often well aware of recognition issues, as well as of the qualifications of various education systems, but smaller employers or those whose activities are limited to their home country may have little if any experience of foreign qualifications. If they receive applications from people with foreign qualifications, they can and should seek advice on foreign qualifications from national information centres, since they may otherwise do injustice to applicants with qualifications the employer knows little about.

This brings us to the next possible outcome: advice to another recognition body. This would be a typical outcome of applications for recognition submitted to national information centres. In fact, it may not even be appropriate to speak of applications in many such cases, because national information centres receive many enquiries about institutions, qualifications and also procedures and issues of principle from higher education institutions and other competent recognition authorities. The advice will often be given in writing, but it may also be given orally, for example in response to telephone enquiries. Advice may also be given to applicants. For example, if some of our acquaintances are unsure about how to submit an application, what information they should provide or even what their chances are of obtaining recognition, they may turn to the national information centre for advice. They may also turn to the national information centre if they feel the decision taken by a competent recognition authority is unfair and they would like to appeal against the decision. In none of these cases can the national information centre make a decision, or change a decision made by another body, but they may be able to provide useful advice. This advice would, however, not be legally binding, and information centres are often careful in specifying this.

The third possible outcome, a recognition statement, can perhaps be seen as a specific kind of advice, since it does not constitute a formal decision with legal effect. Typically, recognition statements would be issued by national information centres or other bodies to applicants who do not apply for a formal recognition decision, but who wish to obtain a written assessment of what their foreign qualifications are worth in terms

---

66. See definitions in Section I of the convention.

of the education system of their host country. Most often, applicants will not specify a purpose in asking for such a statement, and the statement will often be carefully worded so that it provides a broad comparison of the foreign qualification with corresponding qualifications of the system of the country in which recognition is sought, but without going into great detail. Such a statement may, for example, say that the foreign qualification is of the same level and workload as a first degree qualification of the host country and that it has been issued by an institution that belongs to the higher education system of country A. It may also add something about the profile of the foreign qualification, for example to note that the profile is somewhat different from the typical profile of the corresponding degree of the host country.

Let us imagine that one of our acquaintances has a first degree with a somewhat higher number of credits in disciplines not directly related to his or her main field of study than what is normally allowed in the country in which recognition is sought. If, for example, the first degree in question is in political science, it might include 5 ECTS credits in the history of music, 5 in the history of art and 10 in a foreign language, whereas first degrees in the host country typically include only 10 such unrelated credits. There could also be a difference in profile within the main area of specialisation, for example if the foreign qualification in political science contained no credits in international relations whereas this was a mandatory component of a first degree in political science in the host country. Neither difference would affect the level or quality of the foreign qualification, but it might mean that, for certain purposes, the applicant would need to undertake supplementary work to make full use of the foreign qualification, and the recognition status might draw attention to this.

The latter point also draws attention to what happens if, for well-argued reasons of substantial differences, a credentials evaluator draws the conclusion that the foreign qualification cannot be recognised. The credentials evaluator would then issue a negative recognition decision, advice or statement, but the question is how negative this would be. Again, this will often depend on the purpose for which recognition is sought. If the application is for recognition for the purpose of access to a regulated profession, the answer is basically a "yes/no", since one cannot "almost gain entry" to a regulated profession. Nevertheless, even if the decision is negative, the credentials evaluators should assist the applicant by providing a reasoned decision and by pointing to supplementary work that the candidate might undertake in order to obtain recognition.

Let us imagine, for example, that a member of the group we have referred to so often is a medical doctor with access to this regulated profession in his or her home country and wants to practise medicine in the host country. If in the country of origin – meaning the country in which the qualification was earned – there is no requirement for medical doctors to have assisted in a minimum number of births, whereas in the host country all medical doctors must have assisted in at least three deliveries in order to obtain a professional licence, this may indeed constitute a substantial difference. The reason it does constitute a substantial difference may be very pragmatic: perhaps the country of origin is a very densely populated country in which birth is given at hospitals well staffed with specialists, and the whole population lives close to such hospitals, so that generalists never or very rarely have to deliver babies, whereas the country to which the doctor wishes to move is a sparsely populated country in which a large part of the population cannot easily reach specialised hospitals. In this case, a doctor who is not trained to deliver babies may work very well in the first country but find himself in considerable difficulties in the second country.

However, is this substantial difference a valid reason to ask the doctor to start his or her medical studies from scratch? It would clearly be much more reasonable for the competent recognition authority, which in this case is likely to be a professional body, to tell the applicant that regrettably the foreign qualifications cannot be recognised, but that it is very likely they could be recognised if the applicant undertakes specified supplementary work, which in this case would be to participate in three deliveries under approved supervision. In this case, there would still be no formal recognition, but there would be an indication of further work the applicant could undertake and have reasonable chances of having his or her qualifications recognised. In other cases, it may be possible to grant what is called partial recognition,[67] which is to say that the foreign qualification may be recognised as meeting a part of the requirements towards obtaining the corresponding qualification of the country in which recognition is sought.

Let us revisit our group of acquaintances and imagine that one of our friends holds the first degree in political science that we referred to, in which no credits had been earned in the field known as international relations – perhaps because international relations was a separate study programme at her home institution. Let us further assume that the second degree programme to which she seeks admission requires a minimum of 30 ECTS credits in international relations and that further work in this field is required at second degree level, whatever her ultimate specialisation within the second degree. In this case, it seems reasonable to accept that her lack of training in international relations does constitute a substantial difference for the purpose of access to the second degree programme, where further work on international relations will be required, presupposing previous knowledge of the field. However, it would also be reasonable that the recognition decision not be an outright rejection, but partial recognition. The applicant's foreign degree is of a quality, level and workload that satisfy the requirements for a first degree in the country where she seeks recognition, but she will need to do some extra work – perhaps not quite as much as 30 ECTS credits in international relations – to gain access to the second degree programme for which she has applied.

This would be a constructive message to the applicant, and would make her less likely to appeal against the decision. It is fully justifiable in terms of learning outcomes and the quality of the education system of the host country. It also helps avoid personal distress, as in the case of the holder of a degree in dentistry who applied for a doctoral programme in another country and was told that her qualifications could not be

---

67. See paragraphs 8 and 45 of the Recommendation on Criteria and Procedures.

recognised, but she was welcome to study as a beginner in dentistry. It may well be that differences in the qualifications she had earned in her home country and those of the institution in her host country required for access to doctoral studies were substantial, but it is difficult to believe that her complete degree in dentistry from her home country carried absolutely no value in her adopted country.

This reminds us of the value of developing attitudes to the recognition of qualifications that take account not only of the rules and regulations and seek to interpret them strictly, but that also take account of surrounding factors and that seek to arrive at a recognition decision that allows learners to develop their full potential while at the same time ensuring that the public is protected against holders of less than sufficient qualifications and also that learners are not encouraged to enter study programmes and occupations in which they will in all likelihood fail on the basis of their current qualifications.

This also takes us to a consideration of why qualifications are important and what future developments are likely to be. That will be the subject of our final chapter.

15   Qualifications: functions and further development

Qualifications and the purposes of education

As we approach the end of our consideration of the concept of qualifications, it is time to look at the functions of qualifications and some likely further developments. Qualifications are a fascinating phenomenon, and I hope to have been able to keep the reader's interest until this final chapter. Nevertheless, it is important to keep in mind that qualifications are not only fascinating in themselves. They contribute to a broader goal – that of preparing learners for whatever activities they will pursue once they have completed the course of learning they have embarked on, whether that activity be gainful employment, a deeper understanding of themselves or the world in which they live, or a contribution as citizens. Hopefully, learners will be engaged in all three kinds of activities, and other activities as well. They also allow others to understand and assess the competences acquired by learners. We should be careful to specify that this course is a specific "piece" of learning, and not the end of all learning. The day a learner completed all kinds of learning would be a sad day indeed. In the perspective of lifelong learning, this would be the end of life itself.

Qualifications, then, cannot be seen in isolation from the society in which they prepare us to work and live. As this society evolves, so must the form and content of qualifications. Yet, qualifications should be much more than the end point of a course of learning, the only purpose of which is to prepare learners for a specific job or even for a broad segment of the labour market. Qualifications are important in preparing for work, but if that were their only objective, they – as the education that leads to the qualifications – would miss their mark. Qualifications must be seen in relation to the purposes of education.[68] Preparation for work and the economic function of higher education are clearly of great importance, and this is recognised in current debate. The other main purposes of higher education – including that of promoting citizenship – are far less clearly recognised in current debate, and the present chapter aims to put the concept of qualifications into this broader context of the purposes of higher education.

As these lines are written, we are already a few years into the 21st century, yet there is every reason to wonder whether our higher education qualifications are adapted to this fact. Have our descriptions of the knowledge, understanding and skills that higher education should develop been adapted to the likely requirements of the future, or are we still looking back towards the past century? Alternatively, have we been too eager to adapt our qualifications to our immediate concerns without asking ourselves the

---

68. See Sjur Bergan, "Higher education as a 'public good and public responsibility': what does it mean?" in Luc Weber and Sjur Bergan, *The Public Responsibility for Higher Education and Research* (Strasbourg 2005: Council of Europe Publishing – Higher Education Series No. 2) and Sjur Bergan, "Promoting new approaches to learning", article B 1.1-1 in Eric Froment, Jürgen Kohler, Lewis Purser and Lesley Wilson (eds), *EUA Bologna Handbook – Making Bologna Work* (Berlin 2006: Raabe Verlag). This chapter in particular draws on the latter.

difficult but crucial questions about the values on which we would like our societies to be based and how our qualifications help promote those values?

The concept of an educated person has shifted over time, and so have the purposes of study – whether in generic terms or in terms of studying a specific discipline. Just think of Latin. At the time of the Roman Empire, the purpose of learning Latin was for many to master their native language and for many others to gain fluency in the foreign language considered most useful for professional and social advancement. Latin was a *lingua franca* long before the emergence of the language that gave rise to the term. It had the function that English has gained today, that of the most important facilitator of communication between people from a variety of linguistic and cultural backgrounds. However, a working knowledge of Latin as a foreign language was reserved for an elite, much more so than a similar level of English today. In geographical terms, the elite who mastered Latin was also concentrated on a much smaller territory than those who master English today.

In the Roman Empire, public speaking or eloquence was an important part of education and served to prepare young men for careers as politicians and lawyers. Later, when schools became attached to the Church in western Europe, while the language of education was still Latin, the main goal of formal education was religious.[69] Today, those who study Latin are less numerous, and their reasons for studying what is often referred to as a "dead language" are mostly either cultural enrichment, to use Latin as a support discipline for scholarly work in disciplines that require a knowledge of this language or – for a smaller minority yet – as an academic specialisation in its own right.

Yet, even if the specific objectives of education have changed over time, the deeper purposes seem fairly constant. Their relative importance may also have varied somewhat, but it would be difficult to find a time when education did not, at least to some extent, have the following purposes:

(i) preparation for the labour market;

(ii) preparation for life as active citizens in democratic societies;

(iii) personal development;

(iv) the development and maintenance of a broad, advanced knowledge base.

These purposes are not mutually exclusive. Rather, they tend to reinforce each other. I also tend to consider them equally important for contemporary society, even if much of the current debate centres on the first of them: preparation for the labour market.

---

69. Tore Janson, *Latin: Kulturen, historien, språket* (Stockholm 2002: Wahlström och Widstrand), pp. 103–4.

The order in which they are listed should therefore not be seen as an expression of values or relative importance. Yet, the order is not entirely coincidental: it goes from the purpose that is the most debated through one that is increasingly emphasised in public debate through the one that is the least prominent in current discourse to the one that most clearly combines education and research.

Preparation for the labour market

From following current debate, one could easily get the impression that preparation for the labour market is the main or even the only purpose of higher education, but also that it is a relatively new purpose, a consequence of modern society and mass higher education, as opposed to the leisurely times of elite education when personal development was the main purpose. This impression is at considerable variance with reality.

The reason why the early universities focused on the *studium generale*, followed by theology, law and medicine, is not that these were the disciplines most conducive to personal development, but that they prepared learners for the kind of jobs for which higher education was required in medieval society. The earliest universities were strongly orientated to the labour market, but the academic labour market has changed radically since the late Middle Ages, and so has higher education. The *studium generale* was considered to provide the necessary background for undertaking professional studies, and it is perhaps not a coincidence that those three broad fields of professional studies are today typically among the regulated professions in most countries.[70] That the *studium generale* was so considered had partly to do with the emphasis on general culture in a society in which formal learning was the preserve of an elite, and partly with the fact that the opportunities for formal study enabling students to acquire such learning before they entered higher education were not well developed, as we saw in Chapter 1.

However, academic qualifications were not necessarily required even for these professions. In the Catholic Church, systematic academic training for all clergy came in the wake of the Council of Trento in the mid-sixteenth century, as a part of the Counter-Reformation, and led to the establishment of seminaries.[71] Medicine was long thought of in more theoretical terms, with the hands-on parts left to practitioners with strong arms but little or no academic training. As late as 1789, one of the leaders of the early Brazilian independence movement, Joaquím José da Silva Xavier, went by the name of Tiradentes (Tooth Puller), which reflects the contemporary approach to dentistry, a trade he practised along with medicine and commerce.

Today, the labour market demands highly qualified persons to an unprecedented extent. Whether that has to do with the development of mass higher education or whether, on

---

70. In a legal sense, this is not true of theology in all countries. Nevertheless, to enter the priesthood or to practise as a minister, ordination is required in most churches.
71. Marcel Launay, *Les séminaires français aux XIXe et XXe siècles* (Paris 2003: Les Editions du Cerf).

the contrary, mass higher education is a response to the labour market may be of theoretical interest, but need not concern us here. Probably the two reinforce each other and both are linked to the development of society, which is becoming increasingly complex technologically, but also politically and socially. Sometimes, the emphasis on specialisation – not least technological specialisation – can give the impression that the needs of the labour market are limited to increasing specialisation with little or no need for a broader view.

In this case, we would be talking about training and not education. Or, as we have developed the concept in the course of considering qualifications, we could say the needs of society were for subject-specific rather than transversal competences. This would be a very narrow concept of the needs of society as well as of the purposes of education and, as we have seen in the course of our discussion, both kinds of competences are needed. Most readers will probably have no problem remembering teachers or colleagues who had insufficient command of the specific subjects or disciplines that were essential to the job. At the same time, most readers will probably also have met the opposite case: teachers or colleagues who knew their field very well, but were lacking in transversal skills. They were unable to communicate their highly specialised knowledge and understanding to others or to apply it in practical terms.

Preparation for active citizenship in democratic societies

This may seem like a new purpose of education, and if we emphasise the terms "active" and "democratic", it probably is.[72] Yet, if we drop the adjectives, this purpose is probably as old as the notion of education, since the socialisation of children and young people has always been a key concern of both formal and informal education.

The emphasis on active citizenship and democracy reflects profound changes in society and the need for higher education to respond to them. How higher education responds, as well as the extent to which it responds, varies enormously from country to country and even from institution to institution.

"Citizen" and "citizenship" have a double meaning. In strictly legal terms, they denote "belonging" to a state. We may be citizens of Slovenia or of Greece, meaning we carry a Slovenian or Greek passport and expect to exercise certain rights, such as voting, in Slovenia or Greece as well as to enjoy a measure of protection from the government of our country of citizenship if we get into trouble abroad. We also have certain duties in regard to the country of our citizenship, the emblematic one being military service, even if many countries have now abandoned conscription in favour of professional and voluntary armed forces.

---

72. It may be argued that active democratic citizenship was a feature of Athenian society and is therefore not a new feature of education. Even if Athenian democracy was of fundamental importance as a model for European democracy, its democratic character can be contested in our view on grounds of eligibility and participation.

The other meaning of "citizen" and "citizenship" is a societal one, and this is the one that is relevant to our concerns with qualifications. It denotes a set of skills, attitudes and values related to how one perceives oneself as a member of society, and since we are concerned with democratic citizenship, they are the skills, attitudes and values that members of a society should have, for democratic societies to function as such.

If we think back to our school textbooks in civics and related subjects, the chances are that they described democracy in terms of institutions. Citizens elect parliaments, the government is formed by the party or coalition of parties with the highest number of votes and parliaments enact democratic laws by voting, in which the majority decides. Of course, institutions and laws are important, and democracy would be inconceivable without them. They are absolutely necessary, but they are not sufficient. They will not function unless they are embedded in democratic culture.

Democratic culture has to be developed anew in each generation, and education at all levels, formal as well as informal, plays a key part in developing this democratic culture. Emphatically, developing democratic culture is not just a concern for new democracies: we do not need to read many newspapers to see that the old democracies also face formidable challenges in developing and maintaining democratic culture. It includes values as well as commitment. It cannot be developed by those who identify with democratic ideals in principle, but are unwilling to engage in the public sphere. The importance of democratic culture, as well as the essential role of education in developing and maintaining it, was recognised by the heads of state and government of the Council of Europe at their Third Summit in May 2005.[73]

The concepts of subject-specific and transversal competences are relevant also to this purpose of education. Active citizens in democratic societies need to know something about political theory, as well as about democratic institutions and how they work. They also need to develop a basic knowledge and understanding of a wide range of subjects, from economics through natural sciences to history, political science and language. History has no shortage of examples of what can happen when citizens are tempted by easy and fast solutions, whether it be to unemployment, wealth distribution, environmental problems, immigration or other issues.

Our consideration of qualifications is highly relevant to considerations of democratic culture. To be sustainable, democratic culture depends on well-developed transversal skills:
• analytical ability
• the ability to present an issue clearly
• the ability to identify alternatives
• the ability to see an issue from different angles

---

73. See the Warsaw Declaration and Action Plan, available at http://www.coe.int/t/dcr/summit/default_ EN.asp (accessed on 25 June 2006).

- the ability to step outside one's own frame of reference
- the ability to solve and preferably to prevent conflicts
- the ability to debate, but also to draw conclusions and put them into practice
- even the ability to read between the lines– to read the unstated as well as the stated.

One important transversal skill is the ability to identify and then resolve paradoxes; and, as societies, we are not particularly good at it. How else would we strive to make our country ever more attractive, yet be very upset when it becomes sufficiently attractive for people to want not just to visit, but also to stay in our country to live and work?

It is also disturbing to observe the seeming inability of political debate in many of our societies to look beyond the immediate issues. What is expedient in the short run may not be right in the long run. If you are on a diet, it is normally not for the pleasure of starving, but because you think you will be better off in the long run. Yet, while diets are "in", transferring the same kind of reasoning to political debate seems decidedly "out".

Education, at all levels, plays an important role in developing the skills and competences needed to develop democratic citizenship, and this purpose of education is not confined to primary level or even to compulsory education. Higher education is an integral part of the effort, and higher education qualifications are not a guarantee that the holder will have democratic attitudes. True, it is not difficult to think of academics who have done a lot to further democratic culture and who stood up for democracy at great personal risk. These examples include the Weisse Rose, the student group around Hans and Sophie Scholl, as well as the theologians Dietrich Bonhoeffer (Protestant) and Alfred Delp, SJ (Catholic)[74] in Nazi Germany; Portuguese students under Salazar, especially from the 1960s onwards; Chilean students under the Pinochet regime; Greek students under the regime of the Colonels; Academician Andrei Sakharov in the Soviet Union; and the Alternative Academic Education Network under the Milošević regime. The list could be made much, much longer.

However, it is also easy to think of a list of counter-examples of academics who have led or assisted oppressive and dictatorial regimes. This list includes many right-wing German academics and students in the 1930s;[75] many of the leaders of the Salazar regime, who had their roots at the University of Coimbra;[76] the "Chicago boys" – the economists who hailed from the University of Chicago and the Universidad Católica

---

74. Klaus Gotto and Konrad Repgen (eds), *Die Katholiken and das Dritte Reich* (Mainz 1990: Matthias-Grünewald-Verlag).
75. Notker Hammerstein, "Universities and democratisation: an historical perspective. The case of Germany" (Paper written for a Council of Europe conference on Universities and Democratisation, Warsaw, 29–31 January 1992, reference DECS-HE 91/97).
76. Luis Reis Torgal, *A Universidade e o Estado Novo* (Coimbra 1999: Livreria Minerva Editorial).

de Chile and who played an important role in the Pinochet regime;[77] academically trained judges in the DDR (former East Germany) and other Communist states;[78] the leaders of far too many universities and Academies of Science who served the same regimes; the teachers and students at the University of Ayacucho who founded the Peruvian left-wing terrorist movement Sendero Luminoso and those involved with European left-wing terrorist groups like the Rote Arméefraktion (Baader-Meinhof) in Germany or the Brigati Rossi in Italy. Alas, this list, too, could be made much longer.

Developing and maintaining democratic culture is therefore a double task for the higher education community. It must do so for itself and it must do so for the benefit of others.

For itself, the higher education community must pursue its research and teaching in all areas of importance to sustaining our societies. That includes the ethics, values and principles on which we found our societies as well as the mechanisms that make them work. For itself, higher education must also live by the principles it proclaims. *Orthodoxia* – correct thinking – must be complemented by *orthopraxis* – sound practice.

With the wider society, the higher education community must engage. The image of the ivory tower is, I believe, a considerably exaggerated image. Had it been exact, it is difficult to believe that universities would have survived for several centuries. Yet, we often talk about the "society surrounding higher education" and forget that this is not an ocean surrounding an island. It is the very society of which higher education is a part. Our views of qualifications must reflect that, as must the definition of learning outcomes and other essential ingredients of qualifications.

Personal development

In current debate about higher education policies, it is almost never stated that higher education should contribute to the personal development of learners, nor does much thought seem to be given to what, in today's society, should be the characteristics of an educated person. In current debate, the importance and legitimacy of personal development is about as easy to argue as the indispensable role of coffee breaks at conferences to allow participants to network and discuss informally. Yet, we need not go many generations back in time to find that personal development was recognised as an important characteristic of education. This was not entirely disinterested, however, as education entailed social status and was key to the ideal of a gentleman. It was inconceivable that a gentleman could have no or little education, and the gentleman pursued education primarily for his personal development and the maintenance of his social status. It should also be noted that while "education for education's sake" may have been an ideal of high society, many of those thus educated did feel a strong obli-

---

77. Carlos Huneeus, *El régimen de Pinochet* (Santiago de Chile 2001: Editorial Sudamericana). See also María Olivia Mönckeberg: *La Privatización de las Universidades* (Santiago de Chile 2005: Copa Rota)
78. Ulrich Mählert, *Kleine Geschichte der DDR* (München 1999: Verlag C. H. Beck).

gation to put their knowledge to use at the service of society's less fortunate members or in pursuit of more immediately applicable knowledge.

The ideal of pursuing knowledge for its own sake is still alive, even if it is rarely applied in its purest form. The perhaps most extreme example of which this author is aware is that of Henry Cavendish (1731–1810), who made important discoveries in natural sciences but published only a part of them, so that later scientists made the same discoveries and published them much later.[79] Today, the personal development of students is a stated goal of education in many countries, as exemplified by the Norwegian law on primary and secondary education:

Secondary education aims to ... assist students in their personal development.[80]

Even if the value of personal development is not acknowledged much in public debate, individual citizens recognise it by taking courses at different levels of education and in all kinds of subjects and disciplines with no explicit aim other than personal development and enrichment.[81] These courses are often organised by bodies other than traditional schools and higher education institutions, such as the French *universités populaires*. Students normally pay fees for such courses, which are often offered by bodies that do not belong to the education system of the country in which they operate nor lead to qualifications that are recognised within that system.

Incidentally, there is at least one sector of great importance to modern societies for which training in most European countries is entirely or almost entirely offered by private, profit-making providers: drivers' education. This contrasts with the United States, which has a larger private education sector than most European sectors, but where drivers' education has in most states been made a part of the high school curriculum. High schools may, of course, be public or private.

While personal development does not play a prominent role in any current policy debate of which this author is aware, it is at least implicit in the concept of liberal arts education in the United States. In the Bologna context, the Bologna Declaration strongly emphasised preparation for the labour market, the Prague Communiqué clearly brought in the role of higher education in preparation for citizenship, and the Berlin Communiqué, by emphasising the link between higher education and research, brought in the development and maintenance of an advanced knowledge base. Personal development has so far not been mentioned explicitly as a goal of higher education in any of the political documents of the Bologna Process. An early draft of the

---

79. John Gribbin, *Science: A History, 1543–2001* (London 2002: Penguin), pp. 262–75. One theory is that Cavendish may have had traits of autism.
80. Utdannings- og forskningsdepartementet (1998), *Lov om grunnskolen og den vidaregåande opplæringa* (Opplæringslova); http://www.lovdata.no/all/tl-19980717-061-001.html#1-2 (accessed on 25 June 2006). My translation.
81. Given current trends, it may be worth underlining that "enrichment" is here to be taken in the sense of enriching their knowledge and personal development rather than material enrichment.

Bergen Communiqué contained a reference to the four major purposes of higher education, but it was not retained. The reason was not that there was any opposition to any of the four purposes, but rather that the text needed to be shortened and the reference was not considered essential.

Yet, there is at least occasional debate on whether some national education systems are geared more towards teaching students how to do well in examinations rather than to encourage a broad approach to learning and, for that matter, learning how to learn. There is also debate on the purposes of education, with encouraging attempts to emphasise that education is not purely about teaching students a set of technical skills, but also about helping them develop their personalities and the transversal skills that will enable citizens to discern connections and consequences, and to take a holistic view of society and of human existence. It should be an issue for modern societies that while we get more and more highly trained subject specialists, we seem to be getting fewer and fewer intellectuals, that is, people who can put knowledge and understanding in their proper context and subject received truths to critical examination. It may be worth keeping in mind William Butler Yeats' words that "education is not the filling of a bucket but the start of a fire".

As is the case with preparation for the labour market and preparation for citizenship, both subject-specific and transversal competences are important to personal development. The desire to learn is often subject-specific, such as a burning interest in history, physics or a foreign language. Developing transversal competences like communication and analytical skills along with well-reflected attitudes and values – not least intellectual curiosity – are important to developing personalities. They are of course also useful for other purposes, and there is certainly no contradiction between personal development and other purposes of higher education. There is, however, every reason to be explicit about personal development as a main purpose of higher education. Besides, it is only through personal development that all other purposes can be fulfilled, starting with our earliest childhood experiences, which are very much in the realm of informal learning.

Developing and maintaining a broad, advanced knowledge base

In the Humboldtian tradition, on which much of European higher education is based, education and research are two sides of one coin. They go together, and the development of higher education in Europe since the early nineteenth century would have been very different without this tradition. Today, there is development towards a more differentiated view of the relationship between higher education and research.

The relationship is still essential, but higher education can be research-based in one of two ways. There can be a direct link in that higher education teachers are also active researchers and bring the results of their research into their teaching. Alternatively, the link can be somewhat less direct in that higher education teachers have personal experience of research through their training and perhaps also through earlier stages of their careers, and they are therefore able to follow and make use of research results in their teaching, but they may no longer be personally engaged in research. One could also identify a third way in which research and teaching are linked, in which institutions ensure that the contents of teaching and learning are kept up to date by active reference to contemporary research. This relies less on individuals transferring their own research and more on a collective culture of feeding the teaching environment with active research issues.[82]

In reality, higher education in Europe is research-based in all three ways, and there seems to be increasing willingness to acknowledge this. While the development will not be easy, Europe is likely to move from officially having a system of universities that marry research and teaching to one where some universities are active research universities, while others are mainly teaching universities with limited research of their own, but where staff still have had personal experience of research at some point in their career.

Whatever the model, research is essential to modern societies, which could not have developed without advanced knowledge in a variety of fields. Technologically advanced knowledge is the example that most easily comes to mind, since our contemporary societies would be inconceivable without information technology, advanced production technology, infrastructure for road, sea and air transport, the technology that allows companies to supply goods on demand rather than maintain large stocks, the technology that makes it possible to perform various operations at a distance,[83] the technology and knowledge needed to predict the weather and a long list of other technologies. Yet, contemporary societies would also be inconceivable without advanced knowledge and understanding in other fields. We need to understand how societies function, how the human mind works and how language works. We need to understand the consequences of given policies as well as the basic mechanisms governing the relationship between states and other political entities, how these influence co-operation and conflict, and what influences the decisions of voters.

Certain primates spend more than half their time looking for food. When they are held in captivity and fed regularly, they have much "spare time" on their hands, and the effect is often that they are bored and get either apathetic or aggressive. For humans, however, dramatically reducing the time needed to ensure subsistence has had the opposite effect. It has created opportunities for intellectual development or what Lisa Jardine has called "ingenious pursuits"[84] and, in many ways, this is what has made us human beings.

---

82. I am grateful to Lewis Purser for this observation.
83. See Thomas L. Friedman, *The World is Flat* (London and New York 2006: Penguin Books).
84. Lisa Jardine, *Ingenious Pursuits: Building the Scientific Revolution.* (London 1999: Little, Brown & Co.).

263

Humans develop and transmit knowledge, and research is an advanced form of knowledge development; but not all development of knowledge is research, nor is new knowledge necessarily developed within higher education. A farmer, a gardener or an artisan may acquire and further develop highly advanced knowledge within their specialisation and would normally do so without much contact with the world of higher education and research. Nevertheless, maintaining and developing advanced knowledge in a broad variety of fields is an important characteristic of higher education. Transmitting the knowledge and skills required for research is also one of the main tasks of higher education.

The need for advanced knowledge is, therefore, apparent. However, modern societies need a knowledge base that is not only advanced, but also broad, and that is partly because it is impossible to predict what knowledge will be key to our needs and desires five or ten years from now, not to speak of in the longer term. When the need arises, it will often be too late to develop the basis that will enable us to rapidly develop the precise knowledge we need.

The borderline between basic and applied research is not always clear in practice, but the concepts are nevertheless useful. Exactly what basic research will give rise to a practical application is not easy to predict. From natural science, one frequently mentioned example is Guglielmo Marconi's work leading to working radio transmission. At the same time, Ernest Rutherford was doing theoretically more important work on radio waves, but Marconi's work led to more immediate application.[85] From humanities and social sciences, an example is the oil boycott of the early 1970s, when Arab countries substantially reduced their export of oil to North America and western Europe for political reasons. While some European countries had strong traditions of research in Arabic language, culture and history, many did not, and there was little broad understanding of the reasons for the boycott, and few if any in the countries subjected to the boycott had predicted that this could be the result of their policies in the Middle East. The point here is not whether those policies were justified or not, but rather that, whatever their justification, advanced knowledge and understanding of Arabic language, culture, history and contemporary society would have been of great use in assessing possible consequences of those policies and in seeking to diminish the consequences of them.

Challenges in terms of qualifications

Those concerned with the response of higher education to developments in modern societies and the implications for qualifications are living in interesting times.

This book has largely been concerned with exploring the concept of qualifications and its various components. Our understanding of the concept has improved significantly, and in the next few years we can hope to improve this understanding further.

---

85. Gribbin, op. cit., pp. 500–2.

In particular, I am hopeful that we will better understand learning outcomes, that the description of learning outcomes will improve and not least that this competence will be developed among many more higher education policy makers and practitioners in many more countries. To an extent, the development of the European Higher Education Area depends on it, as do the possibilities for improving the movement of learners and holders of qualifications between Europe and other parts of the world. It is important that increasing numbers of policy makers and practitioners in more and more countries move from a legalistic interpretation of concepts to one that focuses on content. Such a move will also facilitate the recognition of foreign qualifications.

Qualifications are not unlike higher education institutions themselves: their forms and the details of their contents need to be adapted to reflect the changes in the societies of which they are a part, but their basic values must be safeguarded. Safeguarding the values is indeed only possible if the form and content are adapted; otherwise higher education qualifications would become obsolete. However, higher education should not only adapt to changes imposed by others. Higher education should influence and even lead the development of society. This is a formidable challenge, but one to which higher education has risen in the past and to which it must continue to rise in the years to come.

That qualifications must adapt is easy to see if we compare the needs and functions that higher education qualifications were required to meet at the beginning of the nineteenth century with those it was expected to meet at the close of the twentieth century. There is little reason to expect that society will not continue to develop, and there is every reason to assume that the development of society will be more and more rapid.

One important challenge is to make sure that higher education qualifications are suited to addressing all four major purposes of higher education. Qualifications that have addressed only one aspect – as can be seen from many examples of qualifications over-focusing on supposed labour market needs in the past – have become obsolete much more quickly than qualifications with a balanced approach to the four purposes. As we saw, there is no fundamental contradiction between the four purposes. Rather, they complement each other: the knowledge, understanding and abilities that help prepare for citizenship or contribute to personal development can also help prepare for the labour market.

It follows that qualifications that focus only on subject-specific skills, without placing them in a broader context and seeking to develop transversal competencies, are likely be short-lived and insufficient. It would indeed be difficult to find such qualifications at higher education level, but there may nevertheless be good reasons for asking whether some higher education programmes provide students with too narrow specialisations. However, the example may be useful in order to underline that the opposite kind of qualifications would also fail the mark.

Transversal competences are important, but they are not everything. The gospel preached by some management specialists – self appointed or otherwise, in the private sector as well as the public – maintaining that managers should be generalists and need not know much about the specific areas in which their organisation or team is working, is hardly conducive to sustainable qualifications, or for that matter sustainable corporations. It reminds one of the quip about a journalist being someone who knows less and less about more and more. Taken to the extreme, this attitude would hold that the less a manager knows about the content of the core area of the organisation's activity, the better. What our societies will continue to need, at all levels, for all purposes and in all walks of life, is well-qualified citizens with solid subject-specific as well as transversal competences.

These, however, will not be written in stone, and they will not last a lifetime. They will need to be updated much more often than in the past, and this is another challenge in the area of qualifications. The development of qualifications frameworks and the concept of learning paths should facilitate this development, but a political will is needed all the same. Our education systems will need to provide ample opportunities to earn qualifications in different ways, at different times, and at different stages of life. This is true for "first" qualifications, but it is equally true of opportunities to update qualifications. This simple statement raises a good number of questions that go well beyond the scope of this book, including the provision for and financing of frequent return visits to higher education by learners who want to update their qualifications or to earn new qualifications in new areas of knowledge, and who will need to combine work and learning in a way that the traditional student would not, in most cases. The fact that many other factors are involved, however, is no excuse for not making the qualifications frameworks more explicit in their functions and purpose, and reviewing those which already formally exist, including the way we allow learners to earn qualifications. Without innovation in this area, the best financial provision in the world to help learners alternate between work and learning at different ages might be to little avail.

Technological developments are likely to change the ways in which we learn and to diversify the typical learning experience in ways that most of us will find difficult to imagine. Not all innovation is necessarily for the better, but it is certain that some innovations will be substantial improvements on the ways we learn today. As we develop qualifications, we must take account of and, if possible, foresee technological developments in order to make qualifications accessible to more learners. Again, it is a question of changing form and content while preserving values. Technologies that help learners earn qualifications with fewer limitations in time and space will be positive developments and should not only be welcomed, but also integrated into our concept of qualifications. Technologies that encourage unquestioning digestion of "facts" and do not contribute to developing learners' abilities to think critically, analyse information and place it in a broader context will do more harm than good. Technologies that further knowledge and skills without an understanding of what these really are should have no place in the education systems of tomorrow. Qualifications and the assessment processes that measure whether learners have achieved them should be designed to require a deeper understanding both of the specific subject and of its broader context.

The educated person of tomorrow will certainly be expected to master technology. Computer illiteracy may be a modern form of illiteracy, but in technologically complex societies it is a form of illiteracy all the same. In the same way, those able to work only in their native language will be severely disadvantaged in a world in which communication across borders is likely to increase. At the same time, cross-border communication is more than language – it is also intercultural competence: the ability to understand other points of view and to step outside one's own frame of reference.

Ultimately, the measure of whether qualifications are well suited to contribute to the development of society is perhaps whether they are suited to answering the seemingly simple question the Chilean sociologist Eugenio Tironi asked of education: "Educate – for what?"[86] The author seeks the answer not in trying to identify trends in the labour market, but in trying to find an answer to the much broader question: "What kind of society do we want?"

The ultimate measure of qualifications, then, is whether they contribute to developing the kind of society in which we would want to live. This is no small task, and it will challenge policy makers and practitioners alike. This book does not pretend to provide the answer to this challenge, but it will hopefully provide readers with a deeper understanding of the concept and contents of qualifications, so that they can better address the larger issues.

---

86. Eugenio Tironi, *El sueño chileno: Comunidad, familia y nación en el Bicentenario* (Santiago de Chile 2005: Taurus).

Suggestions for further reading

To my knowledge, this is the first book seeking to give a comprehensive overview of the concept of qualifications. In so doing, the book draws on literature covering specific aspects of qualifications in detail, but also on works focusing on other aspects of education and research that are still relevant for a consideration of qualifications.

The purpose of the present bibliographical essay is to present the main sources that have been used in writing this book and to offer suggestions for further reading. Much of the material used is available on the Web, which has the advantage of easy accessibility but also the disadvantage that material on the Web is more transient in character than material published in traditional book or journal format. The Web links offered here were operational at the time of writing, but no guarantee can of course be offered that they will remain operational.

Background and the development of qualifications

To my knowledge, there is no published history of qualifications. However, there are many histories of education, and they generally also contain information on the developments of qualifications. I have benefited from Jacques Verger, *Les universités au Moyen Age* (Paris 1999: Quadrige/Presses Universitaires de France; 1st edn 1973) as well as the multi-volume history of European universities published by the CRE (now the European University Association): Walter Rüegg (general editor), *A History of the University in Europe*. This history is also available in French, German and Spanish. The heritage rather than the history of European universities is the topic of Nuria Sanz and Sjur Bergan (eds), *The Heritage of European Universities* (Strasbourg 2002: Council of Europe Publishing).

I have also benefited from the four-volume history of education in France published by Perrin (Paris) in the Collection Tempus as *Histoire de l'enseignement et de l'éducation*: Vol. I *Des origins à la Renaissance (V^e av. J.-C. – XVe siècle)*, by Michel Rouche (2003); Vol. II *De Gutenberg aux Lumières (1480 – 1789)*, by François Lebrun, Marc Venard and Jean Quéniard (2003); Vol. III *De la Révolution à l'École républicaine (1789 – 1930)*, by Françoise Mayeur; Vol. IV *L'École et la Famille dans une sociéte en mutation (depuis 1930)*, by Antoine Prost. All volumes were originally published in 1981 by Nouvelle Librairie de France.

For the history of science, a good overview is provided by John Gribbin, *Science: A History, 1543–2003* (London 2003: Penguin). Marcel Launay, *Les séminaires français aux XIXe et XXe siècles* (Paris 2003: Les Editions du Cerf) discusses the education of Catholic priests at a time when French seminaries were given a stronger academic foundation.

There is comprehensive information on the Bologna Process at the webpage of the ministerial conference in Bergen: http://www.bologna-bergen2005.no/. The webpage of the ministerial conference in London summarises developments to 2007: http://

www.dfes.gov.uk/bologna/. The Council of Europe website has comprehensive information on its own higher education activities and the Bologna Process: http://www.coe.int/t/dg4/highereducation/Default_en.asp.

An overview of implementation of key policies in the Bologna Process is found in *Bologna Process Stocktaking: Report from a Working Group Appointed by the Bologna Follow-Up Group to the Conference of European Ministers Responsible for Higher Education, Bergen*, 19–20 May 2005, at http://www.bologna-bergen2005.no/Bergen/050509_Stocktaking.pdf – a similar stocktaking report will be submitted to the ministerial conference held in London in May 2007; it will probably be available by June 2007 at http://www.dfes.gov.uk/bologna/.

The EUA Bologna Handbook provides in-depth coverage of a large number of topics related to the Bologna Process, including qualifications and qualifications frameworks; see Eric Froment, Jürgen Kohler, Lewis Purser and Lesley Wilson (eds), *EUA Bologna Handbook – Making Bologna Work* (Berlin 2006: Raabe Verlag).

Issue No. 29/2003 of the *Cuadernos Europeos de Deusto* (Bilbao: Universidad de Deusto) contains a number of interesting articles (in English) on developments in higher education policies, many of them relevant to the concerns of this book.

Components of qualifications

A description of the European Language Portfolio will be found at http://culture2.coe.int/portfolio/inc.asp?L=E&M=$t/208-1-0-1/main_pages/welcome.html. The Dublin Descriptors will be found at http://www.jointquality.org/.

The European Credit Transfer System (ECTS) is described on a European Commission webpage at http://europa.eu.int/comm/education/programmes/socrates/ects/index_en.html#2. For brief overviews of the US credit system, see John Harris, "Brief history of American credit system: a recipe for incoherence in student learning" (2002) at http://www.samford.edu/groups/quality/BriefHistoryofAmericanAcademicCreditSystem.pdf and Jessica Shedd, "The history of the student credit hour" in *New Directions for Higher Education* 122 (Summer 2003) at http://virtual.parkland.edu/todtreat/presentations/cetl03/shedd2003%20history%20of%20credit%20hour.pdf.

Information on the Tuning Project may be found at http://tuning.unideusto.org/tuningeu/. The key Tuning publication for the purposes of the present book is Julia González and Robert Wagenaar (eds.), *TUNING Educational Structures in Europe: Universities' Contribution to the Bologna Process. Final Report Pilot Project Phase 2* (Bilbao and Groningen 2005: Publicaciones de la Universidad de Deusto).

For quality assurance, the key website in Europe is that of the European Association for Quality Assurance in Higher Education (ENQA): http://www.enqa.eu/. The standards for quality assurance in the European Higher Education Area, as adopted by ministers in Bergen in May 2005 may be found at http://www.bologna-bergen2005. no/ – go to "Adopted by Ministers", then to "European Quality Assurance Standards". The background report is at http://www.bologna-bergen2005.no/Docs/00-Main_ doc/050221_ENQA_report.pdf.

The best description of learning outcomes of which I am aware is Stephen Adam, "An introduction to learning outcomes: A consideration of the nature, function and position of learning outcomes in the creation of the European Higher Education Area", article B 2.3-1 in Eric Froment, Jürgen Kohler, Lewis Purser and Lesley Wilson (eds), *EUA Bologna Handbook – Making Bologna Work* (Berlin 2006: Raabe Verlag). Jennifer Moon, "Linking levels, learning outcomes and assessment criteria", presented at the Bologna seminar Using Learning Outcomes (Edinburgh, 1–2 July 2004), a very useful overview of learning outcomes and related concepts is at http://www.bologna-bergen2005.no/EN/Bol_sem/Seminars/040701-02Edinburgh/040701-02Linking_ Levels_plus_ass_crit-Moon.pdf.

Qualifications frameworks

The reference publication for the Framework of Qualifications for the European Higher Education Area is the report *A Framework for Qualifications of the European Higher Education Area* by a working group within the Bologna Process, chaired by Mogens Berg (Copenhagen 2005: Ministry of Science, Technology and Innovation). The report is also available at http://www.bologna-bergen2005.no/Docs/00-Main_ doc/050218_QF_EHEA.pdf.

The European Qualifications Framework proposed by the European Commission is in COM(2006)479 final: http://ec.europa.eu/education/policies/educ/eqf/com_2006_ 0479_en.pdf – a previous proposal for the EQF will be found in Commission Staff Document Sec (2005) 957.

There are also a number of descriptions of national qualifications frameworks. For this book, I have in particular used the descriptions of the national frameworks of:

Australia: *Australian Qualifications Framework Implementation Handbook, Third Edition* (Carlton, Victoria 2002: Australian Qualifications Framework Advisory Board) and http://www.aqf.edu.au/aboutaqf.htm

Denmark: "Mod en dansk kvalifikationsnøgle for videregående uddannelser", report from the Danish Bologna working group on qualifications frameworks, p. 5. The report is dated 15 January 2003 and available at http://www.udiverden.dk/Default. aspx?ID=3555 (accessed on 5 May 2006). The report on the Danish Qualifications Framework is provided in both Danish and English, whereas the appendices to the report are given in Danish only.

Ireland: http://www.nfq.ie/nfq/en/TheFramework/

New Zealand: *The New Zealand National Qualifications Framework* (Wellington 2005: New Zealand Qualifications Authority) and http://www.nzqa.govt.nz/framework/index.html

South Africa: http://www.logos-net.net/ilo/195_base/en/init/sa_16.htm

United Kingdom (England, Northern Ireland and Wales): http://www.qaa.ac.uk/academicinfrastructure/FHEQ/EWNI/default.asp

United Kingdom (Scotland): http://www.scqf.org.uk/

Descriptions of further national frameworks are likely to become available as we approach 2010, which is the deadline for the elaboration of national frameworks within the Bologna Process.

In the literature on qualifications frameworks, an excellent paper is Stephen Adam, "To consider alternative approaches for clarifying cycles and levels in European higher education qualifications", background report for the Danish Bologna seminar on Qualifications Structures in European Higher Education, Copenhagen, 27–28 March 2003, available at http://www.bologna-bergen2005.no/EN/Bol_sem/Old/030327-28Copenhagen/030327-28S_Adam.pdf as well as the reports from related Bologna conferences by Sjur Bergan: from the conference on Qualifications Structures in Higher Education in Europe (March 2003) http://www.bologna-bergen2005.no/EN/Bol_sem/Old/030327-28Copenhagen/030327-28Report_General_Rapporteur.pdf and from the conference on The Framework for Qualifications of the European Higher Education Area (January 2005) http://www.bologna-bergen2005.no/EN/Bol_sem/Seminars/050113-14Copenhagen/050113-14_General_report.pdf. See also Sjur Bergan's report from the Bologna Conference on Recognition and Credit Systems in the Context of Lifelong Learning (June 2003) http://www.bologna-bergen2005.no/EN/Bol_sem/Old/030605-07Prague/030605-07General_Report.pdf.

Recognition of qualifications

The three key websites are the one maintained by the ENIC and NARIC Networks http://www.enic-naric.net/, the relevant part of the Council of Europe's higher education pages at http://www.coe.int/T/DG4/HigherEducation/Recognition/default_en.asp and the webpages of the ACE (Admissions officers and credentials evaluators) professional section of the European Association for International Education (EAIE) http://www.aic.lv/ace/.

For the European Region, the key standard setting text is the Council of Europe/ UNESCO Convention on the Recognition of Qualifications concerning Higher Education in the European Region, adopted in Lisbon on 11 April 1997 and therefore also referred to as the Lisbon Recognition Convention. The text of the convention and its explanatory report, with an updated list of signatures and ratifications, may be found at http://conventions.coe.int; search for ETS No.165. The text of the convention and its explanatory report as well as the subsidiary texts adopted under the convention may be found in *Standards for Recognition: The Lisbon Recognition Convention and its Subsidiary Texts*, compiled by Andrejs Rauhvargers and Sjur Bergan (Strasbourg 2005: Council of Europe Publishing – Higher Education Series No. 3).

An overview of key recognition issues in the Bologna Process is given in Sjur Bergan (ed.), *Recognition Issues in the Bologna Process* (Strasbourg 2003: Council of Europe Publishing) as well as in Andrejs Rauhvargers and Sjur Bergan (eds), *Recognition in the Bologna Process: Policy Development and the Road to Good Practice* (Strasbourg 2006: Council of Europe Publishing – Higher Education Series No. 4).

Transnational or borderless education and its impact on recognition issues are discussed in Stamenka Uvalić-Trumbić (ed.), *Globalization and the Market in Higher Education: Quality, Accreditation and Qualifications* (Paris 2002: UNESCO Publishing and Editions Economica) as well as in Carolyn Campbell, "Transnational education" in *Cuadernos Europeos de Deusto* (Bilbao: Universidad de Deusto), 29/2003, pp. 63–78 and in Jane Knight, "Programmes, providers and accreditors on the move: implications for the recognition of qualifications" in Andrejs Rauhvargers and Sjur Bergan (eds), *Recognition in the Bologna Process: Policy Development and the Road to Good Practice* (Strasbourg 2006: Council of Europe Publishing – Higher Education Series No. 4), pp. 139–60. Updated information on borderless education may also be found at the website of the Observatory for Borderless Education, based in the United Kingdom, at http://www.obhe.ac.uk.

María Olivia Mönckeberg: *La Privatización de las Universidades* (Santiago de Chile 2005: Copa Rota) provides interesting insight into the privatisation of Chilean higher education in the 1980s and 1990s, including the implications this privatisation has had for the quality of education and hence, potentially, for recognition. The author, however, carefully distinguishes between the institutions and avoids the trap of considering all private higher education as low quality. To my knowledge, Chilean higher education is the most strongly privatised in the world.

The standard description of joint degrees is Andrejs Rauhvargers, "Joint degree study" in Christian Tauch and Andrejs Rauhvargers, *Survey on Master Degrees and Joint Degrees in Europe* (Brussels 2001: European University Association). The key standard setting text is the Recommendation on the Recognition of Joint Degrees, adopted in 2004 as a subsidiary text to the Council of Europe/UNESCO Convention on the Recognition of Qualifications concerning Higher Education in the European Region. The text is available at available at https://wcd.coe.int/com.instranet.InstraServlet?Command=com.instranet.CmdBlobGet&DocId=822136&SecMode=1&Admin=0&Usage=4&InstranetImage=43872 and in *Standards for Recognition: The Lisbon Recognition Convention and its Subsidiary Texts* (see above).

The Diploma Supplement developed jointly by the Council of Europe, the European Commission and UNESCO is at http://www.enic-naric.net/instruments. asp?display=DS.

A discussion of attitudes to recognition will be found in Sjur Bergan, "A tale of two cultures in higher education policies: the rule of law or an excess of legalism?" in *Journal of Studies in International Education*, 8/2 (Summer 2004).

Higher education and citizenship

Stefan Berger, Mark Donovan and Kevin Passmore (eds), *Writing National Histories: Western Europe since 1800* (London 1999: Routledge) as well as Michael Branch (ed.), *National Histories and Identity: Approaches to the Writing of National History in the North-East Baltic Region Nineteenth and Twentieth Centuries* (Helsinki 1999: Finnish Literature Society: Studia Fennica Ethnologica 6) address attitudes to the writing of history and, hence, to the development of societies. These attitudes are heavily influenced by education.

Robert Stradling, *Teaching 20th-Century European History* (Strasbourg 2001: Council of Europe Publishing) is the key text on the need for multiperspectivity in history teaching – and by extension in the writing of history. The Council of Europe's Recommendation Rec(2001)15 by the Committee of Ministers to member states on history teaching in twenty-first century Europe is the key normative text on this topic.

Sjur Bergan (ed.), *The University as* Res Publica (Strasbourg 2004: Council of Europe Publishing – Higher Education Series No. 1) discusses the role of students in university governance as well as the university as an actor in the broader society of which it is a part.

Luis Reis Torgal, *A Universidade e o Estado Novo* (Coimbra 1999: Livreria Minerva Editorial) is an excellent case study of Portuguese universities under Salazar, while Notker Hammerstein, "Universities and democratisation: an historical perspective. The case of Germany" (Paper written for a Council of Europe conference on Universities and Democratisation, Warsaw, 29–31 January 1992, reference DECS-HE 91/97) is an equally good case study of Germany.

Some relevant material may also be found in works with a more general scope, such as Ulrich Mählert, *Kleine Geschichte der DDR* (München 1999: Verlag C. H. Beck), Klaus Gotto and Konrad Repgen (eds), *Die Katholiken and das Dritte Reich* (Mainz 1990: Matthias-Grünewald-Verlag) and Carlos Huneeus, *El régimen de Pinochet* (Santiago de Chile 2001: Editorial Sudamericana).

Supplementary reading

I cannot quite resist the temptation to include some works that are more peripherally related to the topic of qualifications, but that nevertheless offer insights into intellectual developments and history. In many cases, they also provide delightful reading, as is certainly the case with Arthur Herman, *The Scottish Enlightenment: The Scots' Invention of the Modern World* (London 2003: Fourth Estate). Lisa Jardine, *Ingenious Pursuits: Building the Scientific Revolution.* (London 1999: Little, Brown & Co.) is equally stimulating reading, as is Eugenio Tironi, *El sueño chileno: Comunidad, familia y nación en el Bicentenario* (Santiago de Chile 2005: Taurus). Tironi addresses the development of Chilean society and sees education as an important component of this development.

Thomas L. Friedman, *The World is Flat* (London and New York 2006: Penguin Books) raises challenging questions on globalisation and the role of education in this context. Tore Janson, *Latin: Kulturen, historien, språket* (Stockholm 2002: Wahlström och Widstrand) discusses the influence of Latin and of Roman culture on later European society, with particular reference to Sweden.

Sales agents for publications of the Council of Europe
Agents de vente des publications du Conseil de l'Europe

BELGIUM/BELGIQUE
La Librairie Européenne -
The European Bookshop
Rue de l'Orme, 1
B-1040 BRUXELLES
Tel.: +32 (0)2 231 04 35
Fax: +32 (0)2 735 08 60
E-mail: order@libeurop.be
http://www.libeurop.be

Jean De Lannoy
Avenue du Roi 202 Koningslaan
B-1190 BRUXELLES
Tel.: +32 (0)2 538 43 08
Fax: +32 (0)2 538 08 41
E-mail: jean.de.lannoy@dl-servi.com
http://www.jean-de-lannoy.be

CANADA
Renouf Publishing Co. Ltd.
1-5369 Canotek Road
OTTAWA, Ontario K1J 9J3, Canada
Tel.: +1 613 745 2665
Fax: +1 613 745 7660
Toll-Free Tel.: (866) 767-6766
E-mail: order.dept@renoufbooks.com
http://www.renoufbooks.com

CZECH REPUBLIC/
RÉPUBLIQUE TCHÈQUE
Suweco CZ, s.r.o.
Klecakova 347
CZ-180 21 PRAHA 9
Tel.: +420 2 424 59 204
Fax: +420 2 848 21 646
E-mail: import@suweco.cz
http://www.suweco.cz

DENMARK/DANEMARK
GAD
Vimmelskaftet 32
DK-1161 KØBENHAVN K
Tel.: +45 77 66 60 00
Fax: +45 77 66 60 01
E-mail: gad@gad.dk
http://www.gad.dk

FINLAND/FINLANDE
Akateeminen Kirjakauppa
PO Box 128
Keskuskatu 1
FIN-00100 HELSINKI
Tel.: +358 (0)9 121 4430
Fax: +358 (0)9 121 4242
E-mail: akatilaus@akateeminen.com
http://www.akateeminen.com

FRANCE
La Documentation française
(diffusion/distribution France entière)
124, rue Henri Barbusse
F-93308 AUBERVILLIERS CEDEX
Tél.: +33 (0)1 40 15 70 00
Fax: +33 (0)1 40 15 68 00
E-mail: commande@ladocumentationfrancaise.fr
http://www.ladocumentationfrancaise.fr

Librairie Kléber
1 rue des Francs Bourgeois
F-67000 STRASBOURG
Tel.: +33 (0)3 88 15 78 88
Fax: +33 (0)3 88 15 78 80
E-mail: francois.wolfermann@librairie-kleber.fr
http://www.librairie-kleber.com

GERMANY/ALLEMAGNE
AUSTRIA/AUTRICHE
UNO Verlag GmbH
August-Bebel-Allee 6
D-53175 BONN
Tel.: +49 (0)228 94 90 20
Fax: +49 (0)228 94 90 222
E-mail: bestellung@uno-verlag.de
http://www.uno-verlag.de

GREECE/GRÈCE
Librairie Kauffmann s.a.
Stadiou 28
GR-105 64 ATHINAI
Tel.: +30 210 32 55 321
Fax: +30 210 32 30 320
E-mail: ord@otenet.gr
http://www.kauffmann.gr

HUNGARY/HONGRIE
Euro Info Service kft.
1137 Bp. Szent István krt. 12.
H-1137 BUDAPEST
Tel.: +36 (06)1 329 2170
Fax: +36 (06)1 349 2053
E-mail: euroinfo@euroinfo.hu
http://www.euroinfo.hu

ITALY/ITALIE
Licosa SpA
Via Duca di Calabria, 1/1
I-50125 FIRENZE
Tel.: +39 0556 483215
Fax: +39 0556 41257
E-mail: licosa@licosa.com
http://www.licosa.com

MEXICO/MEXIQUE
Mundi-Prensa México, S.A. De C.V.
Río Pánuco, 141 Delegacíon Cuauhtémoc
06500 MÉXICO, D.F.
Tel.: +52 (01)55 55 33 56 58
Fax: +52 (01)55 55 14 67 99
E-mail: mundiprensa@mundiprensa.com.mx
http://www.mundiprensa.com.mx

NETHERLANDS/PAYS-BAS
De Lindeboom Internationale Publicaties b.v.
M.A. de Ruyterstraat 20 A
NL-7482 BZ HAAKSBERGEN
Tel.: +31 (0)53 5740004
Fax: +31 (0)53 5729296
E-mail: books@delindeboom.com
http://www.delindeboom.com

NORWAY/NORVÈGE
Akademika
Postboks 84 Blindern
N-0314 OSLO
Tel.: +47 2 218 8100
Fax: +47 2 218 8103
E-mail: support@akademika.no
http://www.akademika.no

POLAND/POLOGNE
Ars Polona JSC
25 Obroncow Street
PL-03-933 WARSZAWA
Tel.: +48 (0)22 509 86 00
Fax: +48 (0)22 509 86 10
E-mail: arspolona@arspolona.com.pl
http://www.arspolona.com.pl

PORTUGAL
Livraria Portugal
(Dias & Andrade, Lda.)
Rua do Carmo, 70
P-1200-094 LISBOA
Tel.: +351 21 347 42 82 / 85
Fax: +351 21 347 02 64
E-mail: info@livrariaportugal.pt
http://www.livrariaportugal.pt

RUSSIAN FEDERATION/
FÉDÉRATION DE RUSSIE
Ves Mir
9a, Kolpacnhyi per.
RU-101000 MOSCOW
Tel.: +7 (8)495 623 6839
Fax: +7 (8)495 625 4269
E-mail: orders@vesmirbooks.ru
http://www.vesmirbooks.ru

SPAIN/ESPAGNE
Mundi-Prensa Libros, s.a.
Castelló, 37
E-28001 MADRID
Tel.: +34 914 36 37 00
Fax: +34 915 75 39 98
E-mail: libreria@mundiprensa.es
http://www.mundiprensa.com

SWITZERLAND/SUISSE
Van Diermen Editions – ADECO
Chemin du Lacuez 41
CH-1807 BLONAY
Tel.: +41 (0)21 943 26 73
Fax: +41 (0)21 943 36 05
E-mail: info@adeco.org
http://www.adeco.org

UNITED KINGDOM/ROYAUME-UNI
The Stationery Office Ltd
PO Box 29
GB-NORWICH NR3 1GN
Tel.: +44 (0)870 600 5522
Fax: +44 (0)870 600 5533
E-mail: book.enquiries@tso.co.uk
http://www.tsoshop.co.uk

UNITED STATES and CANADA/
ÉTATS-UNIS et CANADA
Manhattan Publishing Company
468 Albany Post Road
CROTTON-ON-HUDSON, NY 10520, USA
Tel.: +1 914 271 5194
Fax: +1 914 271 5856
E-mail: Info@manhattanpublishing.com
http://www.manhattanpublishing.com

Council of Europe Publishing/Editions du Conseil de l'Europe
F-67075 Strasbourg Cedex
Tel.: +33 (0)3 88 41 25 81 – Fax: +33 (0)3 88 41 39 10 – E-mail: publishing@coe.int – Website: http://book.coe.int